The Creative Turn

Advances in Creativity and Giftedness

Volume 6

Advances in Creativity and Gifted Education (ADVA) is the first internationally established book series that focuses exclusively on the constructs of creativity and giftedness as pertaining to the psychology, philosophy, pedagogy and ecology of talent development across the milieus of family, school, institutions and society. ADVA strives to synthesize both domain specific and domain general efforts at developing creativity, giftedness and talent. The books in the series are international in scope and include the efforts of researchers, clinicians and practitioners across the globe.

Series Editor:

Bharath Sriraman, The University of Montana, USA

International Advisory Panel:

Don Ambrose, Rider University, USA
David Chan, The Chinese University of Hong Kong
Anna Craft, University of Exeter, UK
Stephen Hegedus, University of Massachusetts, Dartmouth, USA
Kristina Juter, Kristianstad University College, Sweden
James C. Kaufman, California State University at San Bernardino, USA
Kyeonghwa Lee, Seoul National University, Korea
Roza Leikin, University of Haifa, Israel
Peter Liljedahl, Simon Fraser University, Canada
Paula Olszewski-Kubilius, Northwestern University, USA
Larisa Shavinina, University of Quebec, Canada

Editorial Assistant:

Claire Payne

The Creative Turn

Toward a New Aesthetic Imaginary

Anne Harris
Monash University, Melbourne, Australia

SENSE PUBLISHERS
ROTTERDAM/BOSTON/TAIPEI

A C.I.P. record for this book is available from the Library of Congress.

ISBN: 978-94-6209-549-6 (paperback)
ISBN: 978-94-6209-550-2 (hardback)
ISBN: 978-94-6209-551-9 (e-book)

Published by: Sense Publishers,
P.O. Box 21858,
3001 AW Rotterdam,
The Netherlands
https://www.sensepublishers.com/

Printed on acid-free paper

All Rights Reserved © 2014 Sense Publishers

No part of this work may be reproduced, stored in a retrieval system, or transmitted in any form or by any means, electronic, mechanical, photocopying, microfilming, recording or otherwise, without written permission from the Publisher, with the exception of any material supplied specifically for the purpose of being entered and executed on a computer system, for exclusive use by the purchaser of the work.

TABLE OF CONTENTS

Acknowledgements		vii
Note for Readers		ix
Introduction: Building Creative Capital		1
Chapter 1	The Creative Turn in Educational Discourse: Reality or Rhetoric?	17
Chapter 2	Young Playwrights' Ink	31
Chapter 3	Deaducation: Why Schools Need to Change	53
Chapter 4	Ethics 'Versus' Aesthetics: Best Frenemies?	73
Chapter 5	Aesthetic Politics and Creative Pathways	97
Chapter 6	Aesthetics and Innovation	113
Chapter 7	Animating Culture Or: Where has all the Magic Gone?	127
Chapter 8	Creative Industries Or Creative Imaginaries?	151
Chapter 9	Our Creative Century: Toward a New Aesthetic Imaginary	171
Index		183

ACKNOWLEDGEMENTS

My deep gratitude to my friends, passionate co-thinkers and vibrant, committed community of creative, arts education, and arts-based researchers and scholars, most especially Enza Gandolfo, Christine Sinclair, Clare Hall, Mary Ann Hunter and Robyn Ewing. Additional thanks for conceptual and editorial engagement with these draft chapters from my generous and valued colleagues, most especially: Mary Lou Rasmussen, Melissa Wolfe, Elena Petrova, Emily Gray, Genine Hook, Julie Faulkner, Sally Newman, Simone White and the Monash University writers group readers of an early draft of The Creative Turn chapter.

Thanks also to the collaborators, participants, and friends who dreamed up and implemented the case studies featured here. Those from *Culture Shack*: Mary Rose McLaren, Andrea Lemon, Brett Reynolds, Sonja Dare, Nantali Indongo, Jon Staley, Kate Kantor, Michael White, Merophie Carr, Maria Vella, Jennifer Barry, Darren Brown, Tin Nguyen, Julie Ung, Vineta Ioapo, Atong Deng, Abul Adub, Aluel Aleer Chut, Mava Valu, Mele Vi, Achai Deng, Piath Thuoc, Sunday Deng, Ana Faafetai, Joy Ioapo, Eseta Ioapo, Andrea Malut, Ayat Malut, Jaclin Dimo, Andrea Dimo, Afreem Sagor, Dona Malaish, Abuk Deng, Linda Deng, Winy Anai Majok, Tran Ho, Akec Diing, Ayen Diing, Quynh Quach, Ben O'Mara, Patrick O'Neill, Sarah Wallace, Nick Donaldson, Demian Shipley-Marshall, Samantha Trewin, Angie Manifavas, John Carreon, Huy Le, and all others inadvertently overlooked – thank you all for your incredible passion! From *Teaching Diversities*, my thanks to my collaborators Bree McKilligan, Lian Low and Greig Friday; to our inspiring advisory group and critical friends, among them Darren Grainger, Dr Greg Curran, Roz Ward, Associate Professor Anne Mitchell, Dr Shanton Chang, Dr Maria Pallotta-Chiarolli, and to those who will remain anonymous who shared their stories and experiences of being 'multi'. From *SAILing into Uni!*: Adiba Jalaly, Achai Deng, Catherine Kuol, Dona Malaish and Vivian Simon, Belinda Crockett, Ruth Klein, the Sudanese Australian Integrated Learning Program including Nik Tan and Sophie Tolich and the students at all campuses; and lastly but certainly not least, those stalwarts of New York City's Young Playwrights Inc.: Artistic Director extraordinaire Sheri Goldhirsch, who always says yes and has been an inspiration to me since I met her at 19 years of age, and continues to teach me about the beauty and efficacy of humbly doing the work despite enormous odds and at great personal cost, and to Brett Reynolds who makes each new generation of young people believe that being a playwright is something noble, worthy and fun. Thanks also to the interviewees included in this book from the many hundreds of Young Playwrights Festival alumni, particularly Tish Durkin, Madeleine George, and Greg Clayman. Thanks to my colleagues in creativity, new media and the arts at the Faculty of Education at Monash University and elsewhere, who sustain me in this often-unpopular work. Thanks to copyeditor extraordinaire Rebecca Miller for both her technical and conceptual engagement in preparing this

ACKNOWLEDGEMENTS

manuscript for publication, and to my wonderful editors Bharath Sriraman and Michel Lokhorst at Sense Publishers, thank you for making a home for this work.

Above all, thanks to Ruth, Luna and Tasha for making this house a home, and for making all things not only possible, but always fun and creative.

NOTE FOR READERS

Figure 1. Melbourne graffiti, #1 (2013).

This book has been designed to be read in conjunction with the digital compendium for the book, found at the website of the Creative Research Hub:

> http://www.creativeresearchhub.com/#!books-and-projects/c619

By clicking on the 'digital assets' button for this book, readers can view the videos, still images, and educational resources that accompany – and are commented upon in – the critical analysis of this text.

The three main projects that provide the empirical data for this book include:

Culture Shack

Sailing into Uni

and

Teaching Diversities

By clicking on these three tabs viewable on the book page, you will be taken to each set of videos and other digital assets as you read.

Enjoy!

INTRODUCTION

BUILDING CREATIVE CAPITAL

The diversion of commodities from specified paths is always a sign of creativity or crisis, whether aesthetic or economic. (Appadurai, 1986, p. 26)

What McLuhan suggested in those seminars is that creativity is the perfect antidote to all fear of change. (Lamberti, 2012, p. 44)

Figure 2. Culture Shack self-portrait Rania (2010).

INTRODUCTION

A student teacher walks into a first-year creativity unit at a popular university. She grumbles that she is "being made" to take creativity ("I haven't got a creative bone in my body!") and she believes this is a waste of time. The lecturer explains that he doesn't have a mathematical bone in his body, but he was still made to take numeracy and literacy in school in order to have the baseline skills necessary to be competent in contemporary society. "Well I'm paying good money for this, it had better be relevant," she fumes, and throws herself into a seat. When the lecturer begins, he starts by sharing some of his creative expertise, beginning with several degrees in fine arts (dance), and professional productions and awards. The student raises her hand. "So is everyone creative or not? Because if you're trying to say you have to be special or something, this is not going to be very relevant to us then, is it?"

DON'T I KNOW YOU . . . ?

The conundrum of understanding, practising or teaching contemporary creativity is that it wants to be all things to all people. Almost all modern lists of creativity, creative thinking and how-to 'becoming creative' books begin with one premise: the creative individual/artist is not special, rather each of us is creative in a special way. This is the basis upon which teachers of creativity in its generalist forms 'sell' the content to unwilling buyers. But, increasingly, industry and education leaders are claiming that creativity is the one skill or disposition that can take us into the prosperous future, so everyone needs it. Therefore, everyone must be able to have or develop it. In educational terms, it is becoming a basic skill. Yet centuries of association between aesthetics, mastery and creativity are hard to dismantle. The contradiction between what the lecturer above *said*, and what he *did*, represents the schizophrenic search for a clear definition of creativity, and how to benefit from it as a commodity.

What is creativity and can it be taught? This question, in its many guises and applications, has been around forever, rather like the student who never graduates. As Deleuze points out, no philosophy of creativity can be considered a historically (Lundy, 2012). Benjamin and McLuhan head-dunk us into thinking culturally about creativity, including its more elusive aspects like unpredictability and reproducibility, two characteristics moving to the foreground as 'innovation' and 'value'. But what, in the end, is it?

These days, it is increasingly difficult to discuss creativity without reference to business, industry and innovation. Why do we love to think of creativity in this way and no longer as that rare visitation of the muse or the elite gift of the few? Is it a democratisation of creativity? Partly. It also may just be part of the recommodification of everything, and now it's creativity's turn. This book explores the possibility that it is taking a turn, what that turn might be, and how it relates to industry, education and, ultimately, changing the nature of aesthetics for our new era. No small task. Perhaps an impossible task. But there is one thing all the experts agree on: creativity is undefinable, possibly unteachable, largely unassessable, and becoming the most valuable commodity in the 21st-century market.

Hartley et al. (2012) tell us that "the abstract noun 'creativity' was first recorded in English in 1875 and was next found in the early twentieth century in phrases such as 'creative education' (1936) . . . the modern usage of creativity therefore is a product of the mid-twentieth century and the modern West" (p. 66). Its most visible modern incarnation a century or so later comes as the split between discourses that name it as creative learning—largely in the UK (Sefton-Green et al., 2012; Burnard, 2006; Craft et al., 2001; Thomson & Sefton-Green, 2011) (more in Chapter One)—creative industries (Australia, the UK and the USA) and creative pedagogies (Canada and Australia). Creative approaches to research continue to expand and improve in both quality and quantity. Yet the turn toward commodification—in educational parlance, 'standardisation'—can be seen across all these areas.

This book is primarily about creativity in relation to education, not industry or management or science or mathematics per se, or anything else it might and probably does apply to in this day and age. Creativity in education is both different from other areas and harder to pin down due to education's inherently risk-averse nature. The writing of this book has arisen partly through my academic research over the past few years, but also from my original training and professional experience as a playwright in New York City. It was at the intersection of my expertise as a professional playwright, my eleven years' experience as a high school teacher, and finally my emerging identity as an academic researcher, that I began to see both parallels and contradictions in the ways that I and many others think about arts, education, youth and creativity. These seemingly compatible notions and discourses include increasingly contradictory components such as aesthetics, expertise, mastery, participation, innovation and industry. On one hand is the nearly unassailable and glitteringly elitist/exclusionary notions of brilliance, genius or creativity: how to define it, do it, teach it. On the other, the murky waters of education, pedagogy and inclusion: arts education. And so this book represents something of a coalescing of movements, discourses and changing practices: arts education, creativity as an economic imperative, and the neoliberal co-option of creativity as innovation.

Often, arts education becomes the tattered handbasket that we are all 'going to hell' in. The arts are there for the purposes of not judging, having a go, not focusing on expertise but rather participation—all of which are honourable and absolutely essential characteristics of the good teacher, yet which in the process almost completely erase the expertise required to be a good artist. Are the two things incompatible? I don't think so, and many before me have argued these points; later in this introduction I will begin with a brief overview of some of them. However, we inhabit an era in which the notions of 'creativity' and 'innovation' are increasingly moving away from embodied education, the arts and social critique—some of their previous social roles. In many ways this might be a good thing—it opens a window of opportunity/possibility that creativity is once again plaguing some very good minds, and it presents a newly-democratised ideology of creativity—

anyone can do it, it can sell, etc. Gone are the 'artist in the garret', La Boheme/ Rent portrayals of creatives who are tragic, rebellious, and who die of love and poverty. Gone too is the notion of the muse. These days the muse, if it still exists or visits this plane at all, can be more readily found at Pixar Studios or in Apple's innovation labs. In my day, many self-respecting playwrights wouldn't be caught dead writing for television—today almost all are, and not just to make a living. Some of the most creative writing in popular culture today can be found in serialised television from HBO, Showtime, and other networks. It is now seen by many as both profitable and highly creative. On the other hand, creativity is being decoupled from the notion of the arts—which (as Hickey-Moody, 2013; O'Brien & Donelan, 2008 and others have recently articulated) is often the last bastion of the 'at risk'—while being increasingly coupled with innovation, marketplace, industry and productivity, and thereby the future hope of all de-nation stated and newly-globalised cultures and societies.

This book articulates a creative 'turn' as moving away from performative/ performed creativity, which has been tied inexorably to an embodied performativity of various kinds. Judith Butler famously developed a notion of performativity as repetitive acts, which constitutes a cumulative gender and sexual identity (1997) over time. This repetition of acts creates the thoughts, values and eventually ritual practices that constitute (in Butler's canon) gender. Here, creativity is similarly irreducible to a single identity or fixed person, but rather becomes exemplary of a series of acts, performed in both embodied and disembodied ways, which eventually lead to thoughts, values and ritual practices culturally constituted as 'creativity'. This set of meanings is changing, and in this book is identified as a creative turn.

Denzin (2003) and others have combined theories of performativity with a critical approach to education and ethnography, in order to articulate a complex understanding of the ways in which classrooms are cultures that are inherently performative, culturally productive, and risky businesses. His notion of seventh moment performative research pushes us to understand identity and research both as serial events, simultaneously both embodied and disembodied, creative and reproductive. The creative turn may be urging us toward a merging of embodied (performed) with disembodied (digital) spaces, ritual acts and identities, and for this Appadurai is endlessly helpful.

THE IMAGINARY

Appadurai famously articulated the notion of the 'imaginary', made up of five 'scapes', including mediascapes, ideoscapes and ethnoscapes. His work was prescient in relation to the current globalised flows engined by digital media and characterised by intercultural border crossings (Harris, 2012). Appadurai's notion of a new 'imaginary' as a social structure-in-the-making, and how his imaginaries and social structures are co-constitutive, is at the heart of my engaging him here. Cumulatively, his 'scapes' serve to constitute the notion of the imaginary as a social field, which is both future-focused and also already existent. Through intersecting scapes, participant-citizens co-create new modes of social organisation and emergence that are based in current capabilities and identities as well as emergent ones; driven by intersubjectivities and also capital flow structures and nation-states. Creativity is one such flashpoint in contemporary global culture, now 13 years into the twenty-first century, just as it was in the 1930s when Walter Benjamin and others began to wonder at the ways in which reproducibility was affecting and would further affect the mystical or undefinable embodied nature of artefacts, including original artworks. The very move to reproducibility changes the original object. The quest for a reproducible creativity today echoes many aspects of Benjamin's argument, which offers some assistance as we try to make sense of our current transit. When Marshall McLuhan famously quoted 'the medium is the message' some years after Benjamin's seminal essay (1936), the sense of cultural anxiety about just how great a role such 'media of reproducibility' would play was evident. Flash forward sixty years from McLuhan, eighty years after Benjamin, and arts and cultural artefacts are only more rapidly reproducible, and creativity less understood. When Apple and Pixar are able to hire some of the brightest creative minds in the world and offer them the place and the means to 'be creative' without a day job, is the market driving creativity or creativity driving the market? This book attempts to grapple with such questions.

I draw on Appadurai's imaginary as a lightning rod for helping to understand a range of changes evident in creativity discourses across multiple fields: education, economics, arts, technology and design, yet he was not the only one to suggest that a creative crisis was on its way. Appadurai borrowed from Anderson in exploring 'imagined communities' (see Chapter Eight), and Walter Benjamin and Marshall McLuhan (Chapter Seven) in considering creative reproducibility and the modern productivity imperative, and I too can't escape a return to Benjamin. Extending Benjamin helps to unpack the creative turn this book seeks to identify, as constitutive of the split between 'performed' and 'digital' or 'embodied' and 'disembodied'. Benjamin and McLuhan both foresaw it and help us to understand why 'creativity and innovation' are now conflated in rampant and proliferating discourses of technology and all things digital, while so often the embodied arts is abandoned or decoupled from explorations of creativity.

In addition, this book is imbued with the soft wash of education theory—in this case arts education theory—but importantly one that is floating in the sea of socio-cultural theory and speeding away from the shore of performance ethnography as it sails toward *reproducibility* and away from *embodiment*. Like the Frankfurt School, which parted ways with Marxism in trying to understand 20th-century capitalism, this book traces some ways in which creativity is parting ways with arts practice in education, signalling a 'creative turn' in understanding the commodity value of education. Through three case studies, I show how this turn both methodologically (in research terms) and epistemologically (in discursive terms) heralds a new way of understanding the role—indeed the need—of creativity in a globalised age of what Benjamin called 'mechanical reproduction' and what we now know as digital reproduction. But I also explore the possibility that creativity itself is changing in nature, not just in role and reception.

Like those in the Frankfurt School, this current creative work is inexorably practiced and theorised against a backdrop of social change, global mobility, and interculturality, and as such is a 'critical' project. As arts-based research can be considered inherently applied, or immersive or generative research, the act and the critical theoretic of any kind of new creativity or new examination of creativity and its relationship to art and innovation, must itself be both action-based and critical. For this reason, this book alternates in its structure between critical theoretical chapters (which seek to unpack the ways in which creativity is changing, in both expansive and more narrowing ways), and case study examples of that unpacking, in order to remind readers that our theoretical adventures must always be tied back to shore.

Beauty Sticks Like Glue

Despite the changes that come and go in discourses of creativity and its cultural positioning, aesthetics remains a constant in the sea of culturally-buffeted creative chaos. Here too Benjamin can play a role in helping us navigate these stormy waters. Chapter Six draws on Benjamin's notion of the 'decline of the aura' and the decay of myth. If the myth-value was lost in the process of mechanisation, perhaps Benjamin would have much to say to Appadurai's notion of a new imaginary in which mediascapes both expand and contract the possibilities for global human creative endeavour. It may well be that in the end this book is not proposing a new aesthetic imaginary, but rather an anti-aesthetic imaginary focused on reproducibility. Yet even as I write this I hear Steve Jobs' creative-innovation-imperialist cry "beauty sells!".

So the role of aesthetics remains firmly and undeniably at the heart of a contemporary turn in ways of thinking about (and doing) creativity. There are of course multiple 'turns' occurring simultaneously, and not all in the same direction. Massumi (2002) and Clough and Halley (2007) for example explore an 'affective turn' that represents new possibilities at the nexus of technology, bodies and politics. Unsurprisingly, most theorising of 'turns' involve changes in understanding of not only cultural but economic conditions. Whether the cultural and economic impact of the current creative shift constitutes an irrevocable influence over the ways in which we understand and pursue 'creativity' remains to be seen, but one thing is certain: creativity is no longer the primary territory of the arts or aesthetics.

Pop-education commentator Ken Robinson has articulated perhaps the most simplistically misleading indicator of this new link between creativity and economics in his oft-quoted definition that creativity is "the process of having original ideas that have value" (2008, n.p.). But less often discussed is the question "of value to whom?"—a question now driving creativity discourses today, in a range of disciplines, fields and sectors. McWilliam defines creativity as "the defeat of habit by original ideas" (n.d.), a definition equally compelling for its simplicity, but does it really tell us anything useful about how to understand, practice or nurture creativity?

This introduction sets the scene for a broad discussion of the ways in which the changing notion of creativity as a 21st-century conceptual framework is impacting multiple sectors, including education, economics and industrial innovation. While cultural theorists and government and industry advisors are quick to theorise the need for creative and innovative capacity-building, the education sector struggles to identify quantifiable ways in which to effectively train the next generation in these skills and capacities, indeed to decide at all whether creativity is valuable to schools as a 'transferable skill', as a holistic time-out from more 'academic' subjects like literacy and numeracy, or as discipline-based tuition in arts-based skills and theory.

To this end, the introduction will offer a brief overview of the places in which creativity is present—and markedly absent—and will set the scene for the chapters that follow, inspiring readers to think more critically about the depth and breadth of our real creative potential as teachers, innovators, workers and lifelong learners. As such, this introduction will establish the ways in which a contemporary discussion of creativity cannot exclude industry any more than it can aesthetics. The structure of the chapters will follow this dual narrative, and borrow from three significant case studies which exemplify different aspects of the aesthetic/industry divide.

THE ARTS AND CREATIVITY: A 20TH-CENTURY MARRIAGE?

Twentieth-century discourses of creativity in education were inextricably linked to the arts: arts education, arts approaches, arts and play, and grew out of a rich period of innovation and educational enhancement from about the 1850s, in which children were increasingly invited to play, imagine and create as part of their education. It was good for all, and focused predominantly on experiences, processes and whole-student pleasure. Then, almost exactly one hundred years ago, Franz Cižek pioneered the child-centred art education movement by casting attention on the pedagogical value of the creativity and imaginations of the young children who became his visual art students, eventually inspiring arts educators across the globe. In an era of largely transmissive teaching practices, Cižek was certainly ahead of his time in recognising the value of both allowing children to experientially express (if not teach) themselves by way of unstructured arts activities, but also in nurturing and recognising its pedagogical value. For Cižek, the arts were a way of knowing.

Others quickly followed in his path, and especially in the first half of the century both creativity and arts education discourses, were characterised by an attention to aesthetics (by those like Dewey, Piaget and Bruner) now almost completely absent. By the second half of the century those like Eisner, Gardner and Heathcote were turning to the transferability of these experiences, skills and ways of thinking. Gardner's educational psychological approach to human creativity distinguished between *domain* and *field*: the domain is a set of practices associated with an area of knowledge; the field consists of the individuals and institutions that render judgments

INTRODUCTION

about work in the domain" (Gardner, 1996, p. 152). Jerome Bruner countered the theories of Piaget and saw art as a 'way of knowing' that made room for multiplicity rather than unification, perception rather than positivism, and embraced a narrative mode over paradigmatic modes of thinking. These thinkers and others, including Shirley Brice Heath (born c. 1950) and Maxine Greene (b. 1917), advocated passionately for the primacy of arts and creative pedagogies at all levels of schooling, often highlighting the benefit of links with industry, creative and otherwise. Many of them integrated their interrogation and advocacy of arts education and creative endeavour with other epistemologies of learning theory, such as Bloom's taxonomy for scaffolded learning. They and their approaches are emblematic of a century that embraced art and the arts in the field of education as vitally important, but often roughly cast apart from other more 'academic' subjects, or in relation to them.

For all intents and (arts education research) purposes, Tom Barone took over the torch from Elliot Eisner nearly thirty years ago and has largely been responsible for keeping the flame burning and aloft above arts education and research. He extended Eisner's argument about the need for a different kind of assessment focused on process rather than product, which most assessment continues to focus on. Then, in 2012, the two big guys of arts education research came together for the broadening out of their attention to methods and methodologies: *Arts Based Research* (Sage, 2011). Here they not only identified the what, where, why and how of arts-based research, and linked it often and well to education, but returned to their shared preoccupation with assessment (see, Chapter Eight: *What are some criteria for assessing arts based research?*). Most interestingly, however, they seemed to fall down the rabbit hole of epistemology in their acquiescence to articulating a schema in Chapter Ten: *What are some fundamental ideas from arts based research?* We seem to live in a time obsessed with a need to schematise, quantify and codify the characteristics of everything, and unfortunately the arts and creativity seem to be included.

Finally, while there are a number of continually-rolling 'new waves' in creativity research and discourses, they are by no means definitive or universally accepted (much as some will claim they are). Ken Robinson has sprung to the front of the pack with his widely watched online videos and popular books on creativity, imagination and education. He is popular partly because his message signalled the rise of the current wave, and partly due to the readability of his texts (both video and book). Behind Robinson's repositioning of creativity into the forefront of popular minds, to my mind there are four major discourses: these include **cognitive and education psychology creativity discourses**; **creative industries** and economies discourses (usually popular best seller formats or 'pop science' written by those in business, technology or urban development); **creative arts and aesthetics**; and **creativity in education** (roughly, arts education and digital and new media, which almost never intersect). Of these, this text primarily addresses the intersection (or not) of arts education and creativity discourses. Those mostly prominently addressing creativity in schools today include: framed as 'creative learning and teaching' (Anna Craft, Pamela Burnard, Ken Jones, Julian Sefton-Green, Pat Thomson, in the UK, amongst others); framed as creative arts partnerships (Maxine Greene, Howard Gardner, and Liora Bresler, amongst others in the USA); and in Australia Mary Ann Hunter and myself continue to work toward re-broadening the possibilities of creativity, curiosity and its applications in secondary and tertiary education. Australia's Centre for Creative industries continues to advance creative industries discourses, but contextualised more within the industrial sector and professional and digital art-making. The differences and similarities between these areas of enquiry and approaches to the study of creativity and education are in large part the topic of this book. Yet always at the centre of this book and these discourses is an acknowledgement of creativity's proliferating characteristics, discourses, and applciation, and the inconclusiveness of its definitions, measurements, and value.

Creativity and Aesthetics in the 21St Century

Recent research in both the UK (Arts Council UK, 2013; Jackson & Shaw, 2006) and Australia (McWilliam n.d.; 2009) has produced significant studies representing majority views within (largely tertiary) education around the interrelated notions of creativity and imagination, and the ways in which creative pedagogies and practices work together for both teachers and students. The links between creativity, teaching and learning, and 'academic success' are fairly consistent across these two national contexts and exemplify a theoretic of creativity put forward by Csikszentmihalyi (1999) and others. Both McWilliam and Csikszentmihalyi use a systems approach to interrogate ways of nurturing and cultivating creativity and innovation in education. Such a system (what Csikszentmihalyi calls domains) identifies both a schema of 'symbolic elements' or rules, and "its own system of notation" (1997, p. 37). This separation of symbolic from semiotic can be linked to Benjamin (more in Chapter Seven), and has been effectively applied within the Australian context by McWilliam. McWilliam's schema and case study represent one effective example of bridging the arts education and creative industries divide that this book in part sets out to do.

McWilliam frames today's creative turn not through a history of arts education in which teachers strove to link pedagogy, assessment and creativity, but through learning and social theorists who were not in the arts. From Florida and Csikszentmihalyi back to Koestler, Perkins and others, McWilliam lists those skills, attributes, dispositions and contexts which have been identified as conducive to creativity. She nails it with her recognition of the shift in education that seeks to "unhook creativity from 'artiness', individual genius and idiosyncrasy', and to render it economically valuable, team-based, observable and learnable, [making] it difficult for those who teach in higher education to step around creativity's challenge to traditional learning and teaching practice" (McWilliam, blog, n.d.). "Creativity," she claims, "has become less mystical." I disagree. The demystification of creativity we so desperately seek as educators, employers, and global economic actors in this conceptual economy is a chimera and a dream.

INTRODUCTION

With the renewed interest in claiming creativity for various sectors, there is a creative explosion of interest in re-examining and quantifying what creativity itself is. Some, like Salehi, see "in the history of ideas about creativity and art, a general continuity of agreement that creation takes place within chaos, and forms where chaos and order meet each other . . . [the] differences arise in conceptions of how to order chaos, who can order it, and what the function of such ordering may be" (2008, p. 282). This is of course the topic of this book, with a specific lens on who those creative powerful may be, who the producers of these new creative economies are, and how they are remapping imaginaries. However, it is clear that simply drawing on an arts-based history of creativity is not enough—these days creativity is squarely in the field of economics.

In ancient Greece, the 'muses' were the inspiration for creativity and the arts, but they were always also associated with a kind of mysticism, uncontainable sensuousness, and impetuousness. They do of course appear in various forms in most cultural mythologies, not only European. Since then, the notion of 'The Muse' has gone through many innovations, yet always feminised, and most often coquettishly choosing to 'visit' an artist or remain aloof, spoiling his chance of creative satisfaction and success. During the Renaissance, the focus shifted to the artist's relationship with the muse (which had become a kind of stand-in for 'inspiration'), and this relationship had the supernatural ability, it was believed, to allow man godlike qualities; if not The Creator then A Creator. Creativity came to be associated with transcendence, visionary abilities, and interpretation of the great mysteries that surround all human experience. Artists became mediums or—as it were—media. Today, creativity is once again found most readily in 'media'—but with a different connotation. Our media also tell us something about our increasingly singular world culture, global flows and knowledge economies; their insatiable need for creative products is linked to instantaneous dissemination in digital markets. The hurdle of 'embodiment' has been addressed somewhat in recent times by the explosion of YouTube, gaming and other video-based tools: not only can virtual creativity and collaboration be three dimensional, it can be loud, moved, and interactive in real time. Streaming is nothing but a digital expression of the spontaneity principal in creativity and collaboration. Once again—no differently to previous eras—the marketplace sets the need and context for our notions of creativity and artmaking. As Salehi reminds us:

> If we accept that the formation of a paradigm is related to the context in which it emerges, I believe that both modernist and post-modernist discourses of creativity have been responsive to the needs of capitalism as a system of nomadic power and of constant de/reterritorialization. Today, the process of commodification plays a vital role in the construction and experience of contemporary subjectivity as well as the notion of creativity subjecting people to free-floating and nomadic forms of control . . . .The Deleuzian world is a state of flux, a constant differentiation. Creation, in such a world, is driven by differentiation. The only way to affirm these underlying processes of differentiation is in 'creative becoming' (2008, p. 283).

The truth is that educators and theorists have been trying to demystify creativity for a long, long time—perhaps as long as we've been around and looking in mirrors (or at least writing about what we find!). The difference today is that our fear of the rapidity of digital change means that we have come to believe that we *need* creativity, not just that it would be a lovely treat. To need something that badly is as dangerous as loving the wrong person—it can lead us down dark alleyways and into deep waters. The problem is not in loving the wild child for a glorious, unfathomable fling; it's in wanting to marry her or him. In education and in industry both, we seem to want to marry creativity and settle down—one might wonder if this is against the very nature of creativity itself? What is the relationship between creativity and aesthetics (Vesna, 2007) in our contemporary context? While it appears to be moving from a central concern with aesthetics to productivity and innovation, this book examines whether or not this appearance can be supported with the evidence available to us now.

At the heart of today's creativity discourse is the persistent question of defining what creativity now is. This book problematizes this search, and what a singular definition of creativity could possibly provide. Why, for example, were Plato and his contemporaries more willing to accept creativity as an indefinable phenomenon, a mystery beyond our full comprehension? McWilliam has advanced the articulation of a definition of creativity for higher education. Yet any argument that attempts to address the 'we' of education—as this one does—must first acknowledge the danger of the 'we'. Is it primary, secondary, tertiary? Is it arts education, creative industries, fine arts, arts-based methods? While such distinctions may seem subtle, they represent cavernous differences in thought, approach, values, and often discourses, epistemologies and histories of practices. This book takes as its 'we' primary and secondary schools, but as they intersect with the growing discourse of creativity, but does not attempt to stake ground in defining creativity (as is done by so many elsewhere); rather it points out the contentious nature of these claims, definitions, and their implications. One reason for this is my resistence to the current need to argue these claims with statistical or other standardized forumulae. While media, policy makers and funders seem to be moving backward in their inability to consider use-value claims with any other way than statistical or other standardized measures, this book resists those imperatives and instead begins by acknowledging the rhizomatic and constantly proliferating definitions and expressions of creativity.

A NEW CREATIVE IMAGINARY

Definitions of creativity are becoming, for the first time, global discourses. Again, no real discussion of creativity, even in education, can fail to acknowledge that it has taken on an increasingly commodity/value/status aspect, as addressed in part by Appadurai. Through his theoretic of the imaginary, Appadurai allows us to see the ways in which things also have social lives circulating in different regimes of value (1986, pp. 3-7). Ken Robinson (2008) would love this assistance in identifying the real nature of 'value' when thinking about creative or aesthetic 'things' and where

INTRODUCTION

they fit, yet importantly, Robinson's quotable approach to creativity and its products and processes sails above such detailed investigations.

In addition, Appadurai's little-used notion of 'tournaments of value' (1986) might offer a way of considering Robinson's question of value in new ways. Might creativity be going through a period that resembles these tournaments of value, a 'turn' in which creativity is inexorably linked with its token value, its transactional value of a marketable good? Appadurai tells us that "what is at issue [in the tournaments] . . . is not just status, rank, fame or reputation of actors, but the disposition of the central tokens of value in the society in question," (1986, p. 21), applying the kind of thinking evident in Benjamin's seminal essay to a contemporary examination of reproducibility. In many ways, 'good' creativity (that is, creativity with value), must now be reproducible, scalable creativity.

Appadurai also productively links the increasingly decoupled notions of creativity and imagination. In his 2003 analysis of cinema and its impact on contemporary global culture, Acland notes:

> For Appadurai, focusing on human creativity, on the imagination, extends the possibilities of acknowledging the accomplishments of people as we struggle to find a way to live in the modern world. His project is to 'show that the work of the imagination, viewed in this context, is neither purely emancipatory nor entirely disciplined but is a space of contestation in which individuals and groups seek to annex the global into their own practices of the modern (p. 41).

Globalisation continues to impact on creativity. One might argue that creative industries generally—not just the contemporary film business—are industries and cultural practices that are contingent upon an intersection or fusing of the global and the local, in ways that highlight their interdependent nature. Co-creating imagined communities of collaborators and consumers through creative endeavour, arts products, practices and locations in contemporary society constitute sites of resistance against neoliberal encroachment and economic rationalist discourses, acting as " . . . an assemblage of practices, people, technologies, times, locations, and ideas. This assemblage resembles what Appadurai calls for in any theory of globalization—a linkage between the mobility of texts and contexts, and one that is empirically grounded" (Acland 2003, p. 43).

Any search for links between commodification, imagination and creativity leads us back to epistemologies of globalisation. For Appadurai, "globalisation is not simply the name for a new epoch in the history of capital or in the biography of the nation-state . . . it is marked by a new role for imagination in social life" (2000, p. 13 in Giri, 2004, p. 21). Such new imaginaries will be addressed further in Chapter Seven, where the relationship between creativity and cultural diversity makes itself felt through a featured case study. While cultural diversity is only nominally acknowledged in popular media that still demand cultural actors conform to the dominant culture, so too do schools represent a limiting 'scape', a diversity 'imaginary' in which students who seek diversity (whether cultural or creative) continue to feel out of place. Chapter Three's attack on 'Deaducation' unpacks this urgent need for schools to change or risk obsolescence. Creativity can or might represent the kind of methodological or pedagogical diversity that multiculturalism held as its ideal culturally. Creativity always offers the possibility of greater diversity, as is discussed further in Chapter Five.

Appadurai and other cultural theorists have focused (not always productively) on aesthetics, a move that has been problematised by Castronovo (2007), Benedict Anderson (2006), and others who seek to look beyond an attention to aesthetic beauty at the expense of equity and inclusion. For Appadurai, who claims that modern consumption culture "seeks to replace the aesthetics of duration with the aesthetics of ephemerality" (1996, p. 84), creativity and innovation have perhaps become interchangeable (think endless iterations of the iPod).

An Invitation

This text invites you to engage with such tangled discursive and epistemological threads, with a recognition that if there is a unifying problematic for today's function of creativity it is that no unified definition or function can be found. The rhizomatic nature of research, education, the media and industry itself suggests that whatever direction we move in is bound to be rhizomatic and web-like rather than mono-ideological or mono-directional. Chapter One's opening gambit identifies the 'creative turn' emerging in the early twenty-first century, one tied to digital technology but with no simple definition. Set against the context of education, this opening chapter serves as an establishment of creativity discourses as they shift from sector to sector. In higher education, creativity and innovation are increasingly conflated and leaving some behind. As standardised testing invades education systems worldwide, creativity's ability to morph and change to the demands of a productivity culture signals its reframing as 'innovation', a core skill and disposition of 21st-century learners and workers, but one that is increasingly inseparable from capital.

As a concrete example, Chapter Two draws upon the unique 30-year history of New York's Young Playwrights Festival (YPF) to investigate some long-term effects of professional creative engagement in adolescence—an opportunity increasingly unavailable in these fast-moving times. Here four alumni from this ground-breaking program draw on their experiences as professionally-produced teenaged playwrights in New York, through a lifetime of professional experience in a range of industries, in order to reflect on the transformative effect of that early experience. In this chapter I draw on Csikszentmihalyi to contextualise these deeply personal experiences, and unpack the increasing difficulty of creative engagement that unfolds over a lifetime. The chapter argues some ways in which educators, industry managers and professional creatives might learn from the YPF about defining success and creativity, and the myriad skills and dispositions that these ex-participants have brought into a wide range of industries, markets and aesthetic endeavours.

INTRODUCTION

Chapter Three's exploration of 'Deaducation' brings this critical meeting of creativity, innovation and aesthetics back to school where it started; to an acknowledgement that schools are falling further behind—not in the literacy and numeracy wars of educational discourses, like the proponents of a new standardisation would have us believe—but in a new version of Appadurai's mediascape that is organically overtaking school and siloed learning platforms through the rise of social media, open universities and the proliferation of online possibilities. The chapter highlights the need for schools to change in response to these innovations, and more quickly than they currently are.

In Chapter Four unpacks the need to see both an aesthetics and an ethics of creativity, by drawing on Deleuze's notion of 'becoming' as a lens for interrogating the nexus of creativity as it straddles the different discourses typifying the education/industry divide. Here Deleuze's notions of contingencies and flow help readers consider the ways in which creativity can productively help make the familiar strange, while also embracing contingency planning as creative industries discourses ask us to do. Central to any Deleuzian discussion of aesthetics and ethics, though, is the notion of 'letting go' as a capacity central to creativity and imagination, and Chapter Four invites readers to let go of static binaries as they consider the ways in which creativity inhabits these sometimes wildly different worlds.

Chapter Five, 'Aesthetic politics and creative pathways' draws on community-based case studies, with the shared features of integrated creative and cultural knowledges as central to the artmaking and research outcomes of the projects. This chapter looks closely at creative research, and some ways in which it can be transgressive while collaborative. Here I have drawn on Massumi's attention to creative relationship rather than aesthetics or outcomes, as a critical lens in helping to understand the power of creative capital in the words and works of the young people discussed in these two case studies. For Massumi, interactive art is intrinsically affective, an exchange that invites the Other in each of us to engage with the centre.

Chapter Six theorises the ways in which educational discourses might be limiting, rather than extending, how creativity is taught, learnt and assessed. The creative industries and economics sectors are setting the current understandings as well as funding structures for creativity, a marketplace imperative for valuing contemporary creative endeavour that will have an unmistakably limiting effect on both creativity and aesthetics, as culturally representative symbols and practices.

Chapter Seven extends Walter Benjamin's view of the 'mechanical turn' in artmaking to shed new light on the ways in which digital re/production is changing the notions of creativity and aesthetics, dissemination and representation. By positioning the current creative turn as a third turn after Benjamin's in the early twentieth century and McLuhan's in the mid-twentieth century, this chapter asks readers to consider the emergence of this new creativity as historically-situated, culturally co-constructed, and inherently economic. To illustrate the ways in which current creativity theorists echo both Benjamin and McLuhan, this chapter draws on a third and last case study: a digital animation project for gay and lesbian youth who purposefully experiment with different aesthetics for the creation and in some cases colonisation of more democratised online worlds.

Building on the 'imagined communities' made possible in new ways through this kind of digital creative use of online technologies, Chapter Eight leverages Benedict Anderson's scepticism of the nation-state to imagine new ways of nurturing creativity in schools that aren't singularly market-driven—as the emerging and powerful creative industries appear to be. Here I critique Appadurai's notion of 'scapes' as falling short in its ability to respond to our current need to create new aesthetic communities that can serve to organise beyond capital/industrial needs.

Chapter Nine asks readers themselves to imagine such new possible futures after the current creative turn, futures that may be characterised by a new aesthetic not yet known. Drawing on the theoretical and case study analyses, which exemplify a range of ways of reading creativity's contemporary commodification, I propose one aesthetic possibility that suggests the ways in which Appadurai's flows and imaginaries might combine fruitfully with McLuhan's futurism to assist us in separating an innovation discourse of creativity from an aesthetic one. In closing, a new 'aesthetic imaginary' is proposed that resists neoliberal productivity discourses and moves instead toward a recognition of the ways in which productive failure, contingency and risk-taking might benefit a creativity that can serve different authentic roles in emerging contexts—some of which we don't yet see or even anticipate. I hope you enjoy the book, but more importantly that you feel engaged enough after finishing it to dream your own aesthetic imaginary and extend this creative conversation in much-needed ways.

REFERENCES

Acland, C. R. (2003). *Screen traffic: Movies, multiplexes, and global culture*. Durham, NC: Duke University Press.

Anderson, B. (2006). *Imagined Communities: Reflections on the origin and spread of nationalism*. London, UK: Verso.

Appadurai, A. (2004). The capacity to aspire: Culture and the terms of recognition. In R. Vijayendra & M. Walton (Eds.), *Culture and public action* (pp. 59–84). Stanford: Stanford University Press.

Appadurai, A. Grassroots globalization and the research imagination. *Public Culture, 12*(1) (winter 2000), 1–19.

Appadurai, A. (1996). *Modernity at large. Cultural dimensions of globalization*. Minneapolis: University of MN Press.

Appadurai, A. (1986). Introduction: Commodities and the politics of value. In A. Appadurai (Ed.), *The social life of things: Commodities in cultural perspective* (pp 3–63.). Cambridge, MA: Cambridge University Press.

Arts Council UK. (2013). *Creative industry finance*. Retrieved from http://www.artscouncil.org.uk/funding/apply-for-funding/creative-industry-finance/

Benjamin, W. (1936/1973). The work of art in the age of mechanical reproduction. In *Illuminations* (pp. 211–244). London, UK: HarperCollins.

Burnard, P. (2006). *Creativity in education*. London, UK: Routledge.

Butler, J. (1997). *Excitable speech: A politics of the performative*. New York, NY: Routledge.

Castronovo, R. (2007). *Beautiful democracy: Aesthetics and anarchy in a global era*. Chicago, IL: University of Chicago Press.

INTRODUCTION

Clough, P., & Halley, J. (Eds). (2007). *The affective turn: Theorizing the social*. Durham, NC: Duke Univ Press.
Craft, A., Jeffrey, B., & Leibling, M. (Eds). (2001). *Creativity in education*. New York/London, NY: Continuum.
Csikszentmihalyi, M. (1999). Implications of a systems perspective for the study of creativity. In R. Sternberg (Ed.), *Handbook of creativity* (pp. 312–335). New York, NY: Cambridge University Press.
Denzin, N. (2003). *Performance ethnography: Critical pedagogy and the politics of culture*. Thousand Oaks, CA: Sage Publications.
Gardner, H. (1996). The creators' patterns. In M. A. Boden (Ed.), *Dimensions of creativity* (pp 143–158). Boston, MA: MIT Press.
Giri, A. K. (Ed.). (2004). *Creative social research: Rethinking theories and methods*. Lanham, MD: Lexington books.
Harris, A. (2012). *Ethnocinema: Intercultural arts education*. The Netherlands: Springer.
Hartley, J., Potts, J., Cunningham, S., Flew, T., Keane, M., & Banks, J. (2012). *Key concepts in creative industries*. London, UK: Sage.
Jackson, N., & Shaw, M. (2006). *Imaginative curriculum study: Subject perspectives on creativity: A preliminary synthesis*. Lancaster: The Higher Education Academy.
Lamberti, E. (2012). *Marshall McLuhan's mosaic: Probing the literary origins of media studies*. Toronto, CAN: University of Toronto Press.
Lundy, C. (2012). *History and becoming: Deleuze's philosophy of creativity*. Edinburgh: Edinburgh University Press.
Massumi, B. (2002). *Parables for the virtual: Movement, affect, sensation*. Durham, NC: Duke University Press.
McWilliam, E. (n.d.). *Creativity is core business*. Retrieved from blog post: http://www.ericamcwilliam.com.au/creativity-is-core-business/
McWilliam, E. (2009). Teaching for creativity: From sage to guide to meddler. *Asia Pacific Journal of Education, 29*(3), 281–293.
Robinson, K. (2008). *Sir Ken Robinson on the power of the imaginative mind (part one)*. Retrieved from Transcript Edutopia: http://www.edutopia.org/sir-ken-robinson-creativity-part-one-video
Salehi, S. (2008). *Teaching contingencies: Deleuze, creativity discourses, and art*. Unpublished doctoral thesis, Ontario, Canada: Queen's University. Retrieved from http://qspace.library.queensu.ca/handle/1974/1209
Sefton-Green, J., Thomson, P., Jones K., & Bresler, L. (2012). *The Routledge international handbook of creative learning*. Routledge Chapman & Hall.
Thomson, P., & Sefton-Green, J. (2011). *Researching creative learning: Methods and issues*. UK: Routledge.
Vesna, V. (2007). *Database aesthetics: Art in the age of information overflow*. Minneapolis: University of Minnesota Press.

CHAPTER 1

THE CREATIVE TURN IN EDUCATIONAL DISCOURSE:

Reality or Rhetoric?

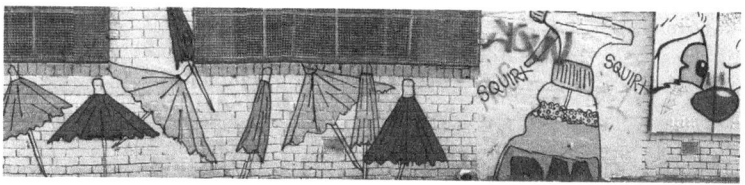

Figure 3. Melbourne graffiti, 1 (2013).

Creativity is a word that comes with baggage. In some circles it hints at genius, in others to dodgy accounting practices. (Smit, in Craft, 2005, p. xiv)

INTRODUCTION

Education as a sector, and as an institutionalised backwater of experimentation, can often feel like one's elderly dog—a bit scruffy and always barking at the wrong stranger at the wrong time. Often with liminal cultural issues, education lags behind—whether it's cultural diversity, pedagogical diversity, or the purpose of organised education at all. Creativity in education suffers a bit from the pedagogical spirit is willing but the institutional funding flesh is weak. This book does not seek to advise the reader about ways of learning creatively, or of innovative approaches to curriculum or pedagogy, or to further commodify creativity so that educators or entrepreneurs might read it for an hour before falling asleep to find new hope for their creative futures. In this book I use education as a flashpoint for looking more closely at a change in the way creativity is both perceived and pursued in contemporary culture. And like your old dog, she may be a bit inappropriate at times, but still has a job to do.

Craft (2005; 2001) and others have convincingly argued the universalisation of creativity research, in particular providing an excellent overview of the ways in which creativity discourses have been politically and pedagogically commodified, and to some degree co-opted from aesthetics and education discourses into economic ones. In this way, any contemporary creativity discourse bears upon the education sector but also more widely. One preoccupation with almost every interrogation of creativity, however, is how these discussions are accelerating in other fields, and slowing down in education. So this is where I will begin.

CHAPTER 1

In his search for a universal definition of creativity, Salehi (2008) concludes that "the literature indicates that there is no widely accepted definition" (p. 26). Yet he, like Cropley, agrees that creativity transcends the kinds of psychological schemas that previous generations have sought to create and offer the world to better understand, serve and nurture creativity. It is more than "a matter of cognitive processes such as knowing, thinking, recognizing, remembering, or puzzling out, but . . . also involves factors such as motivation, personal properties, and feelings" (Cropley, 1999, p. 517), they both claim, but schema for measuring and nurturing creativity continue apace. Some scholars have sought since then to redefine creativity in education as creative pedagogies, creative learning and most recently creative industries, but others continue to pursue a cognitive or capital measure of the elusive creativity. Well into the second decade of the twenty-first century, it seems clear that creativity is becoming a commodity that is increasingly sought but still not well understood.

Creativity as innovation is increasingly present in educational discourses, inexorably linked to notions of productivity, while creativity for its own sake is more vilified than ever. While economics discourses pay homage to creative economies (Peters & Araya, 2010), creative classes (Florida, 2007), and creative industries (Lehrer, 2012), cultural theorists like Halberstam (2011) insist that the risk of failure necessary for true creative exploration is anathema to a global neoliberal culture, including (or especially) sectors like education. In this chapter I introduce the notion that the current discourses of creativity-in-education are actually a shrouded marketplace colonisation of the arts, artistic and creative endeavour and, as such, represent a gentrification of the imaginary. By drawing previous understandings of creativity into a contemporary discourse of productivity and returns, innovation can be framed as a creativity that is market- and product-driven, characterised by product development, industry expansion and marketability. This chapter argues that, within education, these distinctions must be articulated in order to advance the practice and understanding of creativity as an end in itself—a worthy affective endeavour vital to the mechanics of learning and growth—but simultaneously necessary to intervene in the marketplace colonisation of creative practice.

The notion of 'creativity as becoming' (Massumi, 2008) within education is steadily gaining traction, but any real idea of 'creativity as being', is long since dead. While those like Schulman (2012) note the hegemonising effects of gentrification as a spatial, economic and intellectual phenomenon in urban neighbourhoods and also minds, others have noted the ways in which educational standardisation and outcomes-focused learning have gentrified the possibility of failure in learning, cultures and classrooms around the world (O'Gorman & Werry, 2012; Halberstam, 2011; Ahmed, 2010). Creative arts teachers, particularly in secondary schools, have understood the broad value of the creative process for students (especially those struggling) in school contexts, but have made little headway in gaining time, place or status for such endeavours; indeed, they are steadily losing ground. Arts education advocates argue that vital to this creative process are such under-valued and increasingly outlawed activities as daydreaming, provoking, brainstorming and commemorating, and sometimes failing miserably in the conceptual endeavour attempted.

In creative arts classrooms, these failures have been acceptable—indeed welcomed—by those who understand their generative power, not just as part of the 'process' of learning and inventing/expressing, but as ends in themselves. With the slow global spread of standardisation, however, these spaces and places for experimentation are drying up. Trial and failure as sites of creative potential are becoming a thing of the past, like rotary phones, down time, and getting lost. But despite countless efforts to lock down not only the 'what' of creativity, but the 'how' of it, we must remember that "definitions of and assumptions about creativity are unstable, are subject to historical periodic re-interpretation, to new associations, and that these shifts in a general understanding of creativity are very much a political function of the discourses and power systems of their moments" (Salehi, 2008, p. 22). So whether in education or other sectors, this book does not attempt to give an exhaustive literature review of creativity discourses, or to colonise the multiple discourses as they emerge and shift: here I intend to explore some of the implications of this turn, both educational and cultural, and how it may lead us into new aesthetic territory, if only we stop tying it to the past.

Peters and Araya (2010) attempt to distinguish between definitions of 'creative,' including geographical, cultural and occupational, but they are all tied to industry and productive understandings of creative endeavour. Building on the 1990s knowledge economy, and Florida's (2007) articulation of the creative class that characterises our post-industrial culture, this new creative economy portends a shift from production to information, and calls for new "modes of education" (p. xvii) to accompany new modes of knowledge. Yet this new creative economy—reflected in schools—is never far from considerations of material conditions and capital. The *Creative Capital Report (2008)* (in Peters and Araya, 2010) defines "creativity in relation to artistic, scientific and economic creativity" (p. xvii); like Robinson (2010) and Joubert (2001), these are conceptualisations of creativity as 'original ideas that have value'. This chapter problematises the question of who is defining that value.

Ironically, the rhetoric of creativity is increasing in relation to schools and education. Yet the conflation of creativity with innovation is a form of ideological gentrification, in that while appearing to value the arts and creative endeavour it is really redirecting and narrowing the discourse of creativity into productive innovation and marketplace measures of value. And this more than anything signals the death knell of 'arts education,' which remains tainted by its relationship to risk, un-productivity (time-wasting, daydreaming) and 'failure'—all of which are increasingly impossible in a marketplace economy.

As O'Gorman and Werry (2012) tell us, "the right to fail (with all its promise of inclusiveness, generosity, freedom) can only be claimed at an ever-mounting cost" (p. 3). This chapter will not argue against the inevitable: it is clear that the move toward homogeneous success and productivity is (for now) irrevocable. To argue against it in education—arguably one of the most conservative sectors—would be in itself an act of flagrant failure. Rather, in this chapter I argue the possibility that the more standardised schools and the education sector become, the riper they are

CHAPTER 1

for transgressive spaces of alterity, creative resistance and even productive failure. Artists and artistry have always thrived in contradiction to a mainstream which seeks to contain and control them, and real artistry and creativity can be tracked and measured as a counter-movement that thrives in times of conservatism. Therefore, this chapter will argue that the 'standardising turn' in education opens creative possibilities not yet named, and that these possibilities stand in stark contrast to the current discourses of 'creative economies and creative industries'.

First I will argue for a decoupling of the notions of innovation (marketable creativity) and process-focused creativity. Second, I argue that the promotion of innovation in schools and industry is hostile to the notion of creative exploration in its very definition of seeking to 'sell' rather than 'interpret' culture to the masses. Third, I argue that, in order to re-embrace the notion of failure in schools and education, educators must redefine creativity as a necessary but un-'productive' choice for both themselves and their students, and revisit its desperately needed role in contemporary culture, especially as culture is expressed in the microcosm of classrooms.

The F Word (Failure)

> The fetishization of excellence and outcomes, the prevalence of 'audit culture' (Strathern, 2000) and prevailing instrumentalism and vocationalism, all institutionalize, codify and restigmatize failure. Now the encompassing regime of the test eclipses all other ways of understanding and valuing schooling: through standardized testing, student evaluations and bureaucratic measures of school 'performance', the threat of failure is the defining condition under which we (not just students but also teachers and institutions) operate (O'Gorman & Werry, 2012, p. 3).

As learners, teachers, and teacher-educators increasingly frame themselves within consumer cultures, we move away from what Sedgwick calls "the middle ranges of agency that offer space for effectual creativity and change" (2003, p. 13). If we are to reopen the possibility of real creativity in schools, we must remember what real creative engagement feels like, as well as its transgressive potential. Real feeling, like real creativity, always risks failure.

For most who are actively developing a discourse of productive failure in contemporary thought, the value of failure is articulated in relation to process. Educational discourses are challenged here due to their over-reliance upon outcomes-based analysis and assessments. In other words, the notion of failure can be productively adapted to educational contexts and discourses due to its focus on process versus product. This is one of the very core challenges facing educational discourses now. This chapter draws from those theorists in other fields (including but not limited to O'Gorman & Werry, 2012; Power, 2010; Halberstam, 2011; and Bailes, 2011) who are actively recruiting notions of failure in their cultural analyses, and I will seek to do the same here within a context of research in education.

On Daydreaming

Massumi (2008) considers something like daydreaming in examining the ways in which "thought and imagination are the leading edges of [the] exploratory expansion of potential, because they can wander from the particular present posture even without actually leaving it" (p. 11). We can easily acknowledge the value of wandering from the 'particular present' and the productive value of imagination—both necessary traits of the good researcher. Yet as teacher-educators, are we equally willing to push our pre-service teachers into intimate contact with the imagination—the 'not yet'—when all they so often want are facts? Secondary school timetables leave little room for unstructured time at all, particularly the kind that amounts to nothing more than 'daydreaming' and exercising the imagination. In fact, popular depictions of school have always equated daydreaming (Jane staring out the window) with failure: disengagement, waste and sometimes lack of ability (both teacher's and student's).

Yet the need for pauses, escapes, down time and daydreaming have been noted by both education and creativity scholars (while still lamented by teachers everywhere). Daydreaming, or "moments of insight" (Lehrer, 2012, p. 64) are crucial to creative endeavour and anathema to school timetables and standardised curricula. Such free time produces an "ability to notice new connections" (p. 46) for curious learners, and perhaps unsurprisingly, "people who consistently engage in more daydreaming score significantly higher on measures of creativity" (p. 48). How then do schools straining under the demands of increasing performance measures clear an overburdened school day to make room for kids to wander in their minds (much less their bodies)? A new consideration of productivity seems to be indicated.

On Provoking

"Deleuze would always say that to really perceive, to fully perceive, which is to say to perceive artfully, you have to 'cleave things asunder'" (Massumi, 2008, p. 12), as creative artists well know. This is the provocation and failure required for newness of perception that is at the heart of creative endeavour (including in schools). Massumi recognises that "it is the opposite of disinterestedness" (p. 12) and teacher-artists too have argued for the value of down time, outsider thinking and meandering investigation (Harris & Staley, 2011). Failure is the bulldozer that can clear the decks for other, less structured business than the mind-numbing business-as-usual.

Brecht argued the need for taking away the blinding effects of emotion and spoon-feeding an audience (or class) a cathartic version of their lives that they can relax into (Jameson 2000). He believed that laying bare the overriding social conditions governing his spectators and actors lives was a gift of empowerment and the only real way to create agentic change. His expansion of the 'V-effekt' (or 'alienation technique') used theatre to make the familiar strange so that audiences would first be able to *see* their lives, and then *change* them.

CHAPTER 1

In some ways Brecht's approach was what today we might consider good pedagogy, in other ways not. Defining the difference between feeling and no-feeling is useful in educational discussions, in that emotion plays a starring role in the process of learning and motivation: sometimes as an enemy, and sometimes a friend. Teacher-educators now talk about classrooms as places of relationship, acknowledging that without good student-teacher relationships very little teaching or learning is possible. Yet relationships are imbued with (if not made up of) emotion. As teachers we are taught to avoid 'excessive' emotion, subjectivity, to pursue objectivity, and convey only facts, as if this were ever possible. We strive toward reliability, validity and balance. Students have learned this well: they ask us now for 'correct' answers, for data, for the key to unlock high achievement. There is no room for interpretation of what Heidegger called "the unconcealing process" (in Massumi, 2008, p. 73). Many students resent the very call to criticality as too hard or a waste of time.

For creative artists and thinkers, it is the opposite: "our thoughts are shackled by the familiar" (Lehrer, 2012, p. 128) and artists constantly seek states of consciousness in which awareness that "a single thing can have multiple meanings" (p. 129) becomes heightened. Lehrer claims that "the power of dissent is really about the power of surprise," (p. 129) and I would argue the same for creativity. Dissent is innovation, but pedagogy and curriculum teacher education hardly ever teaches the value of dissent, surprise and provocation: and when it does the students often complain that this is not what will 'prepare' them for good teaching—like lesson plans and assessment rubrics.

On Brainstorming

One understanding of the value of brainstorming (often at odds with productivity) distinguishes between brainstorming (most often a collective activity) and daydreaming (usually a singular one). In both pedagogical and creative terms, the benefits of both collectivity and singularity have been abundantly documented. In the context of a discussion about productivity and creativity though, our understanding of group work and outcomes can be more easily problematised.

Schools frequently celebrate an individual learner's "feeling of knowing" (Lehrer 2012, p. 81), yet demand group work in accomplishing set class tasks. Brainstorming is one such activity that remains central to pedagogical strategies, yet resists the kinds of individual assessment required by outcomes-based testing. As a result, brainstorming—like creativity—can be considered one of those activities with acknowledged value, but not measurable value. It is relegated to a 'formative' task or procedure, and its low value or status is subtextually apparent to students. By examining pedagogical practices like brainstorming (a collaboratively emergent activity), we can start to accumulate some recognition of the ways in which classrooms (if not education as an industry) do already recognise the necessity (if not value) of non-assessable, collaborative and generative activities. It is not such a great leap from there to considerations of creativity.

On Commemorating

Some writers (scholarly and otherwise) are now arguing the significant and many ways in which creativity is *not* equivalent to innovation, yet educational discourses continue to conflate them in both policy and pedagogy-related literature. Yet, even more than thirty years ago, scholars were trying to figure out what constitutes 'creativity' (as distinct from other things) in order to be able to teach, foster, or at least facilitate the conditions for it in our classrooms and students. It seems, generally speaking, that it's easier to agree on what creativity is *not* than on what it is. Balkin argues that it's not a synonym for "talent" (1990, p. 29) and asserts that "to create means to do" (p. 29), while Lehrer claims that creative types are also good at "rejecting, sifting, transforming, ordering, and . . . persisten[ce]" (2012, pp. 75-76). Creativity clearly has something to do with making the familiar strange, with combinations of both ideas (content) and approaches (strategies), and "the power of surprise" (Lehrer, 2012, p. 163).

If failure and hope share a connection, surely it can be found in creativity education. If scholars have convincingly argued that failure might signal a new space for hope in a clearly ailing capitalist context, then education is the context in which hope might be found on the blank slate of creativity. If students (and teachers) are allowed time, space and silence (the cheapest of all resources), and if creativity is (as Seelig claims) an "endless[ly] renewable resource" (2012, p. 75), surely the stage is set for innovation and change, and perhaps even —in purely in economic terms—the time is right for a 'creative turn' in education.

The C Word (The 'Creative' Turn)

Such notions of failure do not contradict hope and aspiration, but rather nurture them. In these creative life-worlds, hope can live side-by-side with the possibility that failure is no more than the promise of something better. If a creative turn in educational discourse can be seen, it is surely sitting in the sunny window seat of hope (Dolan, 2005; Giroux, 2002), a place where escape is possible and daydreaming is the business-at-hand.

In a 2009 US survey, Cushman found that a majority of students reported that their teachers almost never speak to them personally about "things that matter", over a quarter said that their teachers don't connect their learning to the "real world", and "only one in four students felt strongly that school let them use their abilities and their creativity" (2010, p. x). Do teachers prevent students from bringing their abilities, interests and creativity into their school-based learning? And if so, why? Perhaps spaces of escape, daydreaming and the possible feel too much like failure in the here-and-now.

CHAPTER 1

The UK's Open University conceives of creativity in education as now inextricably linked with ICT and technological innovation. Creativity and arts education researchers have built on a shift away from products and outcomes and turned to Gardner's notion of multiple intelligences and the role of processual creativity in education as a strategy (it is not coincidental that Craft—Britain's foremost scholar of creativity in education—takes as her definitional basis Gardner's 'creative learning', yet this like much scholarly discourse often remains UK- and US-centric). The shift beginning in the 70s and 80s showed a turn from individual creative abilities (as giftedness) to a more community-learner exploration of creativity as a quality or skill that can be nurtured. This shift might be characterised as "concerned with the ordinary, rather than the extraordinary" (Craft et al., 2001, p. 2). Such investigations and articulations invariably include how-to lists of the skills required for creative thinking and endeavour, including risk-taking, down time and time to play.

Craft et al. highlight the ways in which (mainly British) education discourses of creativity have shifted since the 1990s to focus on marketplace value, where "organizations now have good reason to develop democratic cultures that encourage creativity" (2001, p. 4) and in which education plays a policy role as well as an economic one. Ironically, economists now seem to be reiterating "precisely the pedagogic approaches that were being advocated by educationalists in the 1960s" (p. 4). Since then, Robinson and other educationalists (Thomson & Sefton-Green, 2010; Zhao, 2012; Craft et al., 2001) continue to note the ambivalence of governments, who while wanting to be seen to promote creativity, are seemingly foreclosing its possibilities within educational structures. Craft et al. claim there are three "contemporary discourses concerning creativity and education", including a) the role of creativity; b) the "reconceptualisations of the nature of creativity" (p. 5) and c) the restructure of appropriate (creative) pedagogies.

A wide range of scholars as well as popular writers (sometimes the same) have become engaged with the creativity in schools discussion (or, some say, debate). As Robinson argues, creativity like "education has more than economic purposes" (in Craft, et al., 2001, p. ix). Generally, these scholars/writers fall into two camps: those who believe there is a crisis in schools, that the nineteenth-century model on which they are still largely based must change to accommodate new learning models and contexts, including re-asserting the value of creativity in learning and achievement; and those who believe that schools are not in any crisis at all and that everyone shares an interest in increasing the role of creativity in schools (as long as it has a marketplace value outcome). The good news, clearly, for those of us who feel passionately about the need for creativity in education, is that creativity makes an appearance in both scenarios. Here I refer to this as the 'creative turn' in education, a shift of problematising that shares characteristics with the 'affective turn' that preceded it.

Robinson (2010, 2011, n.d.) has long claimed that schools essentially educate students out of their inherent creativity (both perceptual and activity-based). His now well-known argument is linked to his understanding of schools as industrial age institutions, purpose-built for forming children into workforces. His argument presupposes that all children are creative and both want to and enjoy engaging in creative endeavour. Further, his implicit argument might be summarised as the claim that every individual has an inherent creativity that we would wish to be nurtured and maintained into adulthood if only we were able. Not everyone agrees with Robinson's argument, but his accessible and engaging style of writing and speaking has won him many adherents. Robinson might be considered the exemplar of the first argument about schools and creativity summarised above.

Lehrer (2012) and Sefton-Green (2010; 2011; Thomson & Sefton-Green, 2010) might be considered proponents of the latter argument. They both argue along the lines of the need for, and inevitability and intrinsic value of, a growing creative economy as a characteristic of our 21st-century global context. Sefton-Green argues against the perceived crisis in schooling. He and Lehrer both argue, as do Craft et al. (2001) in the UK that the narrowing of educational curricula works contrary to the notion of collaboration, experimentation, innovation and creativity in schools, all skills generally now agreed as central to economic ascendency.

The economic rationalist influence of those like Florida (2007) and others, however, cannot be underestimated. Their arguments parallel each other, and it is within a globalised neoliberal context that the educational value of nurturing creativity is set. The one commonality here is their agreement about a need for new forms of measurement in relation to creative learning/endeavour/economies. All agree that statistical and standardised measures and outcomes are insufficient tools for understanding, measuring, and ultimately developing creative activities and ways of thinking. For creative educators, this is very good news.

'THE AURA OF THE LIFE BANAL, THE ART OF COOL'

(Massumi, 2008, p. 17)

> This idea of learning as something that can be bought, acquired, and then completed is deeply ingrained in popular culture. It is a comforting model... it is a simple model. Unfortunately, it is false. If it ever worked, it will not work anymore. The promise of the twentieth-century model of knowledge is an empty one today (Cormier, 2010, p. 513).

Change is scary—particularly so for schools and teachers, who hitch their market value to an outdated conception of 'knowing'. Most teachers lament the changes in the education system which render students as 'consumers' and teachers as 'facilitators' or 'service providers', and in my experience this extends from secondary teachers to TAFE to university educators. Yet, is this such a bad thing? Might it be a kind of liberation rather than failure? It is plain for everyone to see that facts, data (both soft and hard) and 'research' are all products that can now be easily acquired for free. For years, we in education circles have paid lip service to

CHAPTER 1

'lifelong learners' but now, perhaps, we have to become them ourselves. Payback is a bitch.

If our students can get 'data' at the touch of a fingertip, then why do they need us? As Cormier (2010) demands, our old models (and I would argue these are multiple models) of knowledge are empty. It is time to find meaning elsewhere. And yet, surprisingly perhaps, the students keep coming. They are not disappearing into a virtual world of free online self-education. Why? Zhao (2012) and others have noted the ways in which test scores do *not* equal real academic achievement or 'good education'. He highlights the danger of an "imagination-depleted education diet" (2012, para. 4). Yet even Zhao makes the mistake of conflating creativity, innovation and entrepreneurship.

The ruling-class strategy of co-opting art and artistic endeavour is not new. Massumi reminds us of the historical examples of both photography (see Walter Benjamin) and before that perspective painting, in which "the aesthetic event-value was captured by that political formation [the court] and translated into political prestige-value" (2008, p. 17). Similar claims might be made now in relation to the prestige-value of 'creativity' and its practical application within education. The contemporaries of Massumi's 19th-century court have realised in our era that creativity can be harnessed and employed for profit. Our 21st-century equivalent to the enlightenment royal court is not government (widely resisted as national curricula continue to roll out) but global marketplaces (who really stand to benefit from such creative colonisation). "The semblance that took off from the framed canvas was *reframed by the court institution, which gave it an abstract function integral to its own dynamic system*" (Massumi, 2008, p. 17, emphasis added). Even moreso (as Benjamin noted), photography prefigured the present moment in educational transformation in its role as a new kind of "marketed commodity object. What is the ghostly force of Marx's 'commodity fetishism' if not a semblance of life lived through consumer artifacts?" (Massumi, 2008, p. 17). Dolan and others argue against the simulacra of life, art and emotion, and her argument might have been a pedagogical one, in believing that "being passionately and profoundly stirred in performance can be a transformative experience useful in other realms of social life" (2005, p. 15). This kind of transferable awakeness is exactly what educational discourses often champion. Emotion and embodiment are central to this kind of experience of being, learning and doing.

Once a more detailed discussion of creativity reaches the skill-base necessary for creating the conditions for creative endeavour, most current discourses agree that the skills necessary for high achievement in standardised testing are often distinct from those that foster creativity. Whereas standardised learning and testing require good rote memorisation (Zhao, 2012), competition versus collaboration, a notion of right answers versus new solutions, and achievement versus innovation, creativity encourages multiplicity, diversity, undirected experimentation and often a lack of resolution. Creativity rhizomatically reproduces itself, and in so doing, reimagines the system in which it occurs:

> New needs and desires are created, even whole new modes of experience, which your life begins to revolve around. You have become, you have changed,

in interaction with the system. . . . It's a kind of double capture of mutual responsiveness, in a reciprocal becoming (Massumi 2008, p. 9).

As both Robinson and Florida note, an education system handed down to us from the industrial age is no longer effective, producing what amounts to students who are proficient in "assembly-line manufacturing" (Florida, 2007, p. 218) of facts and reproduced data. While Henry Ford's production innovation may have been genius for industry, it would never (then) have been articulated as creativity. Today, however, the notions of industrial adaptation and innovation are almost inseparable from the value (if there is any) of creativity, a lack of distinction readily apparent in Lehrer (2012).

While Lehrer draws heavily on market examples of innovation, including the old show pony Pixar Studios, he does not make a convincing case that Apple or Pixar's unprecedented rate of imaginative innovation can be called the same as Auden's poetry. By its very nature as market-driven, and because it seeks to standardise (iPods, iPhones, film franchises) rather than create anything unique and non-reproducible, one might argue that Lehrer's examples are the very antithesis of 'creative'. Like the popularity of Florida's co-option of 'creative', popular understandings of creativity are increasingly linked with business; even conceding the unprecedented economic and cultural influences of Pixar and Apple, one must acknowledge that these are not creative accomplishments but business ones, the supreme marketing strategy of tying aesthetics to consumerism, introducing the product that all people must then want, must then understand and must learn to be able to use. Apple and Pixar designers may be different from artists because they are creating a product required to have mass appeal. Yet such jobs are both the bane and friend of so many secondary teachers like me who tried desperately to lure young people into the arts and found the intrinsic value argument fell on deaf ears. We resort instead to the marketplace argument in favour of the arts, citing more often than not these very jobs. Teachers of arts (like myself) also often serve as role models demonstrating that really the arts don't pay, rather than as positive models of the holistic value of creative endeavour. For students and their parents, an acknowledgment that moderately talented accountants still usually make a better salary than artists is often the only real consideration in career counselling.

For teachers trying to nurture creative contexts in their classrooms, Australia's move toward standardised curricula and testing is also bad news. If Zhao is right that "creative entrepreneurship and test-driven curriculum standardization" (2012, n.p.) are contradictory notions, then Australia must learn from examples in the USA, UK and elsewhere. Sefton-Green (2011) draws explicit links between trajectories of creative learning in the UK and an emerging scene in Australia.

Conclusion (The Fetishisation of Performance)

As this chapter has attempted to show, the room for creativity in schools is being co-opted by an entrepreneurial imperative, colonised by marketplace concerns, and ideologically gentrified to death. The danger is not that schools will lose their ability to invite learners into creative and innovative spaces, but rather that we will teach them that the only productive creative endeavour is a profitable one.

In order to encourage our students and our pre-service teachers—the ones who will ensure an educational future here that is not standardised and returns to truly student-centred learning—to embrace the creative (and supremely pedagogical act of "asking questions and challenging the status quo" (Zhao, 2012, n.p.), teacher educators should consider the ways in which clearly articulated theories of creativity have resonance within educational discourses.

REFERENCES

Ahmed, S. (2010). *The promise of happiness*. Durham, NC: Duke University Press.
Bailes, S. J. (2011). *Performance theatre and the poetics of failure: Forced entertainment, goat Island, elevator repair service*. London and New York, NY: Routledge.
Balkin, A. (1990). What is creativity? What is not?. *Music Educators Journal, 76*(9), 29–32.
Cormier, D. (2010). Community as curriculum. In D. Araya & M. A. Peters (Eds), *Education in the creative economy: Knowledge and learning in the age of innovation* (pp 511–524). New York, NY: Peter Lang.
Craft, A. (Ed). (2005). *Creativity in schools: Tensions and dilemmas*. Abingdon/New York, NY: Routledge.
Craft, A., Jeffrey, B., & Leibling, M. (Eds). (2001). *Creativity in education*. New York/London, NY/UK: Continuum.
Cropley, A. (1999). Definitions of creativity. In M. A. Runco & S. Pritzker (Eds.), *Encyclopedia of creativity* (pp 511–524). San Diego, CA: Academic Press.
Cushman, K. (2010). *Fires in the mind: What kids can tell us about motivation and mastery*. SF: Jossey-Bass.
Dolan, J. (2005). *Utopia in performance: Finding hope at the theater*. Ann Arbor: University of Michigan Press.
Florida, R. (2007). *The flight of the creative class: The new global competition for talent*. New York, NY: HarperCollins.
Giroux, H. (2002). Educated hope in an age of privatized visions. *Cultural Studies/Critical Methodologies, 2*(93), 93–112.
Halberstam, J. (2011). *The queer art of failure*. Durham, NC/London: Duke University Press.
Harris, A., & Staley, J. (2011). Schools without walls: creative endeavour and disengaged young people. *Journal of Arts & Creativity in Education*. Retrieved November 2011, from http://jaceonline.com.au/issues/issue-title/
Jameson, F. (2000). *Brecht and method*. London/New York, UK/NY: Verso.
Joubert, M. M. (2001). The art of creative teaching: NACCCE and beyond. In A. Craft, B. Jeffrey & M. Leibling (Eds), *Creativity in education* (pp. 17–34). London/New York, UK/NY: Continuum.
Lehrer, J. (2012). *Imagine: How creativity works*. New York, NY: Houghton Mifflin Harcourt Publishing.
Massumi, B. (2008). The thinking-feeling of what happens: A semblance of a conversation. *Inflexion*, 1.1 *How is Research Creation?* Retrieved May 2008, from www.inflexions.org
O'Gorman, R., & Werry, M. (2012). On failure (On Pedagogy): Editorial introduction. *Performance Research: A Journal of the Performing Arts, 17*(1), 1–8.
Peters, M. A., & Araya, D. (2010). (Eds). Introduction: The creative economy; origins, categories, and concepts. In D. Peters & M. A. Araya (Eds.), *Education in the creative economy: Knowledge and learning in the age of innovation* (pp. 13–30). New York, NY: Peter Lang.
Power, C. (2010). Performing to fail: Perspectives on failure in performance and philosophy. In D. Meyer-Dinkgraffe & D. Watt (Eds.), *Ethical encounters: Boundaries of theatre, performance and philosophy*. Newcastle: Cambridge Scholars Publishing.

Robinson, K. (2010). *Out of our minds: Learning to be creative* (2nd ed.). Boston, MA: Capstone/Wiley.

Salehi, S. (2008). *Teaching contingencies: Deleuze, creativity discourses, and art.* Unpublished doctoral thesis, Ontario, Canada: Queen's University. Retrieved from http://qspace.library.queensu.ca/handle/1974/1209

Schulman, S. (2012). *The gentrification of the mind: Witness to a lost imagination.* Berkeley/Los Angeles, CA: University of California Press.

Sedgwick, E. K. (2003). *Touching feeling: Affect, pedagogy, performativity.* Durham, NC: Duke University Press.

Seelig, T. (2012). *InGenius: A crash course on creativity.* New York, NY: HarperOne.

Sefton-Green, J. (2011). *Creative Learning: policies, practices, schools and young people.* The Creative Learning Forum/ The Dusseldorp Foundation, Sydney Australia. Retrieved from http://www.julianseftongreen.net/

Sefton-Green, J. (2010). *Creative Agents: A review and research project.* Creativity, Culture and Education (CCE). London, UK.

Thomson, P., & Sefton-Green, J. (2010). (Eds.) *Researching creative learning: Methods and approaches.* London, UK: Routledge.

Zhao, Y. (2012, July 17). Doublethink: The creativity-testing conflict. *Education Week, 31*(36), 26–32. Retrieved July 17, 2012, from http://www.edweek.org/ew/articles/2012/07/18/36zhao_ep.h31.html

CHAPTER 2

YOUNG PLAYWRIGHTS' INK

That's one of the things that Young Playwrights got me prepared for [to] just get over that hump very young, that these people are professionals. They're famous, you know, I can't possibly do this, but you realise that somebody does it; it might as well be you (Carter L Bays in McGarry, 2001, p. 286).

Figure 4. Culture Shack drama workshop (2010).

INTRODUCTION

In this chapter I draw on a sample of interviews with alumni of the 32-year-old Young Playwrights Festival in New York City and the impact it has had on some of its earliest participants, for a birds' eye view of the impact of professional creative engagement with youth across the lifetime. To date there are over 300 Young Playwrights' alumni, and in this chapter I share excerpts from interviews with four diverse alumni, including myself, for the purpose of gaining insight into the broad ways in which such experiences can enhance creative thinking, skills and dispositions in young people, but also how these broad benefits can often go unnoticed, uncredited, unmeasured and unfunded in the organisations that nurture them.

Csikszentmihalyi (2013) recognises the importance of "study[ing] creativity as a process that unfolds over a lifetime" (p. vii) and links such study to his well-known 'systems approach' to creativity. Csikszentmihalyi, like others, continues to debate

CHAPTER 2

and define the boundaries of creativity; but they all agree that to be considered creative within one's context or culture, an individual must impact, change (dare I say *innovate* within) a given domain of endeavour. But innovation within the bounds of what society can understand, approve of (at least partially) and consume continues to be intrinsic to notions of 'value'. By using the Young Playwrights Festival and its long-term effects on its participants as one new measure of its effectiveness, this chapter argues that sometimes the innovation must come in the measurement rather than the methodology. On a larger scale, this text is problematising the shift in the measurement of creativity within education and culture at large, and this chapter is one case study that asks readers to reconsider standard measurements of 'success' in youth playwriting programs/contests/training.

The intersection between professional playwriting and education has often been a dangerous crossroads, scattered with warning signs and blind spots. The literature abounds with studies that approach the process of working creatively with participants from often either a theatre perspective or an education perspective, as though they are mutually exclusive. In this chapter I will argue that this troubled meeting of practices is often falsely binarised—even by some of the people interviewed here. I argue that young people have always understood the pedagogical value of arts engagement, and the power of being heard by the peers and adults in their lives. Those who are interviewed in this chapter make profound statements about the pedagogical value of professional arts engagement, of the impact of relationships on creativity, and the lifelong capital engendered through the creative validation of young people. More than anything, this chapter reaffirms the need for professional educators and arts makers to abandon our outmoded siloed approach to creativity, the arts, creative industries and education (Centrestage .n.d.; Lamb, 1991; Chapman, 1990).

I combine this new data with a previous study (McGarry, 2001) documenting the first ten years of the organisation, and contrast with O'Farrell's study of professional playwrights (1999) and the recommendations of both for professional development and training. Using this case study problematises the notions of 'young playwright' and 'success' as defined by funders, organisers, and other pedagogical and professional adults—and not always to the best advantage of the youth participants. I reinforce some earlier recommendations for bridging gaps between professional and pedagogical programming, their disconnect from policy and funding imperatives, and finally I offer a critique of such standard recommendations for 'best practice' that—in the next chapter—I will expand within a framework of 21st-century creative industries understandings.

Early Days

When the Broadway composer Stephen Sondheim was visiting London's Royal Court Theatre in the early 1980s, he met a dynamic young director named Gerald Chapman who was initiating a new young playwrights festival there that focused on the professional talent of the writers—not a developmental program for kids that treated them like kids. It was important to him that their talent be recognised and that they have a professional experience. Sondheim was so impressed and energised by this, he decided to establish such a program in his native New York. For this purpose, and in his role at the Dramatists' Guild there, he convinced Gerald Chapman to come to New York in 1980 and run the inaugural American Young Playwrights Festival.

The YPI[1] has, almost since its inception in 1981, provided teacher training, student workshops, internet support to teachers and writers globally and, of course, professional readings and productions for a new batch of American young playwrights every year (YPI, 1999; Lamb 1991). They have always made explicit the links between writing, creativity and teaching/learning, so crucial to developing playwrights rather than plays.

In 2001, Frances McGarry, a former education director at YPI, completed her doctoral study of the first ten years of YPI. In it, she interviewed its famous American founder, Stephen Sondheim, and a range of other affiliates—Artistic Director (for over 20 years) Sheri Goldhirsch, former young playwrights, directors and dramaturgs. This Young Playwrights' family is now larger than ever, and working in a range of creative- and 'non-creative' careers. Of those who were involved with YPI in its earliest years, some are dead, some are globally recognised names in theatre, film and television, and some are working in other industries or approaching retirement. As an alumna myself ('*In the Garden*', 1984) in this chapter I will draw on my own experiences and those of three other alumni in order to think more longitudinally about the value of creative arts engagement across a lifetime.

A few common themes emerge in talking to these alumni—all incredibly interesting and successful people, albeit some who haven't written a play since the 1980s or 1990s. Amongst the emergent themes are the centrality of relationships, the 'nature versus nurture' question about where creativity and talent comes from, and the continuum of creative expression across creative industries, professional writing, 'creative writing', other art forms, industry and education. This chapter does not set out to answer questions of how these four interviewees acquired their creative skills, gifts and attributes, and this sample is not generalisable. But by reading them together with the long-view of over thirty years of creative context, some deeply important patterns begin to emerge.

PROFILE #1 – MADELEINE GEORGE (*SWEETBITTER BABY,* 1993; *THE MOST MASSIVE WOMAN WINS,* 1994)

Madeleine George has been a member of the New Dramatists play development organisation in New York City since 2010. She's been writing since 1993 when her first play was included in the Young Playwrights Festival, and has written plays, novels and other works since then. She has won numerous awards (including the prestigious Princess Grace Playwriting Award) and has been commissioned to write plays by some of America's top theatres, including the Manhattan Theatre Club and

CHAPTER 2

Playwrights Horizons. I first met Madeleine during the 1994 Festival. Here is what she had to say when we caught up in May 2013:

Madeleine: In 1993 [as part of the Festival], they gave us tickets to see 'Angels in America.' It had just opened, we were third row— we—me and two other teenagers, no adults with us and we sat in the third row and then the angel exploded through the ceiling at the end and we were showered—like dust got on us, and we got in a cab to go home and we cried. You know we were speechless. Like, I mean of course we all went and saw the high school production of 'Bye Bye Birdie' and loved it when we were kids, but that is not the same. This was like this is the pinnacle of achievement and it's, you could be right next to it. There is no reason why you can't walk right up to that pinnacle of achievement and stand right next to it.

. . . In terms of the commodification of creativity, [one YPI alumnus] is such an interesting case. Do you know that he was the show runner for 'How I Met Your Mother'? . . . [another alumnus] is the music critic for the New Yorker . . . [one is] a speech writer for Ray Kelly, head of the New York Police Department. These are all really interesting jobs. I'm boring in a way, because I have sort of just been slogging in education and theatre, which are very close to that original. I'm a playwright and I'm a novelist and I also run a college program in a prison—those are my three jobs. I would say that [the YPI experience] was determinant, in terms of, I probably would have tried to be in the theatre, but I was definitely never going to **not** try after that. It was a solidifying experience. One very positive and one really a challenge. It's hard to have a solidified sense of yourself as destined to be a playwright when you are 18, for a couple of reasons: one because it's a rough life, and two because you're not remotely smart enough to write a good play when you are 18. It meant that I spent the twenty intervening years basically trying to become the person that I was waiting to become, so that I could be the writer that I wanted to be. And that's been a very long and often quite painful wait.

I was sort of ridiculed by the critics, by 'The [New York] Times' when I was 18 and it took me a long time to kind of unfold from that. It was really rough for me. But the core of the experience was those relationships and to be given difficult feedback by people in a loving way and be able to take it. Everything that was rough and difficult about that experience, the stakes of it, the exposure of it, at the time—it's still rough and difficult. It's the same stuff, you know. But I guess there is something about being taken seriously in that way that is—that it just like puts that foundation underneath you somehow. And I think also because the other thing that's true about the theatre is that it is made of relationships with people.

[The play that was ridiculed was] a feminist play about body image. Okay, it gets done about three or four times a month, it's been published three times, it's been done in like fifteen countries, it has been multiply translated and you know, it's a great thing for me. But, at the time, it was like, pfff, this little trifle about whiney women, basically. Now, it doesn't matter, but at the time I was like 'I will never recover'. I left [the festival] before I was supposed to, I was so devastated. Because I had been so vulnerable. [At the time] I was like 'I have these questions', and I can use [playwriting] to ask these questions. And although I write obviously differently from that first play now, I notice that it forged basically the core of my aesthetic: seeing how I could use text and spoken text in a variety of ways in the same performance piece. Ultimately what I want theatre to do is to basically enquire intellectually while offering a deep emotional experience.

A lot of my worst and endemic personality traits were really fanned by the experience, like that kind of desire for approval, and a wishing to be the winner, and these various other kinds of unattractive qualities. But the actual people that I worked with were so beautiful to me, and so important to me, particularly my directors, Seret Scott and Phyllis Look and also my dramaturg who was with me during the production process in 1993 and again in 1994, so he and I have a consistent, steady relationship. And so one of the, I guess skills or dispositions would be turn and face in the direction of people that you admire, and who will respect your work, not your status. Seret took me to New Dramatists, like she walked me up the street and she brought me into New Dramatists and she introduced me to everybody, and she was like, this is Madeleine and she is going to be a New Dramatist someday, and I am telling you, during the years of being rejected over and over again by them, I thought about that all the time.

There's this kind of odd little kinship structure that happens between people who are in this [YPI] network. And to feel like, oh I am part of this group, I am part of this family of people. That stuff is intangible and it's really important. And it's also the thing that saved me, because I definitely don't think I would have made it, and of course at any moment everything can collapse, but I became involved in a playwright's collective called 'Thirteen Playwrights' . . . that is the reason why I have any stamina at all, because it was like mercifully I was facing in the direction of other writers. I felt like I was in the world of the theatre because I was contributing to this different endeavour, and I just don't see how sending things out, trying to make relationships with agents, begging people to do readings, et cetera that would not have been sustainable for me for that period of time [without it].

Can creativity be taught? The thing about the curriculum is that it's for every kid . . . To tell you the truth, not everybody cares, like not everybody is going to care, not everybody should. Not everybody does have to write a play. It's not for everybody in the same way that a guy could come into my classroom in high school and demonstrate pipe fitting and I could be like, that is amazing, that's so useful, my God, every single house needs that. I think by the time a kid has been strange enough to write a play when they're 15, often in verse or whatever, and they put them in a room with other people who are similarly bizarre, then it's like that kinship. Especially if you're in a small town . . . where everybody is not doing it. I think that those weirdo [kids] are gonna find that thing, you know what I mean? . . . [YPI] is like a beacon and kids who write plays, are weird, they are going to write plays as we know. They are out there writing those plays and then they are looking around ravenously where can I send this? I think that YPI is a profound, life-changing gift.

Lynne Alvarez who was my professor at NYU [New York University] whom I loved, that wonderful playwright, she is gone now, but she once said to me, "Just do it for a while, and then do it longer and then eventually you won't be able to do anything else." [Laughs] . . . and then she said to me, "I still have to wrap presents at Macy's [department store] at Christmas time for extra money," and she was like in her sixties. And I was like, oh my God. But in fact she was right. You just do it, and then you do it some more and then pretty soon it's the only thing that you can do . . . .and that really is not going to, I am sure that it won't change until I die.

PROFILE #2 – ANNE HARRIS (*IN THE GARDEN*, 1984)

When I was 17-years old, my mother called me to the phone one cold winter's night in upstate New York and crackling through the line was a strange Englishman's voice telling me I'd been selected to participate in the final round of this year's Young Playwrights' Festival.

I'd been selected.

I wasn't quite sure what it meant, but of course I was thrilled anyway. I had just graduated and was plotting my escape from my small working class upstate New York town. It's not that I didn't love upstate, I did. It's a gloriously beautiful part of the world, one that many writers, artists and tourists travel to—and sometimes relocate to—regularly. But for me, it seemed too sleepy, too quiet, and too claustrophobic. I had been writing stories, plays and composing music all my life. My English teacher saw my passion for it, and introduced me first to Samuel Beckett and then to the Young Playwrights' Festival. We (he) submitted my first play, called In the Garden, which led to the phone call from Gerald Chapman on that winter's night.

I had enrolled as a mid-year intake at the University of New Hampshire, I was coming out as a lesbian, my brother had committed suicide the year before, and it was the dead of New England winter: Chapman's words could not have come at a better time.

What followed was a series of events that I for a long time referred to as my 'smack' period—the time when my addiction took hold. I went from being a scared kid away from home for the first time, to meeting famous people in New York City, being flown down to the city for rehearsals of my play every two weeks, being offered a scholarship to the Dramatic Writing Program at New York University (first one in the country), and finally launching the life of specialness that I had always known I was destined for.

Then it all ended. Not with a bang, the kind of fitting crash and burn that might make great short stories ten years later, but a slow and humiliating fizzle that never quite seemed to regain that original high. Sure, I had productions, I got an agent, I almost landed several big theatre hits and film contracts—almost. I was an 'emerging writer' with 'promise' for a good ten years, for longer than I could stand it. But when I began to refer to my life in New York as 'this lottery lifestyle', in which I'd bleed over each new play and subsequent draft, send it off with hope and enthusiasm, and then never progress much beyond the developmental reading stage, I knew something might have to change. Not that millions of young hopefuls don't have that same experience; but to start off with Broadway types singing my praises, buying me lunch and university and agent offers pouring in, and then still not quite make it to where I wanted to be, was very difficult to accept.

Such can be the beginnings of squandered lives, the "I shoulda been a contender!" pathetic, the ever-hopefuls, the almost-were. When, many years later, I had a short 10-minute play accepted to be self-produced in the 'Short and Sweet' annual play festival in Melbourne, Australia, and a friend said with sincere enthusiasm "Wow, congratulations! You must be quite thrilled!" I realised I was in danger of becoming one of those bitter people who could never even take one sip, one hit, one tab—the slope slippery enough then to take me all the way downhill. I felt at that moment that playwriting was indeed lost to me forever and I could never look it in the eye again. It has not remained so, but it encapsulates the highs and lows I associate with my YPI experience. It gives an echo of the despair in the question how could I have lost talent? I was talented once, they said so. People who should know!

I had never heard of Christopher Durang when I went to the first rehearsal of my play In the Garden in New York City's iconic Public Theatre in Greenwich Village. Its famous off-Broadway founder (and founder of the New York Shakespeare Festival, both still running after 50 years), Joseph Papp, was still alive then and greeted me at the theatre door. It was 1983, and Durang had a Broadway smash—Sister Mary Ignatious Explains it All for You—starring a gifted actress Elizabeth Franz. Durang was directing my reading, and Franz was starring in it. It was egalitarian, I remember most of all. People just . . . sat around together, smoking, eating, adults and kids, and they talked to us like peers. "How did you do that?" one of them asked me. And then waited for a response. It's hard to explain how or why this was so different than the other interactions I had had with adults, or why it was so formative, but it changed my life. I felt important, and excited, and part of something.

I remember meeting Mandy Patinkin ('You breathed Barbra Streisand's breath!' was all I could say); the roughly romantic Sam Shepard and his luminous companion Jessica Lange at The American Place Theatre, Morgan Jenness who told me stories about working with Michael Bennett on the creation of A Chorus Line, one of the best Broadway musicals in history—all of it left me speechless and tingling.

I remember the first read-through of my play, I remember where everything was in that room and the quality of the light, of talking to Joe Papp and Stephen Sondheim who seemed then like sophisticated, arty and sweet old men (though now I think they weren't so old!). I remember the first terrifying rehearsal of my play, of the warmth and humour between Chris and the two actresses he was directing. I was momentarily hurt that in response to my dark and depressing family drama, these three howled with laughter throughout the entire thing! Had I known his own work better then, I would have understood and been flattered. I remember sitting in the theatre seats in the dark, choking back tears because I felt they were making fun of my play, until the end of the read-through, realising they had uncovered a most effective and enlightening way of seeing this play but also dealing with tragedy. I remember thinking 'this is why theatre must be collaborative—because I can't see everything, just one perspective, even if I am the writer.' It was probably my first experience of 'critical literacy', of taking apart a text (my text!) and seeing that it has many lives that aren't always apparent at first, and all of which are powerful.

I was completely star-struck by the glamour, the talent, the coolness, the incredible wealth, the glitter around me; I had grown up in a poor working class family in the country, buying my school lunch with food stamps and getting my brother's hand-me-down clothes. This was a world that completely captivated me, and I seemed more susceptible than most to the impossibility of its opportunities to make me into something I always thought I might be. I loved the rehearsals, the words and the process of preparing my play for production also, but it was the glamour that overwhelmed me. I remember leaving rehearsals at lunch break and wandering around Greenwich Village and Soho, just quietly, like it was my special secret. I wanted it all, I wanted this life. It was a blessed time for me, and I would never give it back.

By the time my play came to production, I had experienced both an incredibly fruitful and frustrating professional theatre experience. I struggled with revisions and a change of directors, all of which was terrifying and depressing. When the festival was finished, we finalists were brought to the Central Park

West apartment of Mary Rodgers (daughter of famed composer Richard Rodgers) for a debrief. The debrief really consisted of the adults chatting amongst themselves, and us young people being terrified to make anything dirty (the entire apartment was white—white leather couches, white plush carpet, white everything), and scandalised by the Black maid who wore a strange 'maid costume' which seemed both comical and horrifying, something out of a 1940s film.

My reviews had been mixed, and it was frightening being reviewed in New York papers. I remember my people from upstate coming down for the opening night—including my parents, and my English teacher who had submitted the play on my behalf—and telling me over and over I was going to be famous, which I both resisted and craved (and which came back to torment me ten years later when I still wasn't). I remember getting the offer from the Dramatic Writing Program at New York University to come on partial scholarship, which seemed like the biggest benefit to me and my family who would have had no other way of my ever going to a school like that. And of course, by then, New Hampshire couldn't hold me.

There was always a narrative in my head that you can't really teach people to write. So I had assumed I would just go and do it. What the scholarship bought me was not so much entry to NYU, but to life in New York City. It was a wonderful institutional frame for going alone as a young person to live in that vibrant fantasy land, a safe base from which to run wild.

What I found once I arrived in the program at NYU was a sense of alienation. I was desperately poor and most of the other students were well off; I worked three jobs to afford the rest of what it cost, while most of my classmates hung out in the Department or partied, creating friendships that ultimately saw them employed (but I didn't realise how these things worked at the time). I probably also felt that I would be at least as good, or better, a writer than them, having come from this great national success. My overriding feeling was one of being lost, of confusion with the ever-present self-recrimination: if I was good enough for that, why isn't it working now?

One of the teachers there—a man who has gone on to considerable influence in that department over the years—confronted me the first day of class in front of all my new peers, and said "So! A Young Playwrights' winner! Well, let's see what you're made of!", and everything I wrote in that class got read aloud, and almost all of it got lambasted by him and the other students. It was devastating.

While being at NYU amongst other writers should have been in itself a dream come true, I suffered. I wrote constantly but never seemed to hit the mark, even when my intuition told me so. I eventually stopped feeling special, stopped feeling talented, and found myself increasingly frustrated throughout my twenties. Those at home felt disappointed that my early promise was not

CHAPTER 2

being fulfilled. I myself didn't know what exactly to do: there was no clear career path for playwrights after that initial experience. I went to NYU for the relationships and the scholarship—but neither seemed to help me in the end, and the bills were mounting. Eventually, I dropped out.

Like other Young Playwrights' alumni, I didn't really stay in touch with the organisation, didn't find ongoing mentorship from the directors and actors I had met, and didn't know how to ask for it. I became a teaching artist for YPI, but it wasn't really what I wanted. I helped set up and run the alumni association for a few years, with another alumnus called Charlie Schulman. The actress Lola Pashalinski told me once during those years that "you can't make a living in the theatre, but you can make a life". There was a point at which I realised I knew a lot of theatre people in New York, and had written a lot of plays, but just couldn't figure out how to make them work together. Now looking back I wonder if it is possible or really YPI's responsibility to keep the supporting their alumni. They can't do everything.

Overall, being a participant in the YPF was a positive experience, and one I have treasured. However, it has left scars and I believe delusions that have taken me a lifetime to overcome. What I saw of the New York theatre scene at 17 was not what I experienced later: glamour was replaced by hard work and fierce competition. While it was an incredible experience of feeling 'seen' as a creative artists by adults, by professionals in the field, becoming 'unseen' at least balanced the experience to a wash. I think also it was harder to enjoy or want a 'small' production after that, a bit of an unrealistic taster. But the self-doubt was probably its worst legacy, self-recriminations like, "maybe it was just because I'm not talented enough that it all dried up . . . did they actually see anything in me, or just needed this kind of play to balance the program that year?" "They saw something in me, but didn't stick with me." The 'fall from grace' was how it felt, a long slow fade to LIGHTS OUT.

Did I learn much about playwriting? I learned that productions are collaborative, that plays almost always go through many drafts, that theatre productions are expensive, that they are compromises and that work happens because of relationships—people know each other, want to work together, or things don't happen. I learnt (like others in McGarry and elsewhere) that professional artmaking is scary and stressful, that it is very exposing, and heart-wrenching when it doesn't work (Herrington & Brian, 2006). That it takes a lot more effort and crafting than is apparent on opening night, and that making 'good art' is hard, and there are no straight roads to a perfect goal. But that when it works, there is nothing better in this world, that it makes sense of things in a way nothing else can, and that it brings us together as humans in a way that is truly intergenerational, democratic, intercultural, and deeper than one can imagine who has never experienced it.

PROFILE #3: GREG CLAYMAN (*Mutterschaft,* 1990)

Greg is a media executive with News Corp Global Media, has been the Head of iPad Newspaper at Twenty-First Century Fox, Inc. since 2010, and was an Executive Vice President of Digital Distribution and Business Development for MTV Networks. I spoke with him in July 2013:

Greg: [My YPF experience] was a very personal experience. I had just graduated high school . . . So it was a very engaged experience, at a very young age . . . And so the more immediate—most immediate effect with that was I had a model . . . It gave me a model for how that process worked and then that was something that I continued throughout college. I can talk about theatre, about the life of creativity: I can remember the design of the stage really clearly and I thought it was . . . I was impressed with all the different pieces that went into that. And I'd be like, oh, my God, that's perfect or wait no, that's awful. There was a giant Klimt painting on a wall that scrolled down onto the floor and a huge orange beanbag in the middle of it. It was all very modern and I was like, Jesus, this is much cooler than anything I would have thought of. I mean, oddly enough, my house now looks like that [laughs].

I don't know that I would have ended up working in creative fields had it not been for [the YPF]. I have spent my life since then working with professional creative people. In fact, I would say many of them with more exposure in the world of television, film, online than I ever would have as a playwright. I think creative culture versus theatre arts is a very key distinction because the thing about theatre arts is, it is a small world.

I have been involved in creative industries my whole career . . . one of my first jobs out of school was for Time Warner and doing publishing in the publishing world. And basically working with creatives to find ways to move them into new technology; at the time it was CD-ROMs. I was at MTV Networks for a while, working with creatives. In fact, the more we talk about this, I think the notion of creative people and being able to understand their language and speak it and feel like I was a native speaker of it too . . . I feel like it gave me a connection to theatre and the theatre world and the performing arts in a way that I wouldn't have had otherwise. That is I sort of feel like an insider. A lot of people are interested in theatre and they go see plays, they talk about them, they read it, they study it, they took courses in college. That's all well and good but it's not experiential. And I mean if you're like, yeah, I know how this actually works, I've been that guy, I've seen this, and that feeling of being an insider has given me the sort of tools, I think, to appreciate the theatre arts and performing arts on a different level.

CHAPTER 2

There was the notion that you had all these amazing resources. I had lots of great times with Michael Mayer, who was my director. I am still in contact with him and go to see his plays. I don't know that it would have had the same gravitas had it been [outside of New York City and Broadway]. You've got a lot of amazing writers sort of submit their stuff and they pick some of the ones who are amongst the best. The play was already written when you got there, so it wasn't like—the rewrite process was important to me and was an awesome experience. But I feel like it wasn't about nurturing new talent. It was about finding great talent and bringing them in.

I know a lot of people who are in creative industries and fewer people who are in creative arts. I'm surrounded by creative industry people every day—writers—and I don't think they're any less artistic than people who have chosen the theatre or dance as their medium. Maybe the answer is no [laughs]. Maybe I don't see much of a difference. It's sort of an old sore where you've got the whole notion of like the creative artist toiling away and doesn't care about money and is doing it because they're compelled to versus some writer working for a studio being paid by the man to churn out. So, that being said, I've dear friends on both sides of the aisle and the folks who are writing for television I don't think are any less creative than the folks who are writing for theatre. It's just that they practise a different medium. And often jump back and forth.

If you go back to Dickens he was writing as many words as he could in a serial fashion for a newspaper because that's how he was getting paid. It's easy to look at a work now and say look at this beautiful thing and it's all in one piece or whatever. But he was writing commercials, he was a commercial writer. And he was getting paid for everything. He was being paid by a newspaper and if it sucked week to week, it was like, 'Hey, Chuck, why don't you liven this thing up a bit? We're getting complaints.'

You are talking about resources and talent. That didn't exist anywhere else [beside the YPF]. You were talking about some of the greatest directors who've, literally—gosh the year that I was in, I think three of those directors have gone on to win Tony's. Talent in terms of actors—you would see the folks who are in the plays, you would go and see in movies and television shows every day. I mean, this was . . . these were great, great, great actors who gave their time.

I mean Sondheim. You're talking to Sondheim about your play and he said, 'Yeah, I loved it'. And you're like – 'Jesus Christ!' That to me was such an important draw and just a part of the experience. If it's just a bunch of well-meaning teachers and social workers, I don't think it'll have the same pizzazz.

Anne: What I hear you talking about are kind of success imperatives. Part of what is awe-inspiring about that experience for a young person is not just to have adults valuing our work. It was to have famous adults or gifted or recognised—successful—adults recognising our work and going—and go—yeah, the holy shit factor comes partly from the fact that it's not your mum. It's a famous person.

Greg: Yeah. That's right.

How do you measure success?

> We don't promote a methodology for teachers. Unfortunately, most teachers do teach in a traditional and accepted way. That's one of the reasons for the Young Playwrights Festival, it's so that our outreach program is not about teachers—it's about playwrights teaching young playwrights because only a playwright really understands what a play is. *(Sondheim in McGarry, 2001, pp. 282-283).*

Like Madeleine, myself, and many other YPF alumni, Greg sees the function of the YPF as recognising already-evident 'creative talent' and introducing those young people to a community of like-minded others, and in some cases professionals, who might facilitate the young playwrights' professional (and creative) emergence. Since their time in the festival, the YPI has introduced a wide range of other training programs for kids who have never written a play but would like to, such as the *Urban Retreat* in New York City and schools-based training across the country (and overseas).

In contrast to other New York playwright development organisations like the New Dramatists, YPI has remained focused on the very young ones, usually with limited experience (YPI, 1999). Other YPF alumni interviewed by McGarry in 2001 described similar experiences of loss associated with the aftermath of their YPF experience, and perhaps this is why the New Dramatists' model offers a 7-year association, in recognition of the need for longer-term engagement. Young Playwrights Inc. has also tried to nurture these ongoing relationships more since their early years, but all organisations must limit their programming. At its founding in 1981, the American YPF's mission was to "identify and to nurture new generations of talented writers for the theatre . . . as active participants in the highest quality professional productions of their plays" (McGarry, 2001, p. 1). This mission has changed over the past 30 years, to be sure, reflected in its name change to YPI, to encompass delivering educational products as well as (sometimes in lieu of) professional theatrical products.

Professionalism has always been central to the YPF, ever since its original incarnation at London's Royal Court Theatre. Gerald Chapman believed passionately that the words of young people deserved as much professional respect as the words of adults, and that they should be considered equally legitimate as art, and not simplistically divided into 'theatre' and 'theatre for young people' (Chapman, 1990).

CHAPTER 2

McGarry interviewed several of the alumni for her study of the first ten years of YPI, which included valuable reflections on the need for collaboration and development of the scripts as part of the YPI experience—that "learning to collaborate is an intrinsic part of preparing the play for production" (2001, p. 150)—as did O'Farrell's (1990; 1988) studies of professional playwrights which equally noted the benefit of input during revision. In both O'Farrell's and McGarry's studies, playwrights noted the necessity of hearing the work aloud, and the value of this public reading being in a safe but professional setting. The promotion of such skills and dispositions are widely regarded as part of the crossover appeal of creative approaches in schools, despite the waning timetabling of arts activities and subjects.

The great benefit of having long-term Artistic Directorship and staff means that the YPI can critically reflect on and respond to changing contexts in theatre, as well as in education, and their funding structures. What began as a glamorous project of a few Broadway-based theatre makers in New York City evolved into a nationwide professional development and arts education supplier. When they started, the YPI was alone in the USA; now, there are countless young playwrights' festivals around the United States and worldwide (including Australia). YPI has come to represent in some ways the ongoing tension between a growing theatre-in-education of various names, types and orientations, and playwright professional development, which seems to have decreased. YPI's own 'outcome' statistics reflect this need for shift: if measured by the number of alumni who remained primarily playwrights, there are few. Measured by those who have established themselves as professional creative writers in other genres and sectors, the statistics are only slightly higher; measured as those who continue to be impacted by, and professionally incorporate, the diverse skills they developed in that "magical experience" (McGarry, 2001, p. 7), however, the numbers are over 90 per cent. This may indicate one reason why playwriting programs in schools have increased, while funding for programs like the YPI have decreased—as these transferable skills become more widely recognised as broadly valuable, generic 'creativity' and 'arts/literacy' components are incorporated into curricula overall, while playwriting-specific organisations like YPI may be aging out.

So what is the most reliable, fairest or most legitimate measure of the success of programs like YPI? Many funders hold YPI to a measure that counts only the number of playwright graduates still writing plays. Even Stephen Sondheim's anniversary report on the official YPI website summarises their success in terms of writers working in commercial film, television or theatre:

"Today, we receive as many as 1500 plays from all fifty states. Furthermore, we discovered on our 10th anniversary that more than 80 percent of our winners were still actively writing plays. To pick just two, there is Jonathan Marc Sherman, whose 1988 entry, Women and Wallace (written when he was 18) was produced for television by PBS; and Kenneth Lonergan, who was one of our winners in 1982 and whose plays This Is Our Youth, The Waverly Gallery, and Lobby Hero have been widely acclaimed, and whose screenplay for You Can Count on Me (which he directed) was nominated for an Academy Award. (YPI online, n.d.)"

Yet we know these are not the only successful outcomes of this long-running program. McGarry notes how, implicit in YPI's "mission to discover new writers, the intention becomes problematic; in that, is its goal to preen young playwrights for the profession, or to discover new writers?" (p. 210). Importantly, she asks the question that has plagued many teachers and young playwright programs: "does the play become the product or does the playwright?" (p. 210). Current research (Taylor & Littleton, 2012; Sawyer 2011; Sefton-Green, Thomson, et al., 2011) champions multiple ways in which educators and artists may no longer have to choose between the two. My own recount and McGarry's both note that "through YPI's emphasis on professionalism, [and] reviews by New York City critics, the potential for harm to the young playwright exists and therefore creates a conflicting conundrum" (McGarry, 2001, p. 210). The tension is more than just a 'professional' versus 'amateur' assessment criterion, but reflects tensions present elsewhere culturally (industry, education).

In all four personal accounts included here of YPF experiences, professional and creative relationships emerging as a central measurable benefit of the program. Through descriptions of our professional and 'kinship' relationships in the theatre community, we all attest to the value of the professional aspect of those early experiences, as painful as it sometimes was (what profession isn't?). Current funding regimes can be more ruthless in defining what constitutes success, however. While in Sondheim's day the focus was squarely on sampling the 'real Broadway' milieu within the London and New York theatre scenes, today's young playwrights (not just via YPI) are encouraged to think longitudinally about acquiring playwriting and related skills *for the marketplace or career pathways*. From an administrative perspective, there are additional concerns: in conversation with these alumni and with Artistic Director Sheri Goldhirsch (Harris, 2011; 2012), it is clear that the success of organisations like YPI can (and should) be measured in much broader and longer-term ways too. The Young Playwrights' organisation has that rare ability to look back on its professional theatre engagement with young people over more than 30 years, a history increasingly valuable and rare in today's world of arts and culture.

PROFILE #4: TISH DURKIN (*FIXED UP*, 1984)

Tish Durkin has been a journalist and foreign correspondent for over 25 years. She has written about the war in Iraq for publications such as the *New York Observer*, the *Atlantic Monthly* and *Rolling Stone*. She was a political columnist for the *National Journal*, covering Washington DC, Syria, Jordan and Kuwait. As a staff writer for the *New York Observer* from 1997 to 2000, she covered Hillary Clinton's bid for the Senate and the New York mayoralty of Rudolph Giuliani. She now lives in Ireland with her husband and two children.

CHAPTER 2

Tish: . . . I remember [recently] looking at the news as I'm basically cutting up sausage for my son and I'm thinking, 'You know, I used to know the head of Hamas in Syria.' An interesting time for a while there. And I was at Nelson Mandela's inauguration and . . . I mean I had a great career. All the good parts, like everything that's interesting about my career had to do with the people I was writing about. In between it's like 'And then I opened up a can of soup and drank it straight out of the can. There was no oven.'

I always knew I was going to be a writer but I couldn't decide whether it was going to be journalism or more so-called creative writing. Even [during the YPF] I did have this idea that I didn't have anything to write about. I hadn't had that many experiences, or the perspective—of course lots of ordinary experiences become the gem of great literature—but I just knew that I wasn't prepared for anything like that, I knew there was a whole world. So I ended up a journalist and I was in journalism for 25 years . . . which is the greatest job you could possibly imagine. And then 9/11 happened and I went to Syria and Kuwait for a while . . . and ended up as Baghdad was falling and hilariously enough given the aftermath I thought, oh, my God, I'm missing the war. I didn't realise it was going to go on for another 10 years! I got arrested in Syria . . . and ended up going to Jordan and just randomly with people that knew each other rented two taxis for the 17-hour drive to Baghdad. There were four guys plus myself. I later found out they had a coin-toss over who had to take me because of the extra space in the car. One guy lost the toss and he ended up being my husband. We got married New Year's Eve of 2004, living in Iraq most of that time. I was 38 when I got married, and instantly became pregnant. We moved to Spain . . . and then had two children in two years, which changed my life.

My son turned out to have really severe autism so for the last three and a half years that has really been the defining theme of my life, so it's slowed down. I mean I've written quite a bit about autism and all that, but my days as a gunslinger [laughter] are kind of over, but I'm still writing. Coming full circle I've gone back to doing more creative writing because: (a) I've got tons of experiences. I no longer have that problem of never having [anything to say], now that I'm almost 50.

I'm working on a couple of scripts. My goal was to have this little assembly line: something you send out and then when they come back and say, 'Well, this is not the right thing' then you have something there right away. So now I have two basic play scripts at different stages. I have a television thing at an earlier stage, and a book, a novel. I would say that I have a very active, at least in my head, creative life going on and a fairly disciplined creative routine going on that I've just developed in the past two or three years.

Journalism's great because it teaches you, number one, not to be so precious . . . You're writing for totally different audiences, totally different lengths, styles, subject matter . . . As a writing exercise writing about something that is frothy and that you don't really care about is infinitely harder than writing about finding a dead body on your doorstep in Baghdad because all you have to do is say—you write down "I found a dead body on my doorstep" and people are like, whoa [laughter]. You can be quite a bad writer; less is more. I mean you sort of say I knew somebody whose doorbell rang at 5 o'clock and there was a package and she opened the box, it had her brother's head in it. How much creativity or verbal ability do you need to have people go [whoa]?

But in [playwriting I learned] to show things rather than say things all the time. To this day I love cutting, it's my favourite, favourite part. Unrestrained first draft and then pshh pshh: it's wonderful. You can always take it out, it's very freeing. You don't have to worry about getting it so perfect. Professionally [the YPF] interrupted my trajectory because I was always thinking about being a journalist and then I was like, well maybe I'll do this other thing [playwriting] . . .

A kid who enters that contest [YPF] is going to be someone who already considers themselves, or is considered by a teacher, a pretty good writer. I think [the YPF] probably does both [nurture and attract good writers]. My parents did a very good balance between encouraging it without pressuring it. But I think in the long run [my YPF experience] was very good. It opened up the possibility that there are other forms of writing . . . . I think to myself, at one point I did have Stephen Sondheim, Pete Gurney, Wendy Wasserstein, like really serious people, saying you're good at this, you're funny, you write good dialogue and I thought—as recently as last year I thought—well, you know maybe they were right. And I don't know that I would've had the confidence to just say, "Okay. I'm going to give up the rest of it" and start this assembly line that we've been talking about, had that experience not happened to me . . . I have a frame of reference that I did not have once . . . things come in and out of your mind and characters—I don't think I would've thought of writing scripts.

If you are talking to somebody from a [government] arts funding body, well, what's their mission statement? If their stated goal is to . . . make sure that people become playwrights then that might not be the [best goal]. We as a culture have to remember that everything is cause and effect. It's like saying there's no point in having a really great athletic program unless a certain percentage of your kids are in the Olympics. And that's never been really true, and it's not measured that way. There's an awful lot that can be gotten out of these types of things regardless of the explicit outcomes, by being too results-oriented.

CHAPTER 2

It's about possibilities. I think it's about exposure. I think a huge thing as you've mentioned is being taken seriously by adults, and being criticised by adults, constructively criticised. I think every kid needs that, because it was so thrilling to have these bigwigs telling [me] 'you're great'. But I remember sometimes it was like having cold water splashed on you too, in the kindest possible way. They say, 'Well what's that doing there? Why do you have this whole speech in there?' and you go bah-bah, bah-bah, bah-bah. Whereas your usual teacher would be like 'Oh, you're such a genius'. So the rigour of it I think is a very good thing. I mean most kids who study ballet do not end up in the Kirov. It does not mean they shouldn't be studying ballet. So I definitely think it was a good thing . . .

I don't think [standardised testing is] an entirely bad idea because you do have to have some testing, you do have to have some results. But when you talk about the nexus of the whole idea of creativity and management, all these management books and everything is all results-oriented. And that makes sense for a business: if the business is not making money it's going to be run into the ground. But with creativity if somebody writes ten books — is that better than somebody who writes one book if the one book you've written is Tolstoy? It's not so easy [to measure].

And I think sometimes, even though I'm very much in favour of schools having basic [skills]- a school at which the kids graduate illiterate is just not a good school period. But if you think about who's a good teacher, well, one teacher may have the kids doing better on their math and verbal skills, and another teacher may spend an hour and a half after school talking to a kid whose parents have split up, keeping that kid from quitting . . . it is immeasurable. Now so many high schools are measured by where the kids get into college. A kid who gets into—goes to a so-called top school because they've been pressured into it and groomed for it from the time they were 12 and has a nervous breakdown when they're 40, is different than someone who got in there because they were passionate about the cello.

Anne: Okay, in the ironic but not unlikely event that in five years from now you are running your own show about a foreign correspondent, who looks a lot like you, and someone writes an article about you saying it was always obvious and in the cards because you were a Young Playwright when you were 18, what would you say to that?

Tish: Well, you know what I would say? I would actually be very happy for the Young Playwrights Festival to get that press—I think back on it very very fondly. It's not like the world is suffering from too many of these [playwriting] programs that we need to stamp out the [YPF Artistic Director] Sheri

Goldhirsches of the world! Maybe it was always obvious [that I would be a writer] but I would agree with the idea that that YPF were among the first to have a clue. And that's true of everything. That's true of history. You look back at who won the war and then you retrace it and it's all obvious, but when you read stuff going into the war it's not so obvious. Nothing is ever obvious until we're all dead, I mean really.

Creative Pedagogies, Creative Possibilities

In the early years of the YPF, according to McGarry, "when a Festival [was] over, the YPF staff maintain[ed] contact with the young writers. Of the thirty-five fledgling writers represented in the first four seasons, thirty have been heard from again," (2001, p. 64). This level of intensive involvement has not been possible in the ensuing years. As my own narrative described, it is hard for playwrights, mentors, administrators and teachers to stay in touch unless there is a galvanising activity around which to gather. In the case of the YPI, several initiatives were begun over the years, including an alumni association, playwriting workshops (with the more 'successful' alumni), *Writing On Your Feet!* artists-in-the-schools workshops taught by alumni, and other teaching/writing gigs like the *Urban Retreat* which has been offered by YPI every year since 1989.

While Sefton-Green (2011; 2010) and others (Caldwell & Vaughan, 2012; Centrestage, *n.d.*; Herrington & Brian, 2006; O'Farrell, 1990; Gibson & Ewing, 2011) have extolled the virtues of 'creative partnerships', artist-in-schools as a model has worked for a number of years in many diverse contexts. And I'm not suggesting here that I don't believe it's an effective structure, because it can be—all other conditions being equal. However, there are increasing numbers of teachers who come to education from a creative arts background and who consider themselves *both* artists and teachers—a highly compatible dual-identity. Yet most evaluations of teaching-artist programs binarise teachers and artists as though teachers are never trained as artists, and artists are never trained as teachers (Caldwell & Vaughan, 2012). This is not the reality.

Increasingly, teachers and teacher educators are working across disciplines and sectors. Economic imperatives are driving skills and identities together in new and not always unpleasant ways; innovation is occurring in pedagogical and creative ways in digital technologies, creative industries and education management. While some within both education and the creative industries support a siloed approach to this work, more are jumping the great divide, as evidenced by a range of recent publications on the value of skill-based analyses of creative approaches within a range of fields, including business, science, education and industry (Seelig, 2012; Iiyoshi & Kumar, 2008; Sawyer, 2011, 2007).

While developments in digital technology may not directly affect all aspects of creating plays and other forms of writing-for-performance, they are certainly

CHAPTER 2

changing the way they are developed and disseminated, including multimedia performances, new hybrid forms, and a plethora of online distribution and critical collaboration and review channels. Such sites of interaction in fact make possible my current study of the long history of YPI through its alumni in all walks of life—a task that would have been nearly impossible at any earlier time. But all these developments are merely examples of the many ways in which young people are not only participating in increasing numbers in both amateur and professional arts-making, but are connecting with others in their fields of endeavour—all of which support that original mission of the YPF, and its current work in New York and abroad.

RECOMMENDATIONS, THEN AND NOW

While it's clear that no one organisation can provide everything needed to either support young people who want to write creatively for the theatre, or the schools and organisations that support them, the YPI is unique in its role as the first and still the oldest training ground for young playwrights in the United States. From this vantage point, YPI offers a unique perspective on creativity, young people, and how to nurture not only confident voices for the 21st century, but also crucial creative skills. In summary, the top five flashpoints from the dozen alumni I have interviewed to date, and from the organisation itself include:

FLASHPOINT (1): Playwriting (distinct from improvisation, rehearsed acting, or writing for the page rather than performance) for secondary students is "strongly supported" (McGarry, 2001, p. 205) and impacts literacy, expressive and creative confidence and connectedness. The processes of revision, artistic collaboration and public outcomes of original work is a powerful motivator in learning.

FLASHPOINT (2): The centrality of relationships forged through collaborative professional arts activity (like the Young Playwrights Festival) is "qualitatively different than school-based experiences, except where the teacher is a practicing playwright or trained in the art of teaching playwriting" (McGarry, 2001, p. 208), and is irreplaceable for youth participants, even when challenging or upsetting.

FLASHPOINT (3): Professional engagement is of most benefit to the youth participants in the development of skills in self-direction, revision (not limited to literary, but in general), lateral thinking (through creative collaboration) and persistence (especially in challenging collaborations).

FLASHPOINT (4): The 'nature vs. nurture' question about where creativity and talent come from is not a pivotal one in measuring the value of creative arts programs and organisations, as they thrive through a combination of *attracting* those individuals who already show capacity or talent, and democratically *nurturing* the abilities of all young people who present to the program, in order to improve their creative interests, skills and dispositions.

FLASHPOINT (5): There is a clear continuum of creative expression across creative industries, professional writing, 'creative writing', other artforms, industry and education that should be maximised by more productive 'crossover' activities and collaborations, rather than encouraging more siloing into artforms, disciplines and funding streams.

McGarry's (2001) study of the first ten years of the Young Playwrights Festival compared O'Farrell's (1990) recommendations with its own by looking closely at the ongoing successes of the YPI and the changing needs of education and community sectors. Today, an increasingly digitally-based creative industries sector is changing the face of professional creative employment and the conceptual framing of what it means to be working as a creative innovator. YPF alumnus Greg Clayman sees one measure of creative success or effectiveness to be the scope of dissemination or influence of the creative product (audience share)—a difference (but a changing one) between playwrights and creators of digital content today. Sawyer (2007; 2011) and others continue to advocate for a broader understanding of the ways in which creative pedagogies can benefit all classrooms, including informal and public learning contexts. The work of Young Playwrights Inc., as well as of the two other case studies discussed in this book, foreground innovation and the long-term development of broad creative skills, thereby demonstrating the value of such hybrid creative approaches. The unique 32-year history of Young Playwrights Inc. offers a rare glimpse into the impact of early professional creative training across the lifetime, a longitudinal approach largely ignored in the measurement of creative capital and the creative capacities of individuals and organisations.

NOTES

[1] In this chapter I will refer to the organization by two acronyms: YPI (Young Playwrights Inc), which encompasses the range of educational, developmental and presentational programs offered by them, and YPF (Young Playwrights Festival) which is the annual festival of new plays only.

REFERENCES

Caldwell, B., & Vaughan, T. (2012). *Transforming education through the arts.* Melbourne, VIC: Taylor & Francis.
Centrestage (no author). (n.d.). *Teaching playwriting in schools. Teachers' handbook* (p. 26). Baltimore, MD: Centerstage. Retrieved from http://www.centerstage.org/Portals/0/PDF/06PlaywrightsHandbook.pdf
Chapman, G. (1990). *Teaching young playwrights.* Portsmouth, NH: Heinemann Educational Books.
Csikszentmihalyi, M. (2013). *Creativity: The psychology of discovery and invention.* New York, NY: HarperCollins.
Gibson, R., & Ewing, R. (2011). *Transforming the curriculum through the arts.* Melbourne: Palgrave Macmillan.
Harris, A. (2012). *Ethnocinema: Intercultural arts education.* The Netherlands: Springer.
Harris, A. (2011). *Teaching diversities: Same sex attracted young people, CALD communities, and arts based community education.* Carlton: Centre for Multicultural Youth.
Herrington, J., & Brian, C. (2006). *Playwrights teach playwriting.* Ann Arbor, MI: Smith & Kraus.
Iiyoshi, T., & Kumar, M. S. V. (Eds). (2008). *Opening up education: The collective advancement of education through open technology, open content, and open knowledge.* Boston, MA: Institute of Technology Publishing.

51

Lamb, W. (Ed). (1991). *Hey Little Walter and other prize-winning plays from the 1989 and 1990 Young Playwrights Festivals.* New York, NY: Dell Publishing.

McGarry, F. L. (2001). *A history of the young playwrights festival: The first decade (1981–1991).* (PhD dissertation). New York, NY: New York University.

O'Farrell, L. (1990). Involving theatre professionals in the drama curriculum: Playwrights on playwriting. *Youth Theater Journal, 4*(4), 3–6.

O'Farrell, L. (1988). *Teaching the playwright's art: A research report.* Kingston: Queen's University, ERIC ED 292 131.

Sawyer, K. (Ed.). (2011). *Structure and improvisation in creative teaching.* Cambridge, MA: Cambridge University Press.

Sawyer, K. (2007). *Group genius: The creative power of collaboration.* Cambridge, MA: Perseus/Basic Books.

Seelig, T. (2012). *InGenius: A crash course on creativity.* New York, NY: HarperOne.

Sefton-Green, J., Thomson, P., Jones, K., & Bresler, L. (Eds.) (2011). *The Routledge international handbook of creative learning.* London, UK: Routledge.

Sefton-Green, J. (2011). Judgement, authority and legitimacy: evaluating creative learning. In J. Sefton-Green, P. Thomson, K. Jones & L. Bresler (Eds.), *The Routledge international handbook of creative learning* (pp. 311–319). London, UK: Routledge.

Taylor, S., & Littleton, K. (2012). *Contemporary identities of creativity and creative work.* Denver: Littleton.

YPI. (1999). *Writing on your Feet! playwriting curriculum guide.* New York, NY: Young Playwrights' Inc.

Young Playwrights Inc (homepage). Retrieved from http://www.youngplaywrights.org/sondheim-says/

CHAPTER 3

DEADUCATION

Why Schools Need to Change

Figure 5. Melbourne graffiti, #2 (2013).

Deadliness always brings us back to repetition: the deadly director uses old formulae, old methods, old jokes . . . they do not start each time afresh from the void, the desert and the true question—why clothes at all, why music, what for? A deadly director is a director who brings no challenge to the conditioned reflexes that every department must contain (Brook, 1968, p. 39).

These are days when no one should rely unduly on his 'competence.' Strength lies in improvisation (Benjamin, 2002, p. 447).

INTRODUCTION

Contemporary education is obsessed with competencies. One might argue that any system concerned primarily with achieving 'competence' rather than 'brilliance' is already in trouble. As the spread of 'creative economies', 'creative industries' and 'creative classes' moves from western nations to more diverse global sites, educators must confront a daunting challenge; namely, that to remain relevant to a rapidly changing marketplace global economy, education and government policy must recognise the need to teach for an unknowable future and a knowledge economy that requires, above all, greater flexibility than we can now imagine. This is a task

CHAPTER 3

being confronted in all sectors, not just education. The question is: why is education responding both so slowly and so badly?

The profound disconnection between, on the one hand, education policy documents in multiple national contexts that continue to stress educating students for 'creative futures' and, on the other, the business-as-usual of standardised national curricula demands a new consolidating vision for education's future. Through organisations and programs like *Young Playwrights' Inc.* (Chapter 3), *Culture Shack* (Chapter 5), and *Teaching Diversities* (Chapter 7), young people themselves are already articulating this new vision, as they build their own creative strategies for navigating their complex local and global, embodied and digital lifeworlds. Yet why is the education sector not taking sufficient notice? Young people never set out to become 'competent' in using social media and other digital technologies, in dating, in the arts, sports or other hobbies they may pursue. They set out to be the best, or to have fun. School often educates them out of this by sheer boredom or, what some argue, is teaching them to stop dreaming big and to settle for less (Robinson, 2011).

Scholars of curriculum and pedagogy, and policymakers too, might argue that young people themselves are not responsible for vast populations of students with diverse capabilities and therefore can't see the 'big picture' that leads to standardisation. While the serious limitations of setting the goalposts on competencies with schematised rubrics for measuring everything of value in the development of a student's mind is already clearly evident in the United States and United Kingdom (Harris, Smith & Harris, 2011; Hursh, 2007; McNeill, 2000), still more countries are moving toward this singular and reductive measure of success.

Many have already argued the ways in which education is changing, either toward a standardised sameness or toward more dispersed, public pedagogies (see for example Dimitriadis, Cole & Costello, 2009). Others have drawn links between the rise of the charter school movement and other non-normative institutionalised alternatives for incorporating a more holistic and creative approach to learning and knowledge-creation. All of these developments could be indicators that institutionalised education as we know it may have reached its 'use-by' date, that it has come to the end of its pedagogical road. Crazy? Perhaps not. Many now agree that both the quantity and quality of the learning that occurs interpersonally and online in students' so-called real lives now rivals that which occurs in schools. Often in 'youthspeak', what all but the most elite and well-resourced schools can offer young people is a dull replacement for time spent online, in professional engagement like internships or paid work, or with friends. If schools are no longer the source of knowledge accumulation, what are they? This chapter links this potential 'identity crisis' in education with a crisis in theatre that was identified by famed director Peter Brook, who cautioned against the high cultural costs and dangers of allowing theatre—another vital but alleged elitist, bloated and out-of-step industry—to become 'dead'.

DEAD(LY) THEATRE AND THE FUNCTION OF CULTURAL PRODUCTION

Peter Brook is one of Britain's most renowned theatre directors and innovators and is still innovating at age eighty-eight. Apart from his theatre and film work, he has contributed to global cultural life through teaching and writing. Perhaps his most famous text on theatre is *The Empty Space*, written in 1968. It is not only a text about theatre—its rituals, its history, its function—but is also about the social role and necessity of theatre as a tool of cultural critique and production, and the ways in which it both constitutes and reflects the times in which it is made. Arguably, this is true for all art. But I draw on him here to suggest that it may also be true for other tools of cultural production, like education.

One remarkable feature of Brook's book is how contemporary it still feels, not only in regard to theatre but to culture more generally. In his discussions of the stultifying effects of American capitalism, we can see the long lead-up to the current reign of the profitability imperative: a low-wage productivity that pervades the US and global others. Now, 45 years after this book's publication, it is easy to see how such economic rationalism has spread from 'the arts' in the United States to just about every industry and sector worldwide, including education. I extend Brook's articulation of a Deadly Theatre, and apply the frame to education. Brook's discussion of aesthetics and methods can be transposed to a critical exploration of creative curricula and pedagogy. The limitations within theatre that Brook defines in 1968 are now clearly evident in the education sector, and Brook (and theatre in general) has much to tell us about how we might redress these patterns to find a middle ground between productivity and creativity.

Brook calls 'bad' or lifeless, safe, repetitive theatre 'Deadly Theatre', and laments its pervasiveness. His critique can be mistaken for some contemporary critical analyses of education, in that, " . . . it is only if we see that deadliness is deceptive and can appear anywhere, that we will become aware of the size of the problem" (1968, p. 9) – a size much greater in education for after all everyone must go to school. Brook's analyses were not the cynical words of a tired and jaded director: his message was that we can reverse this trend, and to a great degree in the intervening 45 years, he has done so. One might say, '*but theatre still seems pretty dead today, so he failed!*' But theatre—like education and any other tool of cultural production—is always context-specific and historically contingent. Creativity is equally so, suggesting that the pervasive current search for an absolute commodification or definition of creativity is less a neat equation and more an indicator of the times in which we live. Brook tells us that great, living and creative art (as with great education), does not have

> . . . any absolute meaning. They are the reflections of a critical attitude of a particular period, and to attempt to build a performance today to conform to these canons is the most certain road to deadly theatre—deadly theatre of a respectability that makes it pass as living truth (p. 13).

CHAPTER 3

This call to resist calcification in outmoded traditions, texts, rules and systems is an ongoing tension in educational contexts. Education, like theatre, constantly draws on classical texts and forms, but Brook stresses the need to break and reinvent them. Improvisation, in its deepest and intellectual sense, is key. In a living education, as in a living theatre, "we would each day approach the rehearsal putting yesterday's discoveries to the test, ready to believe that the true [play] has once again escaped us... but the Deadly Theatre approaches the classics from the viewpoint that somewhere, someone has found out and defined how the play should be done" (p. 14). Dead approaches to teaching and learning are the same. Whether these airless definitions of 'how schooling should be done' come from previous canonical texts, curriculum documents and programs, standardised tests, or policy-of-the-day, creativity seems to be rushing out of teaching at an increasingly rapid pace.

Differentiating between arts and creativity—or even aesthetics and creativity—is crucial for a clear examination of the ways in which standardised contemporary education is suffering the loss of both. Policy and curriculum discourses have devolved in the past ten years into debates about content. Content is not the issue. In Brook, you won't find much about *what* to do to make good theatre because, of course, good theatre is about an approach, a vision, and a way of doing. Good theatre makers can produce ground-breaking theatre that allows us to see ourselves and our cultures afresh, and can be made out of anything and everything. Education is the same. There is no magic list of skills and attributes that make up a 'good education'. The very difficulty in defining it is what continues to present our greatest challenge, and it is only by looking to others—like Brook, in associated industries which have themselves persevered through adversity and cultural crises—that we can begin to take stock of the depth of the challenge to educators who wish to continue working creatively.

But whether testing and standardisation may be killing (or has killed) a living creative education is only a part of this picture, and there is a great body of literature on critical education and educational social reform that continues to argue these points convincingly (Dimitriadis, for example, continues to do it better than most – see Dimitriadis et al., 2009). This chapter represents a re-examination of creativity in schools from a new perspective that first recognises a need to identify its absence, but not to end there. Even education theorists like Dewey (2001) wrote about the need for newness, in subject matter that becomes "dead and barren" (pp. 118-119), as distinct from real lived experience and life circumstances. We have known this for some time, and have seen the resulting artificial attempts by teachers to 'make' education feel more attractive, relevant and worthwhile. Such efforts so often remain unsuccessful by a disregard for the situatedness of the work – in both educational terms but also cultural ones. So how can we understand the current 'creativity explosion' in educational policy, and its increasing absence in classrooms? (For a discussion of the somewhat narrow ways in which 'creativity' is apparent in the higher education sector see Chapter Eight on 'creative industries').

The role of a director (and a teacher too perhaps) is, as Brook tells us, a strange role . . . in a sense the director is always an imposter, a guide at night who does not know the territory, and yet he has no choice—he must guide, learning the route as he goes. Deadliness often lies in wait when he does not recognize this situation, and hopes for the best, when it is the worst that he needs to face (1968, p. 38).

How often do educators turn our faces to the worst? Yet that is exactly where we need to start in order to revitalise education that speaks to this age. Brook takes a closer look at some important ways in which the decoupling of the arts and aesthetics from creativity and education robs us of a rich overlapping history in which both creative and pedagogical answers can be found. This decoupling is driven by a commodification of creativity, one in which creativity-as-innovation is fundable and teachable, but creativity-as-aesthetics is not. To better consider the conditions for this link between economics and creative education, we return to Brook's vision for theatre. He warns that deadly theatre (and any deadly industry?) always harbours many functionaries in its making and dissemination that enervate its creative drive:

> . . . there is always a deadly spectator, who for special reasons enjoys a lack of intensity and even a lack of entertainment, such as the scholar who emerges from routine performances of the classics smiling because nothing has distracted him from trying over and confirming his pet theories to himself, whilst reciting his favourite lines under his breath . . . unfortunately he lends the weight of his authority to dullness and so the Deadly Theatre goes on its way (p. 10).

Does Brook's deadly spectator bear comparison with Deadly Students or even Deadly Parents in the field of education? Certainly there are those who like things to remain business-as-usual in all walks of life. Education scholars, policymakers and journalists can sometimes appear as Deadly Critics, invested in the critique and not necessarily the innovation of institutional practices. Yet they alone are not to blame: like Walter Benjamin, Brook reinforces the inextricable nature of effective, well-functioning cultural products/productions like theatre and education and their nature as socially embedded. Indeed, their dependence on the society from which they have emerged is central to their efficacy. When and if "the day comes when the gap between [them] and the life of the society around [them becomes] too great" (p. 15) can be an indicator of their irrelevance, but also at times their ability to sit critically outside the cultural and institutional structures they were created to reflect. The roles of theatre (and all the arts) has always been to critically reflect, but education has the somewhat schizophrenic social function of being both cultural critique and cultural reproducer. The degree to which those in either field claim or model "nothing needs to change" (Brook, p. 17) can serve as an indicator of the vitality of its current stake.

Deadly Education and the Economic Imperative

The global trend of instituting a national curriculum—a wave which has already swept Europe and the United States—is now reaching the shores of Australia and its

CHAPTER 3

effects are the same: debate, revolt and, largely, business as usual. A living education, like a living theatre, is by its nature mortal, finite and relative: "In the theatre, every form once born is mortal; every form must be reconceived, and its new conception will bear the mark of all the influences that surround it . . . in this sense, the theatre is relativity" (p. 16). If creativity in education is a marker of relativity to its economic context, the message may well be that economies have always been intrinsically related to the making of art and cultural reflexivity, but have not dictated it.

But artmaking and education both need to maintain a degree of independence from their economic frameworks in order to fulfil their social functions. The difficulty in both fields is that they straddle culture as both insider and outsider (re)producers. In artistic terms, this is an age-old debate; in educational terms, it has yet to be articulated. If education—like art—is simply a function of reproduction for the state (think Nazi art, Stalinist schools), they both cease to either critique or extend current institutional and economic frameworks. In totalitarian regimes this is desirable, as maintenance of the status quo against the popular will is a necessary component of control and governmentality. In democracies, and certainly in capitalist growth economies, it is a sign of certain death. Capitalism depends upon expansion, and expansion cannot occur if only the status quo is maintained; hence the contemporary economic obsession with 'creativity and innovation'. This represents a somewhat schizophrenic cultural context in which western global economies recognise a need to use educational structures to increase productivity and recognise that in order to increase productivity mere manufacturing and reproduction/distribution will not suffice. However, creativity and innovation (even in centralised educational contexts) bring with them a degree of social critique, and this is a threat to the productivity imperative. They go, and have always gone, hand in hand:

> There is a deadly element everywhere; in the cultural set-up, in our inherited artistic values, in the economic framework . . . As we examine these we will see that deceptively the opposite seems also true, for within the Deadly Theatre there are often tantalising, abortive or even momentarily satisfying flickers of a real life (Brook, 1968, p. 17).

Brook identified this contradiction in theatre nearly five decades ago, and the same can be seen in education today. For all the educational rhetoric and resources invested in the pursuit of 'good' schools and good education, in creative terms " . . . the most deadly element is certainly economic" (1968, p. 17), and even elite schools can demonstrate this deadly element equally or moreso than their impoverished counterparts. Brook argued that the economic constraints of trying to create good theatre with insufficient development time (for example, in New York City, where high costs mean shortened development periods) were detrimental to the creative process, if not always to the product. He was suggesting that good art and creativity takes time. Good education too takes time, and certainly nurturing creativity in schools takes time. It is an investment that sometimes pays off, but not in ways that are compatible with contemporary educational testing and environments (see

Chapter Two on the Young Playwrights Festival for more). Yet perhaps ironically, the need for slow creativity is more familiar to industry environments (think Pixar again, or design firms) in which spaces for play, for entertainment, for down time, for socialising and for fresh air are increasingly evident – despite the so-called productivity imperative in schools. If industry is the driver for the standardisation turn in education, why then have we not recognised the central elements of *time* and *environment* in nurturing cultures of creativity?

Brook touched a neoliberal nerve when he cautioned, "time is not the be-all and end-all . . . time can also be used very badly: it is possible to sit around for months discussing and worrying and improvising without this showing in any way whatsoever" (p. 18). Is this what education systems are afraid of? Is it really just a fear of waste, and if so, why? There are daily examples of the ways in which huge sums are wasted in pursuit of improved results in countless industries; indeed, some may argue that the introduction of national curricula and systems of standardised testing are one such failed experiment in spending taxpayers' dollars. The persistently mixed results of the fast-track Teach for America program and its spin-offs (Teach First in the UK, and Teach for Australia amongst others) attests to the capacity of governments to trial expensive experiments without productivity guarantees (see for example Zeichner 2010, Maier 2012, and Heilig & Jez 2010 in the USA; Ofsted 2008, Muijs, Chapman & Armostrong 2012, and Wilby 2012 in the UK; and Scott, Weldon & Dinham 2010 in Australia). No one wants to be accused of wasting money or time, and yet it happens every day with barely a raised eyebrow. So why the worry about creative education and the arts?

The secret to re-enlivening education with creativity is more elusive than a simple matter of time or resources. As Brook rightly reminds his readers, "occasionally in the theatre what one loosely calls chemistry, or luck, brings about an astonishing rush of energy, and then invention follows invention in lightning chain reaction . . . but this is rare . . . " (p. 18). How can we create the conditions for that elusive 'rush of energy', that million-dollar chemistry in classrooms? If it is too difficult to identify the skills and capacities requisite to nurture creativity, perhaps our best bet is to try to identify the characteristics of the *context* of a Living Education, a Living Theatre of learning, in which that elusive thing may be invited to occur.

Productive Risk-Taking as Good Business

Many have written elsewhere about the need for productive risk-taking in nurturing creativity (Carlisle & Jordan, 2012; Craft, 2011; Harris & Staley, 2011) and the increasing lack of such opportunity in mainstream schools. Yet disengagement discourses and inflammatory media coverage of the 'crisis in our schools' never looks at the shrinking space and time for risk-taking or even daydreaming. In a productivity-driven environment, the need for such 'empty spaces' is almost completely overlooked. Rather, teachers now bear distinct similarities to Brook's director in commercial theatres in which "the director must deliver the goods or be fired," (p. 18) and it is impossible to talk of teaching and learning without measures of productivity or what Brook calls delivering 'the goods'.

This turn toward productivity shows that "the artistic consequences are severe . . . each of these parts is brutalised . . . in a sense everyone is continually in danger" (Benjamin in Brook, 1968, p. 19), and that imposing an economic imperative on both theatre and education - as similarly generative endeavours - creates similar tensions. But there is a contradiction in how well it appears to work:

> . . . in theory, this tension should lead to an atmosphere of fear, and, were this the case, its destructiveness would be clearly seen. In practice, however, the underlying tension leads just as directly to the famous Broadway atmosphere, which is very emotional, throbbing with apparent warmth and good cheer (1968, p. 19).

Warmth and good cheer, that is, for those who find a place in this competitive system obsessed with outcomes. Brook's choice of the word 'apparent' is telling. Whether or not you share his view, the efficiency of this productivity machine in a neoliberal context is undeniably reassuring to funders. Education is no different: the productivity imperative means that numbers of results are more reassuring to consumers than quality of results. In such an atmosphere, little thought is given to those who might be excluded, or the quality of work or experience that is lost. Profitability and continually accelerating productivity is not sustainable, nor is it the whole picture, as Brook signals above with his acknowledgement of the difference between what is seen versus what emerges in practice.

Within education, cracks are beginning to appear. Across the globe, two competing imperatives are hurtling toward each other in a contest for primary position: that is, global flows and elites, in which school choice and international qualification transferability is of primary importance and, contrastingly, a growing tide of rebellion, in the United States, Australia and other sites of standardisation, against the subordination of schools to standardised curricula, tests and international measures that erase student-centred learning and locally-relevant pedagogies. All shifts, turns and revolutions are temporary, as is the creative turn and the education revolution that it seems to herald. The signs of imminent change are clear in growing resistance to the narrow and fragmented testing that has already begun. This burgeoning resistance movement is inexorably linked to creativity. Remember here that Brook's critique of theatrical machine culture was followed by an explosion of theatrical creativity in New York, London and elsewhere across the globe in the rich period following this contraction. For example, Judith Malina's Living Theatre was formed in New York City in 1947, but took flight in 1968 (the same year as Brook's text) as a reconceptualisation of what a vibrant non-commercial theatre could be. Working in a multitude of ways against the economic imperatives lamented by Brook, the Living Theatre continues to this day (http://www.livingtheatre.org) and serves as a reminder of the interrelationship between the characteristics of Deadly Theatre and something more. In the ebb and flow of cultural production, there are no absolutes. Similarly, a Living Education is occurring all around us already, yet remains invisible to many working in Deaducation, as both un-educational and uncreative, and demands a closer look.

In neoliberal environments, both creative and educational progress is inhibited. As schools become increasingly regimented, time-poor and test-rich, there is no longer room for the free and trusting collaboration required for both real learning and creativity. In "such conditions there is rarely the quiet and security in which anyone may dare expose [him]self . . . I mean the true unspectacular intimacy that long work and true confidence in other people brings about" (Brook, 1968, p. 19). Profitability fights risk at all costs—literally!—and in this way erodes the room for and possibility of experimentation. If the kind of experimentation that Brooks was discussing in theatre back in the 1960s was one of the first casualties of this erosion of real time, real experimentation and real collaboration between hungry minds and souls, the dawn of the 21st century sees this risk-aversion gaining traction in sectors such as education, in which, "from all sides the same answer – the risk is too great, too many disappointments" which leads to a " Deadly Theatre dig[ging] its own grave" (p. 21). Deadly Education—or Deaducation—is similarly digging its own grave, and this may open the way forward for a dismantling of education as we know it, forcing the need for real educational innovation.

Productive Risk-Taking as Good Education

Brook's lengthy description of the impalpable but crucial exchange between actors and an audience bears striking resemblances to a teacher and class. In this way, the mysticism in a 'creative classroom' can move away from dead conversations about pedagogy and curriculum and move instead further toward relationship and learning. We can refocus attention on what is actually happening for the students, rather than always, relentlessly, teachers. What if the following were a famous teacher's description of a classroom interaction rather than a theatre performance?:

> As he spoke the first name, the half silence became a dense one. Its tension caught the reader [teacher], there was an emotion in it, shared between him and them and it turned all his attention away from himself on to the subject matter he was speaking. Now the audience's concentration began to guide him: his inflexions were simple, his rhythms true: this in turn increased the audience's interest and so the two-way current began to flow. When this was ended, no explanations were needed, the audience had seen itself in action, it had seen how many layers silence can contain (1968, p. 25).

So what are the characteristics of a 'good' learner, or teacher? Many agree that teachers are not actors, that teaching is not a performance, and that students 'see through' what are presumed to be false masks or contrived performances. But what

CHAPTER 3

if teaching is exactly like acting, in its best sense? What if acting—when it is a form of Living Theatre—is indeed art, a tool for reflecting back to us our own foibles, vulnerabilities and passions: isn't this precisely what a good teacher must do? And what of entertainment, or fun? Some believe it is the key to effective learning and teaching, a necessary component of intrinsic motivation in lifelong students who find learning 'fun'. Yet certainly we are living through an educational moment in which all vestiges of fun are being rapidly leached away through relentless teaching to the standardised tests that predominate, including a return to high-stakes rote learning. In such times, it is of no surprise that the media (and many industry funders and drivers, including the ubiquitous Mr Bill Gates) continually return to teachers' deficits to lay blame for poor learning outcomes. If we let Brook note the interrelationship between actors and their audiences, we might find similarities to critical educators' approaches to good teaching. He says, "occasionally, an actor can completely dominate any house, and so, like a master matador, he can work the audience the way he pleases . . . usually, however, this cannot come from the stage alone" (p. 25). His effort to define a living theatre of the 1960s offers us much nearly fifty years later: if education is to come back alive, it will not be from the 'stage' alone.

Critical teacher educators continually repeat the old adage, "be the guide on the side, not the sage on the stage", and yet universities continue to build lecture theatres (with 'stages') and scholars are persistently required to embody 'expert' postures. It comforts consumers, makes them feel as if they are getting their (enormous amount of) money's worth. Yet what is it they are getting? The current obsession with creativity as an elusive element in the learning-teaching-producing triad is an unarticulated recognition that current educational trends and the industries they fuel are becoming increasingly emaciated as we move maniacally toward a kind of productivity that removes all the relationality and time for experimentation that is a pre-requisite for creativity, artistry, innovation and indeed good mental health. Brook could have been talking about present-day education when he described a theatre in the capitalist 1960s that had "many sloppy meanings . . . in most of the world, the theatre has no exact place in society, no clear purpose, it only exists in fragments" (p. 27). If Brook could easily be talking about education in the 21st century, he could also just as easily be characterising creativity.

He tells us that "deadly acting becomes the heart of the crisis" (p. 28) of deadly theatre (just like deadly teaching becomes the heart of Deaducation). Like 'lifelong learning', teachers seldom have time for deep professional development or innovation. Gaining further credentials is not the same as lifelong learning or creative or pedagogical development. Yet that is what professional development has often become, perhaps uncoincidentally alongside the corporatisation of teacher education.

Yet what exactly characterises a good, living, creative teacher can still be elusive. By adapting Brook's definition of a good director, a creative teacher is flexible and constantly adapting, adjusting and experimenting based on the empirical evidence she or he perceives. The living teacher is still characterised in part by mastery, but not mastery alone:

> flexing muscles alone cannot develop an art; scales don't make a pianist nor does fingerwork help a painter's brush: yet a great pianist practises finger exercises for many hours a day, and Japanese painters spend their lives practising to draw a perfect circle (p. 30).

But while mastery in art forms like theatre has been examined and reflected upon for centuries by those like Brook, how many of us really reflect as deeply, as honestly and as passionately on teaching as an art, as a true act of creative exchange? More than skills or tools, as today's professional development is defined, today's 'good teacher' may be grounded in effective relationships, collaboration and adaptability. By looking critically with Brook we can see productive parallels between the roles of 'living' theatre and 'living' education.

> Four hundred years ago it was possible for a dramatist to wish to bring the pattern of events in the outside world, the inner events of complex men isolated as individuals, the vast tug of their fears and aspirations into open conflict. Drama was exposure, it was confrontation, it was contradiction and it led to analysis, involvement, recognition and, eventually, to an awakening of understanding (pp. 35-36).

The characteristics of creative work are at odds with the current climate of educational standardisation, productivity and reproducibility. In dramatists' terms, "Shakespeare was not a peak without a base, floating magically on a cloud: he was supported by scores of lesser dramatists . . . sharing the same ambition for wrestling with what Hamlet calls the forms and pressures of the age" (p. 36). Creative teachers, too, wrestle with the forms and pressures of our own age; they cannot be produced like iPads from a conveyor belt of teacher education in which all look and function the same. The frustrating and fantastic truth is that great teachers are as rare as great artists. And a living education is as elusive and costly as a living theatre, but to become so requires that it be continually reinvented in relation to the times and places in which it exists.

The particular challenge of our current time is to continue the search for such complexities in a climate of economic rationalism. Indeed, the questions cannot be asked outside of a consideration of the material conditions in which we work. The productivity constraints which prevent us from defining great teachers, like great artists, should not compel us to ill-define them. Rather, it should compel us "to look at the problem [of creative mastery] more closely and try to find out what exactly the special Shakespeare qualities are" (p 47), in the context of our own neoliberal times. By imagining that the creative genius in the classroom can be likened to one in the theatre, Brook—like so many creativity scholars today—

attempts to address the definitional problems of his time within a particular economic context. What he suggests may nevertheless have transposable application to our own:

> Shakespeare used the same unit that is available today—a few hours of public time ... The technical devices ... were the ones the author was compelled to develop to satisfy his needs: and the author had a precise, human and social aim which gave him reason for searching for his themes, reason for searching for his means, reason for making theatre (p. 36).

These strategies and compulsions of Shakespeare are also present in today's dynamic classrooms, and they are inextricably linked to economic imperatives. Robinson has defined 21st-century education systems very similarly, and famously compared their outdated institutions to schools constructed to reflect Victorian industrial economies as a basis for arguing the urgent need for structural change. Brook *did* revolutionise the theatre—if only for a while—and his work and analytical writings influenced new generations of practitioners of *living theatre*. Robinson's call for an education revolution that moves vigorously toward creativity and sustainability and away from factory and assembly-line models of education has not yet been answered, but educational and creative innovations in online learning, digital technologies and open classrooms may be giving contemporary teachers the tools and aims with which to create creative and educational change, just as Shakespeare did in his time.

Brook's deadly critics are comparable to deadly policymakers, and they work against the interests of theatre-makers. He describes the distinction between his three types thusly:

> the critic who no longer enjoys the theatre is obviously a deadly critic, the critic who loves the theatre but is not critically clear what this means, is also a deadly critic; the vital critic is the critic who has clearly formulated for himself what the theatre *could be*—and who is bold enough to throw this formula into jeopardy each time he participates (p. 33).

Similarly, what we might identify as deadly policymakers work against the vitality of educators who would pursue dynamic innovation and context-specific curriculum and pedagogy. Despite the constant lambasting of teachers in the media, teachers increasingly have little or no power in defining what the core business of of their classroom work is. Like critics, policymakers often don't come from teaching backgrounds, but instead often from business or academic backgrounds. They - who so often speak on behalf of teachers and educational change - are more often like Brook's deadly 'actor', so enmeshed with their idealistic visions of what education *used* to be—or, worse, *should be*—that they are essentially of no use at all. All the while, the creative teacher who inhabits the stone cold middle ground of education, with her eyes firmly fixed on a better world and prepared to pursue it fearlessly, and who recognises that it must by its nature be a journey into an unfamiliar land, is the kind of critic-advocate-interlocutor that creative education surely needs.

SLOW EDUCATION

Figure 6. Culture Shack, hip hop workshop (2010).

It is not all bad news. That the current system seems fixed against this kind of educator represents a fissure, a crack, a kind of potential, a promise of change and—dare I say it?—innovation: a positive sign to be celebrated. Too often in the current climate we waste all our energies and time on lamenting what education is not rather than pursuing what it surely can be. The very fact that there is such widespread dissatisfaction is a clear indicator that the time for change has come. This change is inexorably linked to both speed and aesthetics. *'Speed and aesthetics?'*, you may ask. Yes. Just as Marshall McLuhan dared to suggest that 'the medium is the message', our acceleration of creativity or creative processes has aesthetic implications as well as economic ones—in other words, not only is the medium the message, but the speed of dissemination determines the process.

At its most basic level, this can be seen readily in the ways the consumption of television products have changed in recent years. No longer content with the 'slow food' system of waiting for network television to decide on, develop and distribute our television products, viewers are now driving the industry through global release models (think Netflix series *House of Cards*) with online access to television shows, replacing the staggered international release model of film and television that has predominated. Increasingly, critics and consumers are commenting on the ways in which modern television (and online) series more closely resemble a Dickensian serialised novel of the 19th century than a weekly drama or comedy installation from 1950s American TV. As McLuhan (and to some degree, Benjamin before him) foreshadowed, in the age of digital media the medium (form) has not only come to dictate structures of creative products, but their content as well. Now, the same pattern can be seen in education. Increasingly teachers, students and parents are no longer content for the 'big studio bosses' (akin to policymakers and education funders) to decide, develop and distribute our education products and are taking

CHAPTER 3

matters into their own hands. But this has implications for both speed and aesthetics/content in the education as well as the entertainment sector.

Certainly television and other media forms have impacted perceptions of both good education and good entertainment (including theatre), and no doubt they will continue to do so. Brook identified some particular ways in which the pervasive characteristics of television in particular have 'degraded' audiences' judgments of theatre and art, and in the contemporary context we can argue too that this altering derives in part from social media and online digital formats. Brook suggested that "the influence of television has been to accustom viewers of all classes all over the world to make instant judgement . . . the steady discrediting of non-theatre virtues is now beginning to clear the way for other virtues" (p. 37). His attention to the acceleration of productivity and its formal implications echoes Benjamin, but also leads us to consider that potential for, not a return to something past but perhaps, a slower, more exploratory approach to creativity, the arts and education.

In Pursuit of Inertia and Creative Leaps in Learning

If education can remake itself in ways that are more compatible with creativity, it must slow down, dig deep and return to an experiential, experimental relationship with learning rather than the increasingly "rush 'em in and rush 'em out" outcome-oriented schooling described by Dimitriadis, Cole & Costello (2009, p. 362). If teachers, administrators and policymakers are able to recognise or re-embrace its slowness, maybe we can make room once again for the kind of creativity that Brook describes. Creativity requires exploration, productive risk-taking and self-guided experimentation. In industry-driven educational contexts, creativity-as-innovation dictates imperatives of 'success' and demands 'productivity' (for more on this, see Chapter Five), goals that are contradictory to the necessary 'slowness' and open-ended conditions of creative exploration. In such a 'dead' and airless educational climate—as in 'dead theatre'—standardisation (or sameness) forecloses both pedagogical and creative opportunities. Brook's call to breathe new life into theatre can be taken as a starting point for imagining a resuscitated education system: that is, in favour of the 'slow-ification' of education, borrowing processes and characteristics from the 'slow food' movement (Slow Education, n.d.; Slow Food, n.d.). This necessity for a return to slowness and exploration amongst students and teachers is a move not only to return to an understanding of the real nature of creativity, but also toward a more sustainable reconceptualisation of education and indeed of aesthetics—a linked creativity and aesthetics which encompasses all areas of radical and risky exploration.

> . . . and I noticed something about the way the ball moved, so I went to my father and [he said to me] ' . . . .this tendency is called inertia but nobody knows why it's true. He knew the difference between knowing the name for something, and knowing something" (Feynman, n.d.).

Scholars have noted the ways in which two global growth trends—toward so-called creative economies and creative classes (Florida, 2012) and simultaneously toward standardised assessment in education—present a seeming contradiction (Sefton-Green, 2011; Costantino, 2011; Grossman & Sonn, 2010; Vaughan, Harris & Caldwell, 2011; Caldwell & Vaughan, 2012) for educators, scientists and sociologists. But creative pedagogies are nothing new, and even creative agents (teaching artists in schools to some) have been around nearly as long as Shakespeare (Centrestage, n.d.; Herrington & Brian, 2006). Yet creative pedagogies and real creativity are not the same; as Feynman understood, understanding something and having a name for it are two different things.

Seelig (2012) calls creativity the 'endlessly renewable resource' and, like many other creativity theorists from a broad range of disciplines and sectors (Taylor & Littleton, 2012; Sawyer, 2011, 2007; Michalko, 2001), attempts to define the skills and qualities associated with creative genius or at least creative productivity. That there is a quantifiable (as well as qualifiable) aspect to this 'new creativity' is no accident: if Seelig is correct, creativity could well be 21st-century employers' newest best friend. But in order to hire for it, and in order to educate for it, one must first understand it. And so in the last five years an increasing number of texts (including webinars, YouTube videos, TED talks and also policy documents) have contributed to the growing discourse on creativity and its possible role in classrooms and industry. The link there is also no accident: classrooms are increasingly tied to the demands of industry and the critical funds made available by industry. Educating 21st-century citizens is now synonymous with educating, not for 'good citizenship', but for productivity, industrial leadership and—yes—profit.

The State of Play in Schools

> I hope we will even learn how to see what we are not able to describe in words, much less measure. And, through the consciousness borne of such an attitude, I hope we will be creative enough to invent methods and languages that do justice to what we have seen. (Eisner 2012, p 121)

One may ask why so many are turning to school-community partnerships for arts-based expertise, as though it's not the realm of schools but rather what 'outsiders' bring from the 'real world'. See, for example, the many well-documented partnership models in Australia, the UK and USA, including Arnold Aprill and his Chicago Arts Partnership, Maxine Greene and the Lincoln Centre Institute for the Arts in Education, Creative Partnerships in the UK (now defunct) and Australia's recent formalisation between the Australian (national) Curriculum and The Songroom artist-in-schools and online program (for more see Sefton-Green et al., 2011). And while the big handbooks in this and other scholarly areas remain overly-focused on the European, British, Canadian and American contexts, Australia, Asia and other regions are not far behind. The clear message is twofold: that creativity is driven by marketplace

CHAPTER 3

concerns and arts education experiences in schools are being increasingly outsourced to consultancies, and no longer the domain of teachers. We seem to have come a long way from Bruner's framing of 'art as a way of knowing', knowledge as multiple rather than unified, and Bloom's championing of scaffolding and 'categorisation' (narrative mode versus paradigmatic modes of thinking) as cognition develops. Now the arts are simply an enrichment activity offered by outside 'experts', others whose main 'business' is the arts not learning. This approach, while valuing the expertise of artists, suggests that the 'teaching' is inherent, whereas the arts (for teacher-artists) is not. While it may offer some short-term means for injecting more discipline-specific arts hours into the school day, these models only reinforce the separation between a marketised conception of creative arts, and an emaciated notion of teaching and learning.

Creative play in schools—in its pure sense—has lost its way. As an activity in which learners are 'allowed' to meander through an experience—any experience— which has recognised educational value, play has been somewhat sidelined by the headlong rush toward competitive results leading to university entrance. The alternative is narrated in Dickensian terms evoking workhouses, unfulfilment, poverty and despair. The sad truth is, this may not be so far from the truth. The result is that even creative play is hurtling toward commodification by a global education system that really doesn't understand it, but is frightened enough of this unknown global future to take notice. Our response, it would seem, is to standardise even the unknown.

Eisner is still articulating the possibility of a new kind of schooling, and history may just be catching up with his visionary stance. His long-time battle in favour of the creative assessment of process rather than product is needed more than ever in this marketised educative moment of 'technical rationality' (2002, p. xiii). Since Eisner famously argued with Bruner in favour of assessments of creative pedagogies that measure process rather than products, the debate has raged about how—if we are to allow that creativity has any *academic* place in schools at all—process should be measured. The debate continues today, with Sefton-Green and others extolling the virtues of artists-in-schools program (or, in the UK, *Creative Agents* and *Creative Partnerships*), all of which seem to overtly or subtextually suggest that teachers really have no idea about real creativity, and artists have no real pedagogical skills if they haven't been to teachers college.

Resuscitate to Educate?

But education needs something more. Whether it is being nurtured by external agents, inter-sector professional and community collaborators, or teachers from a range of disciplines within schools, creativity is on the rise. A quick review of maths education literature in particular, shows the ways in which creativity is taking an increasingly dynamic role in those classrooms. Science and health scholars too are noting the ways in which their areas of study are benefitting from creative approaches

Figure 7. Culture Shack, Samoan crew (2010).

to learning and research. But is there a difference worth noting between, say, baking a cake in chemistry class, and timetabling for discipline-based arts education in schools? Many educators and policymakers think the answer is no.

The only indication bucking this trend is coming from the students themselves. And, largely, it can be seen in digital technologies more readily than elsewhere. There are two clear indications that creativity in technology is alive and well: 1) young people are driving it themselves and 2) adults are afraid of it. In gaming, animation, video tools and social media, young people are driving their own learning through creative exploration and invention and, in most ways, schools are playing catch-up. Just as the slippery notion of 'creativity' is being increasingly deployed in policy and curriculum documents, so too are terms like 'digital', 'technology' and 'ICT'. Similarly, however, the kinds of ICT that are filtering into these 'accredited' documents and websites are often all too safe, simplistic and disconnected from the interest young people have in using digital tools creatively (Erstad & Sefton-Green, 2012; Thomson & Sefton-Green, 2010). What schools and policy-writers *are* understanding though, is that young people *will* learn, just not always in the ways in which teachers and parents feel comfortable (O'Mara & Harris, 2013; Iiyoshi & Kumar, 2008). This divide—generational as well as creative—is pivotal in unpacking the creative/standards hyperbole that at times sounds so contradictory. But equally clear is that the creative arts and creative strategies give young people an expressive and personal way back in to education and engagement when little else works (Harris & Staley, 2011; O'Brien & Donelan, 2008; Edutopia, n.d.).

Sefton-Green, Thomson et al demand of school reform that, "if we do not start with a clear and articulated imaginary of changing learning in classrooms—and this does not mean simply doing what has always been done better than at present—then there will be little actual change in learning" (2011, p. 415). It is certainly possible that Robinson has not gone nearly far enough in his call to move schools out of a 19th-century model of education. In fact, the very way we understand the relationship underpinning 'to educate' may be obsolete. Not only through the rapid advancement of digital and online technologies, but also due to the evolution of global communities and information movements overall, the notion of 'learning' is perhaps a better or more accurate way of describing a contemporary acquisition of knowledge than is 'educating'. Does anyone really educate anyone anymore? For that matter, did we ever? To save, to educate, to empower—verbs all charmingly out of date to a 21st-century palate.

Creativity is, in its essence, a form of self-education. The simultaneous exploration of aesthetic alongside philosophical, affective and conceptual concerns is not only authentic (it integrates current knowledges of the student, which are also completely integrated in her or his everyday life) but dynamic—it is naturally flexible rather than self-consciously so. As Eisner (2002, 2012) and others have argued for more than forty years, it is inherently interdisciplinary and related to everyday concerns as well as historical and theoretical ones. So why aren't we using more of it in schools?

Research and knowledge itself has taken a rhizomatic turn and will continue to do so in the information age: structures of knowledge are increasingly arboreal rather than hierarchical (Denzin, 2003; Cormier, 2008). Schools will eventually be dismantled by their own obsolescence if they don't change. The advent of massive online open courses (MOOCs) and other open learning and open information-sharing platforms (creative commons, open access journals, etc.) advance this inevitability. While many feel that MOOCs are not yet what they claim to be, social media has shown us that real market share capture begins with free giveaways—the oldest trick in the book. It is reasonable to assume then, within the first two decades of the new century, that education itself will find its own way to become user-pays and universally available. The "culture of scarcity" described by Dimitriadis et al. (2009, p. 368) which previously plagued arts teachers is now permeating whole schools; indeed, some argue, systems of education worldwide. Like universities, the function of schools has itself shifted—from its own brand of aesthetic training to one of productivity.

If this is true, the status-value of schools will advance (aligned with standardisation and testing, branding as readily-identifiable global elites), and the affective education—an education of feeling and aesthetics—will become personalised through online information sharing systems, creating different global communities. Creativity will dominate these new sites of learning, and 'old-school' schools will become the sites of a kind of 'deaducation' that increasingly resembles the factories and charnel houses of other lines of production. So which schools need resuscitation? Not globally elite schools, which increasingly represent entry points into global economic and social networks for those who can afford them. It is the local unnetworked schools that are threatened to become even further impoverished, the certificates they offer increasingly worthless. Young people will learn online about places and things they cannot afford to access in 'real life', and their work and their aesthetics will come to resemble their groundedness in local realities and markets. Brook tells us:

> When we say deadly, we never mean dead: we mean something depressingly active, but for this very reason capable of change. The first step towards this change is facing the simple unattractive fact that most of what is called theatre anywhere in the world is a travesty of a word once full of sense . . . we are too busy to ask the only vital question which measures the whole structure. Why theatre at all? What for? (p. 40).

Can we ask ourselves Brook's question about schools too? Why school at all, and for what? This question may be necessary for finding a truly creative education or, put another way, a place for true creativity in education. But as long as policymakers concern themselves only with globally distributable, globally-rankable and globally-exportable products and workforces, education systems (like creative ones) will continue to accelerate, with the resultant proliferation suggesting a kind of pedagogical superficiality. Slowing down doesn't in itself promise a better kind of education, or an increased opportunity for creative exploration and productive risk-taking, but it sets the conditions for doing so.

REFERENCES

Benjamin, W. (2002). *Walter Benjamin: Selected writings 1913–1926* (Vol. 1). Boston, MA: Harvard.
Brook, P. (1968). *The empty space*. New York, NY: Athaneum.
Caldwell, B., & Vaughan, T. (2012). *Transforming education through the arts*. Melbourne, VIC: Taylor & Francis.
Carlisle, O., & Jordan, A. (Eds). (2012). *Approaches to creativity: A guide for teachers*. McGraw Hill Education/ Open University Press.
Centrestage. (n.d.). *Teaching playwriting in schools*. Baltimore, MD: Centerstage. Retrieved from http://www.centerstage.org/Portals/0/PDF/06PlaywrightsHandbook.pdf
Cormier, D. (2008). *Rhizomatic education : Community as curriculum*. Retrieved from http://davecormier.com/edblog/2008/06/03/rhizomatic-education-community-as-curriculum/
Costantino, T. (2011). Research creative learning: A review essay. *International Journal of Education & the Arts, 12*(review 7). Retrieved from http://www.ijea.org/v12r7/
Craft, A. (2011). *Creativity and education futures*. London, UK: Trentham.
Denzin, N. K. (2003). *Performance ethnography: Critical pedagogy and the politics of culture*. Thousand Oaks, CA: Sage.
Dewey, J. (2001). *The school and society & the child and the curriculum*. Mineola, NY: Dover Publications, Inc.
Dimitriadis, G., Cole, E., & Costello, A. (2009). The social field(s) of arts education today: Living vulnerability in neo-liberal times. *Discourse: Studies in the Cultural Politics of Education, 30*(4), 361–379.
Edutopia. (n.d.). Retrieved from http://www.edutopia.org/student-playwrights-project-playwriting
Eisner, E. (2012). *Reimagining schools: the selected works of Elliot W. Eisner*. New York, NY: Routledge.
Eisner, E. (2002). *The arts and the creation of mind*. New Haven: Yale University Press.
Erstad, O., & Sefton-Green, J. (2012). *Identity, community, and learning lives in the digital age*. Cambridge, UK: Cambridge University Press.
Feynman, R. (n.d.). *Inertia and fathers. The world institute of slowness*. Retrieved from http://www.theworldinstituteofslowness.com/sloweducation

Florida, R. (2012). *The rise of the creative class – Revisited* (10th Anniversary Ed.). New York, NY: Basic Books/Perseus.

Grossman, M., & Sonn, C. (2010). *New moves: Understanding the impacts of the song room programs for young people from refugee backgrounds*. Melbourne: Victoria University.

Harris, A. (2012). *Ethnocinema: Intercultural arts education*. The Netherlands: Springer.

Harris, A., & Staley, J. (2011). Schools without walls: Creative endeavour and disengaged young people. *Journal of Arts & Creativity in Education*. Retrieved from http://jaceonline.com.au/issues/issue-title/

Heilig, J. V., & Jez, S. J. (2010). *Teach for America: A review of the evidence. The great lakes center for education research & practice*. Boulder, CO: Educaiton and the Pubilc Interest Center/Univ of Colorado.

Herrington, J., & Brian, C. (2006). *Playwrights teach playwriting*. University of Michigan: Smith & Kraus.

Iiyoshi, T., & Kumar, M. S. V. (Eds). (2008). *Opening up education: the collective advancement of education through open technology, open content, and open knowledge*. Boston, MA: Institute of Technology Publishing.

Maier, A. (2012, January–February). Doing good and doing well: Credentialism and Teach for America. *Journal of Teacher Education, 63*(1), 10–22.

Michalko, M. (2001). *Cracking creativity: The secrets of creative genius*. Berkeley, CA: Ten Speed Press.

Muijs, D.,Chapman, C., & Armstrong, P. (2012). Teach first: Pedagogy and outcomes. The impact of an alternative certification programme. *Journal for Educational Research Online, 4*(2), 29–64.

O'Brien, A., & Donelan, K. (2008). *The arts and youth at risk: Global and local challenges*. Melbourne: Cambridge Scholars Press.

Ofsted. (2008). *Rising to the challenge: A review of the Teach First initial teacher training programme*. London, UK: Crown/Alexandra House.

O'Mara, B., & Harris, A. (2013). *Intercultural collaboration in a digital age: Culture Shack and ICT pathways with migrant and refugee-background youth*. Race, Ethnicity and Education.

Robinson, K. (2011). *Out of our minds: Learning to be creative* (2nd ed.). Boston, MA: Capstone/Wiley.

Sawyer, K. (Ed.). (2011). *Structure and Improvisation in creative teaching*. New York, NY: Cambridge University Press.

Sawyer, K. (2007). *Group genius: The creative power of collaboration*. Cambridge, MA: Perseus/Basic Books.

Scott, C., Weldon, P., & Dinham, S. (2010). *Teach for Australia Pathway: Evaluation report phase 1 of 3* (April–July 2010). Melbourne: ACER Press.

Seelig, T. (2012). *InGenius: A crash course on creativity*. New York, NY: HarperOne.

Sefton-Green, J., Thomson, P., Jones, K., & Bresler, L. (Eds.). (2011). *The Routledge international handbook of creative learning*. London, UK: Routledge.

Sefton-Green, J. (2011). Judgment, authority and legitimacy: evaluating creative learning. In J. Sefton-Green, P. Thomson, K. Jones & L. Bresler (Eds.), *The Routledge international handbook of creative learning* (pp. 311–319). London, UK: Routledge.

Sefton-Green, J. (2010). *Researching creative agents for the creative partnerships national program (UK)*. Retrieved from http://www.julianseftongreen.net/?page_id=4

Slow Education. (n.d.). Retrieved from http://sloweducation.co.uk/?m=201109

Slow Education/Slow Food website (n.d.). Retrieved from http://www.slowmovement.com/slow_schools.php

Taylor, S., & Littleton, K. (2012). *Contemporary identities of creativity and creative work*. Denver: Littleton.

Thomson, P., & Sefton-Green, J. (2011). *Researching creative learning: Methods and issues*. UK: Routledge.

Vaughan, T., Harris, J., & Caldwell, B. (2011). *Bridging the gap in school achievement through the arts: Summary report*. Melbourne, VIC: The Song Room.

Wilby, P. (2012). *Teaching's man with a mission to free young Britons from 'slavery'*. Retrieved October 30, 2012, from The Guardian: http://www.theguardian.com/education/2012/oct/29/social-mobility-teach-first-programme

Zeichner, K. (2010). Competition, economic rationalization, increased surveillance, and attacks on diversity: Neo-liberalism and the transformation of teacher education in the U.S. *Journal of Teaching and Teacher Education, 26*(8), 1544–1552.

CHAPTER 4

ETHICS 'VERSUS' AESTHETICS

Best Frenemies?

Figure 8. Melbourne graffiti, #3 (2013).

A creator who isn't seized by the throat by a set of impossibilities is no creator. A creator is someone who creates his own impossibilities, and thereby creates possibilities. It's by banging your head against the wall that you find an answer (Deleuze, 1992, p. 292).

Live within your century but do not become its creature (Schiller, 1965, 61).

INTRODUCTION

Any consideration of aesthetics and ethics must not completely ignore the long and complicated history of previous investigations, perhaps starting with Friedrich Schiller and his 1794 text *On the Aesthetic Education of Man*. In it (and elsewhere), he argued that art and aesthetics are invariably a political affair, and—like Rousseau —that the aesthetic characteristics of art can and should remind us of our higher nature. Such classical idealism may still have relevance today, particularly for education which continues to grapple with the question of whether we should be educating young people for what our society *is* or for what we want it to be. Schiller, of course, saw aesthetics in the service of education for what it can be. Unfortunately, the current 'creativity explosion' (Osborne, 2003) and 'creative imperative' (Jeanes & De Cock, 2005) bear little similarity to these ideals.

The current commodification of creativity and its ubiquity can be considered a kind of new 'pedagogical imaginary' (Harris & Lemon, 2012), contributing to "a new research imaginary" (Weis, Fine, & Dimitriadis, 2009, p. 437) in education, for diverse audiences, research styles and collaborative sites. As Jeanes & De Cock (2005) remind us, "one could be forgiven for getting a little confused, as it appears that creativity is both ubiquitous and severely lacking in today's institutions" (p. 7). We are now in the strange liminal state of vastly different sectors and actors sharing a disarmingly overlapping creativity discourse: from economics, to management, from technology to mathematics and pure sciences, to education, the arts and humanities. The purpose of this chapter is to critically examine some of the ways in which ethics and aesthetics don't always fit together in creative research, arts-based research or creativity education. Nearly one hundred years ago, John Dewey (1934) addressed the issue, framing it as 'process' versus 'product': the same wrestling with binary distinctions that Deleuze made famous in his considerations of 'being' versus 'becoming' (1992; 2001).

As teachers, and as researchers, we often want our students to 'have an experience', which is a great and noble ethics by which to live. On the other hand, the artist and the consumer both want a satisfying aesthetic experience; yet describing what constitutes such an experience is difficult due to its changeable and elusive nature. There is no 'laundry list' of creative skills or creative success or a creatively successful product in any artform—a state of affairs which is anathema to current educational competencies and skill-based teaching. There is no standardised test, as it were, for the perfect creative benchmark, which is precisely part of its inherent nature and contemporary allure. This chapter examines some challenges in conducting creative research, including the often-binarised ways in which audiences receive this work, despite researchers' intentions to transcend such old-fashioned opposites as 'ethics' and 'aesthetics'.

So in trying to typify, and then teach, nurture or even schematise a creativity that conservative sectors like education can get behind (with funding, policy, etc.) in these neoliberal times of increasingly global standardisation and efficiency, adjectives and definitions like 'chaos', 'emergent' and 'generative' can be scary. It is important to note that no matter how far creativity seems to be moving from arts and arts education in the current climate, aesthetics remains firmly embedded in both commodified and uncommodified creativity (Jeanes and De Cock, 2005). I will say more about this later, but I mention it here so that readers will hold in their minds the puzzle of why perhaps aesthetics remains an integral part of all creative endeavour, as well as what this might tell us about what is most central to our continuing need for creativity and creative arts in our societies, and systems of education, which remain caught in waves of unprecedented flux. Although the aesthetic might be changing, or—as I argue here—although there is a 'new aesthetic imaginary' different from the ones we have turned to before, what remains is the high value still placed on matters of aesthetics. When and if this is in tension with an ethics of creativity is the topic of this chapter.

Artists and art theorists have ceaselessly searched for satisfactory definitions of what constitutes 'art' that were inextricably tied to matters of aesthetics. When considering creativity, however, the question of ethics is always present when arts processes or products are concerned, because where there is an activity (i.e., process), a relationship is also implied: the direct involvement of the maker, but also the face-to-face or other intended or unintended involvement of audience or collaborator through production or sensory experience. Therefore, a consideration of ethics is always present and inextricable from the process of artmaking. Yet if this is so, why then is an aesthetics of creativity so severely understudied and as under-theorised as an ethics of creativity?

More often, creative arts have their own resistant ethics such as 'revolution', 'porn', 'camp', and 'art for art's sake!'. When have you ever heard 'education for education's sake'? Not perhaps since Rousseau argued for the self-determination of the titular character in his treatise on (boy) education, *Emile* (1762), has education for its own sake been so in style. Today, the idea of education for the love of it, or to expand one's mind, or to become a better person, has long since passed. These days—perhaps even more than in Dickens' *Hard Times*, with its treatment of Industrial Age education utilitarianism—education must be tied to facts and lead to a job. So when we talk about ethics and aesthetics in education, can they even be discussed together?

Turning first to aesthetics, this chapter will draw on three of Deleuze's core ideas: the rhizome, 'lines of flight' and 'being and becoming'. Deleuze's poststructuralist philosophy informs more a traditional aesthetics of creativity in education, rather than a contemporary one in which the aesthetics of educational creative arts must be slick, beautiful, accomplished and performable/presentable. His notion of 'being and becoming' as an emergent creativity of self and educational practice is also, perhaps, outmoded and romantic under current educational and education research regimes. There is no time for becoming under the new, standardised world order. Learners must already 'be', and their work must already be 'accomplished' and 'arrived', with no lines flying anywhere including in the arts where assessment is inextricable from outcomes.

Dewey, on the other hand, might be pleased about the ways in which current discourses can be seen to be returning aesthetic and creative practices to the 'everyday', back from the mystical or spiritual elite. As he suggests, as creativity becomes better understood (or believed to be) by the general public, its appeal and pervasiveness grows; while it remains on the "remote pedestal" (p. 6) of the few, art is not seen as central to culture. Like Benjamin, here Dewey is talking about popular arts, like photography, movies and new forms of music. There are plenty of comparable examples today, and false binaries between 'real' art versus 'marketplace' art or 'design' like that of Pixar's or Apple's are not productive. Rather, creativity

CHAPTER 4

and art—contra Robinson's claim that it must have 'value'—has often flown in the face of accepted aesthetic merit (think Dada, hip hop, abstract expressionism, iPhones), which will be discussed further in Chapter Six.

An application of Deleuze and Dewey's theoretics of creativity in education is nearly impossible, due to the standardisation increasingly pervading educational institutions and the sector overall. Through a collaboration lens that uses mutuality as a core ethic of the research process, the creative research approaches drawn on in this chapter are in the service of relationship, of 'becoming' and of the power of liminality, all of which take time, are messy, and have the freedom to remain unresolved. As examples of this conceptual exploration, I will use some examples of my own performance writing and some filmic research products—both ethnocinematic and non-ethnocinematic—to flesh out these differences. This chapter ends with a new consideration of whether the obsessive contemporary search for a creativity measures, in which ethical and aesthetic concerns seem doomed to alienation, provide the best approaches for improving processes *and* products.

Instrumentalising Ourselves Out of a Practice

If this book is an examination of the changing definition (if not nature) of creativity in the present moment, both Deleuze and Appadurai have important but distinct things to tell us about the shift. Appadurai (and his links with Benjamin) are discussed in Chapter Six, but in this chapter I will look at some of Deleuze's notions of creativity and the way his articulation of rhizomatic 'lines of flight', and its relation to 'being and becoming', has significance for understanding both creativity and imagination and their relationship to letting go, and letting go in multiple directions (which most creative individuals, activities and environments do).

Salehi (2008) and others (Hickey-Moody, 2013; Jagodzinski and Wallin, 2013) have noted some of the ways in which creativity is increasingly linked with consumption, neoliberalism and productivity (Salehi, p. ii), and the usefulness of Deleuze's singularities with regard to arts processes and products. Here education systems can be included among systems of consumption and productivity. Scholars have long noted the limitations of fine arts degrees in that, while they can productively teach technique, histories and discourses, real creativity seems innate or at least partially so. Salehi attempts to schematise what is teachable in matters of creativity in saying that "we can teach the enjoyment of chaos and the confrontation of it . . . we can teach resistance . . . we can teach a love of complexities . . . we can teach play" and that these "should be taught as explicit professional objectives, not as 'creativity'" (p. iii). Such a recognition of the differences between the systemic desire to identify and teach transferable skills versus the still-mysterious presence and essence of creativity itself has been articulated by Csikszentmihalyi (1990, 1999) as, among other things, 'flow'.

ETHICS 'VERSUS' AESTHETICS

Deleuze & Guattari's (1987) notion of the rhizome has been adapted by Denzin (2003) and others (Cormier, 2008; Carrington & Iyer, 2011) as a particularly 21st-century approach to research and the rise of digital technology, to diffused and dispersed sites of public education, and to the increasing distance between 'formal' and 'informal' education and research practices. Deleuze and the rhizome are both useful here in helping us to think newly about creativity and the wider context of creative necessity in our transition to global knowledge economies, as well as how to prepare for them, what skills and dispositions they demand, and where they may eventually take us as researchers and educators. Dewey earlier attempted to articulate a new theory of aesthetic experience and, in doing so, differentiated it from art. This chapter will extend Dewey's consideration of aesthetics with the help of a Deleuzian sense of creativity as becoming, in order to explore the question of ethics versus aesthetics in creative endeavour.

In an earlier text (Harris, 2012a) I documented a collaborative ethnocinematic video project involving myself and Sudanese-Australian young women. In it, I argued that at the heart of an ethics of intercultural arts-based research should be a commitment to a collaborative, process-focused project with a shared aesthetic. Too often, arts based approaches are now simply serving as new data-gathering methods, or quantitative research 'value-adding' aspects, both of which diminish the important distinctions between arts-based and other research approaches. In my experience, while presenting that early work to academic audiences, I encountered a great deal of criticism from those advocating for a slick end-product (which they characterised as 'professional') as a primary aesthetic requirement of film-based research. Citing audience expectations when consuming arts (research) products, these colleagues argued that if arts products are not finished, beautiful or polished, audiences will be disappointed and the participants devalued—thereby undermining both the product and, ultimately, the process.

I disagreed then and I still do. Rather, I continue to argue the value of process overriding the product—slick though it may at times be—in a field of consumables awash with marketised product-development that will always out-glamour anything that most amateurs can do. This is precisely the argument long-since made against performance and other qualitative research products: that they are 'amateurish' and devalue 'real' art and artists. I argue instead against the use of limiting evaluation tools—whether for educational assessment or as research measures—to examine these products. All things cannot be equally profitable, yet this is increasingly the kind of marketisation and capitalist value that is driving universities. As many have argued against the '19th century industrial revolution' model of schools, here I am critiquing a similarly outmoded 20th-century production model of creative research outcomes.

This book develops an argument for the ways in which we might approach creativity and its evolving presence in research and educational contexts. Typical of this shift, I borrow, repackage, suggest or problematise other theorists and my own notions of the 'good creative education'. Deleuze & Guattari (1987) have

77

shared with us some suggestions as to how creativity is inextricably linked with the rhizome, and have identified certain common characteristics which may contribute to our examination here:

Characteristics of the Rhizome

1 & 2: principles of connections and heterogeneity
3: principle of multiplicity
4: principle of signifying rupture
5 & 6: principles of cartography and decalcomania (as a map with multiple entry point, not as a 'tracing mechanism' (pp. 7-13)

Here Deleuze & Guattari might be describing the new creative turn; that is, their articulation of the rhizome has indeed spread to other areas of social endeavour, most notably from a social to private context. Any new definition of creativity then may seek to address the singular vision of creativity as always new, never productively reconstructing the old. More recently, Zhang (2009) and others (Sawyer, 2003; Osborne, 2003; Jeanes & De Cock, 2005; Zhang et al., 2009) have extended Csikszentmihalyi's claim that creativity is more about creatively (and often collectively) seeking new problems, rather than merely responding differently to older ones. The difference between Deleuze's articulation of historical hierarchical orders as 'arborescent' versus rhizomatic planes which run parallel to each other may have some corollaries with the difference between ethics and aesthetics in creativity.

Decoupling art and creativity may be part of the rhizomatic opening (or 'becoming') of this new understanding of creativity. Salehi "challenges the regimentation of art and creativity and is able to foster a notion of creativity in conversation with, or resistan[ce] to, identity, the nation-state, and capitalism" (2008, pp. 15-16). If Deleuze suggests that society moves from discipline to control, by means of the control of language and knowledge production, creativity has clearly already turned this crucial corner, as multiple sectors and discourses vie for creative control.

The Rhizome: Lines are Flight, Words are Weapons

Deleuze articulates that one of the three ways of controlling discourse is by controlling the right to speak. Similarly, for Salehi, discourse production and control are of course central to academic work and that "creativity study, like all others, contains, provides and controls the rules for the production of its own discourse, i.e., for the formation and dispersion of statements" (2008, p. 18). The discourse of creativity is certainly being advanced most rapidly at the present moment by economists, not artists or educators. Neuroscientists, pop psychologists, entrepreneurs, tech gurus and corporate leaders all publish, lecture and TEDTalk on the 'real how to' of creativity, or what Harvard Business School's Teresa Amabile calls actionable creativity (2011); that is, they articulate the commodification of creativity.

ETHICS 'VERSUS' AESTHETICS

For Foucault, *enunciative* control is a powerful tool in knowledge economies, with far-reaching effects: "institutions are able to exert power over the emergence of knowledge in a discipline" (in McNabb, 1999, p. 210) and knowledge and discourses are (always contextually and) historically situated. For Salehi, Foucault's articulation of knowledge informs creativity in that "it is discourse, not subjects, which constitutes knowledge" (Salehi, 2008, p. 18). Foucault—like Deleuze—examines the sense-making of the rules and regulation of discourses, a largely unexamined area of enquiry in both the ethics and aesthetics of new creativity.

Certainly there have been interlocking dominant discourses on creativity studies over the last fifty years and more, in a range of disciplines. What distinguishes this creative turn from earlier ones is the convergence of these discourses in unprecedented ways. The similarities between searches for definition, teachability, transferability and measurability are closer than ever. The products, however, remain widely divergent. Within education, the 'creative turn' represents not only a shift from process to product (outcomes), but also from aesthetics to a capitalist ethics of production. Glowacka & Boos (2002) draw us back to Schiller and his lifelong concern with ethics and aesthetics. For him, an education overly-focused on reason (his binary, not mine) and inattentive to nature/affect/beauty will end badly; the ideal must not be productivity or reason alone, but rather education must seek to "find a way of reconciling the demands of reason, unity and universality with the demands of nature, multiplicity, and particularity" (p. 21). Schiller's solution of an aesthetic education that integrates these two poles attempted to actively respond to his political times, which was in many ways not so different to a contemporary recognition of education's commodification, and a firm grounding of creativity within capitalist and neoliberal discourses.

In today's context, Salehi claims that his "central contention is that contemporary discourses of creativity reinforce and contribute to the hegemony of capitalism" (p. 23) due to their increasing ties with productivity and 'innovation' (a catchphrase for 'productive creativity'). Truly, "even creativity (in the form of 'creative' knowledge) is increasingly valued as a commodity in this economy . . . [wherein] newly created concepts are seen as 'things' to be sold or exchanged; all our imaginings of becomings are measured through capital units" (Jeanes & De Cock, 2005, p. 8). Could it be, finally, that the contemporary 'creative turn' is a kind of creativity that is "limited to that of reproduction" (Jeanes & De Cock, 2005, p. 9), and that the creative explosion is an expression of an 'acceleration of capitalism' or consumerism? Perhaps the real question that concerns both an ethics and aesthetics of any new creative turn is one that asks whether the reproducibility of the creative product is what ultimately divests it of any significance or transcendent power (see Chapter Seven, on Benjamin).

As Osborne says, "any such moral or rationalistic avowal (of creativity) runs the risk of turning the value of creativity into something like 'fashion', the endless repetition of permanent change under conditions of permanent imitation" (2003, p. 512). It is this acceleration of capitalism which demands an "increase in the rate at which we manufacture . . . even in such innovative ways as by making creativity itself a consumable package" (Salehi, p. 23). Here I argue that the acceleration itself presents contradictory 'lines of flight' when making the conditions for creativity, if we take as a given that creative experimentation requires something like risk-taking and rhizomatic exploration. Some scholars (Salehi, 2008; Jeanes 2006; Jeanes & De Cock, 2005) would have us believe that the insatiability of late capitalism is antagonistic to any form of 'true' creativity, yet those like Csikszentmihalyi link it to this acceleration of social and global flow.

For Salehi, "the preliminary question of 'what is meant by creativity?' informs discussion of how the current notion of creativity functions in the world of late capitalism and, more importantly, the issue of how creativity can be fostered to help us to resist the logic of commodification and capitalism" (p. 23). Like many other creativity researchers and commentators, I have found that most books, articles, online media and reports I've reviewed begin with attempts to define creativity, including categorising into major categories or streams. Any literature review of creativity from Aristotle until the modern era (which arguably began around 1950) will uncover schemas for measuring aspects and attributes of creativity (Mayer, 1999) that do not bear repeating here and which have seemingly got us no closer to understanding what makes some people have it and some not. Nevertheless, we may use such definitions and schemas for attempting to develop a 'concept of creativity' (Salehi, p. 25). Tarif and Sternberg's (1988) schema includes the following categories, 'creative persons, creative products, creative processes, and creative environments', and is a tool which may indeed assist in understanding other era's contexts for the emergence of creativity. But I argue that the task is not now to define, measure and reproduce creativity schemas, but rather to understand more fully how creativity's service to present market needs is redefining it. Whether creativity is teachable, mystical or reproducible remains, I would argue, an unresolvable question.

More importantly for my purposes, this book interrogates the question, "what does it mean to speak of creativity as not something in itself, but as a discursively operational tool in the capitalist kit (now)?" (Salehi, 2008, p. 23). This typifies the dark side of a creative turn in the current era. It is in this way that creativity can be seamlessly conflated with 'innovation', and shunted away from notions of 'art'. Central to this argument is the pervasive definition of creativity as something "new, useful and valuable" (Magyari-Beck, 1999, p. 433) or alternately "novel or original and worthwhile or appropriate" (Colman, 2006, p. 179) or, not simply culturally-situated, but "valuable or influential, useful or generative" (Stokes, 1999, p. 297). Such definitions echo Robinson's definition as "the process of having original ideas that have value" (Robinson, 2006). Such definitions leave unquestioned the context of to whom it is valuable, and in what way is this value measured.

Educational discourses, increasingly, share definitions like that of Selye's that creative productions are "generalizable" (1962, p. 420 in Salehi p. 30). Unquestionably, the great majority of creativity scholars share this focus on the use value of creativity and its outputs, including, amongst others, Gruber and Wallace, 1999; Boden, 1999; Martindale, 1999; and Stokes, 1999. Martindale in particular defines usefulness as what is "appropriate for the situation in which it occurs" (1999, p. 137), which is surely insufficient to constitute an object or action as 'creative'. For Cropley, "effectiveness refers to the domain in which creativity is studied ... for example, being effective in aesthetics is unlike being effective in business. Creativity has an ethical element because a new idea cannot have a negative connotation and be considered effective and relevant to the field" (1999, p. 30). Yet who defines this 'negative connotation'? It is, as suggested, always context-specific. Salehi (from Cropley) problematizes it further:

> after World War Two, *novelty* was the only known constant factor in creativity discourse by researchers in aesthetics ... A novel weapon of mass destruction is not effective in terms of creativity. In addition to novelty, usefulness and effectiveness, ethicality is a criterion of creativity according to some researchers (Cropley, 1999a, p. 30 in Salehi, p. 30).

Increasingly, those who are writing and thinking (and controlling discourses) about creativity do not refer to or draw from arts educators, even seminal ones such as Eisner, Bresler and Gardner. The spread of productivity definitions and characteristics of creativity is having an effect. Many arts educators claim that creativity must have a product, not just a thinking process and not just an unthreadable series of capacities such as problem-solving (or extended by Zhang [2009] as 'problem-creating'). For others, this unexamined dark potential of the creative turn toward commodification is an urgent necessity. Jeanes & De Cock assert that "in effect we are seeing an *engineering* of the creative process; one that is repeated for its own sake ... and in this process of fixing creativity—of territorializing creativity—we are losing the very ability to be truly creative" (2005, p. 9). Yet in the circular pursuit of the authentic, we might return again to the question of what is 'true' creativity?

So here theorists of creativity, aesthetics and arts education are defining and using quite similar schemas for understanding what creativity is, and how to measure it. Later in this chapter you will see that those in business and management are increasingly picking up the creativity and creative economies discourses, and yet the distinctions between economics-focused discourses and educational ones remain just as large as ever. What we can agree on is that "over the last century, the understanding of creativity has changed enormously, from creativity as a form of self-expression in the 1950's to creativity as an element of successful technological and economic ventures in recent years" (Salehi, p. 25). Educators are still trailing behind this creative shift, and in the next section I argue that researchers using arts-based and creative approaches may be too.

Creativity as Becoming

In Deleuze's ontology of becoming, standardisation of the kind present in contemporary educational policy and discourses can be understood as 'differentiation', even as it is an instance of "the real ... in a state of flux" (Williams, 2000, p. 203) being obscured by the illusion of fixity and identity. For governments all around the globe, this illusion of fixity has become central to pedagogical and institutional educational identities. Creativity is a becoming in which "indeterminacy is the problematic relation of ideas defined as structure of other ideas" (Deleuze, 1994, p. 182 in Williams p. 203); in education, this tension presents itself as the structure of the ideas of transferability (through standardisation) and global mobilities (through access to hegemonic academic success imperatives), rubbed against the ideas of productive risk-taking and individuation central to creative exploration. If ethics (in research contexts) is about process, it is also largely about safety, and safety—as creativity experts agree—is anathema to creativity and innovation in any sector or field.

Many researchers (Sternberg, 1999; Albert, 1990; Csikszentmihalyi, 1990; 1988, amongst others) have found that highly creative people engage with challenging, risky problems for the pleasure of the engagement (and the risk), and are "driven by opportunities to solve challenging, boundary-pushing problems" (Collins & Amabile, 1999, pp. 300-301). Further, Csikszentmihalyi argues that the approach among psychologists, who "tend to see creativity exclusively as a mental process . . . cannot do justice to the phenomenon of creativity, which is as much a cultural and social as it is a psychological process" (Csikszentmihalyi, 1999, p. 313). Williams argues that a Deleuzian response to the indeterminacy of architectural design processes that "go[es] from problems—which would seem to ask for solutions—to a problematisation, which involves the realization that certain problems cannot be resolved once and for all . . . must become part of the creative process" (Williams, 2000, p. 204). Zhang (2009) argues the same within education learning systems, that the benefit of problem-solving is equally in problem-proposing rather than in finding absolute solutions—which seem to benefit no one but policymakers. Williams posits, finally, a kind of Deleuzian ontology of becoming relevant to his focus on architecture, but useful for our discussion of a new aesthetics in education:

a. any actual form is changing *at any given time*;
b. the relation between forms is *necessarily difficult and complex*;
c. the relation takes place within a *constantly changing* context (2000, p. 207).

By this measure, one difficulty of incorporating any possible 'creative turn' in educational discourses is this difficult and constantly changing nature of the *relationship* between creative products and their place. We return to Deleuze's question that "even if this creative imperative to take account of the pure event can be resolved technically, it still poses an ethical problem . . . if an openness to innovation, change and indeterminacy is to condition creative acts, will they not become endlessly destructive?" (in Williams, p. 216). The possibility (or fear) of endlessly destructive creative pursuits or ideas is ever-present in secondary schools that use structure, control and standardisation to avoid the unknown, the uncontrollable ethics of creativity.

ETHICS 'VERSUS' AESTHETICS

A pursuit in which "we must avoid the illusion of control in objective representations; [in which] we must let our real singularities guide our creative efforts" (in Williams, p. 217), is one in which both diversity and creativity would take educational precedence over sameness, measurement (rather than chaotic curiosity) and order. If Deleuzian singularities can be applied to the search for creative productivity schemas, then it is absolutely crucial to develop not only new pedagogies but also new modes of learning (Jagodzinski and Wallin, 2013).

The Ethics of Creativity as Innovation

Creativity within commodity contexts is "creativity that will lead to innovation" and "thus creativity becomes a value in itself" (Thrift, 2002 in Salehi, p. 88). If there is an ethics of the new creativity it may be able to be summarised by its decoupling from traditional aesthetics and recoupling with innovation. Csikszentmihalyi and Deleuze both highlight the flow and procedural aspects of creativity and the stimulation of difference. "For Deleuze, the concept of difference—thinking differently, becoming different and the creation of difference—is key to maximising the potential of life" (Jeanes & De Cock, 2005, p. 3). It seems everyone is seeking a one-size-fits-all solution to the creative challenges of the 21st-century global economy. As creativity discourses spread throughout economic, scientific and educational sectors, employers and educators increasingly believe that "the new ethos for success is built by a package of/for creativity, one full of formulas and techniques" (Salehi, p. 79). This pervasive 'creativity explosion' (Osborne, 2003) has become a commodity in a wide range of sectors, where experts are now competing to "identify, measure, and classify creativity, and to offer techniques to lead people to be more creative" (Salehi, p. 80). If indeed "people make their own culture . . . with commoditized materials" (Willis, 1999, p. 154), surely the commodification of the materials is also co-constitutive with creative practices themselves? While Willis (1999) uses the term *symbolic work* to identify the "active and productive nature of practices of consumption" (p. 154) rather than their pacifying and manipulative function, I argue that his *symbolic* work could be replaced with *creative*. For, as this book argues, creative work is increasingly produced for mainstream consumption in unprecedented ways.

Yet if "the desire to be creative seems today to be compulsory in many domains of life" (Osborne, 2003, p. 81), then surely this desire is inextricable from a Foucauldian governmentality. Csikszentmihalyi's articulation of the 'creative identity' as a kind of 'everyman' reflects this shift toward a democratisation of creativity through its control. That everyone can now be 'creative' in ten easy steps further embodies the shift from production to knowledge economies, in which "education is the mode of access to power" (Salehi, p. 83). This simultaneity of the rise of creativity discourses with that of information productivity and global economies is one example of how a new "motivational structure of [economic] activity in a post-industrial society is described in terms of creativity rather than labour" (p. 83). Thus, creativity becomes

83

CHAPTER 4

a core activity of these new global economies that seek to feed insatiable markets. The shift can also be recognised and articulated as "commodity-based capitalism [which] is being replaced by knowledge-based capitalism, within which elites/ intellectuals are the dominant source of wealth for companies and societies" (p. 83).

History as a process of 'deterritorialization' (Deleuze and Guattari, 1983) is now reflected in a similar kind of deterritorialisation of creativity. It is no longer the domain of the arts, but was it ever completely independent of the marketplace? From the necessary commission-based work of Michelangelo to Frank Lloyd Wright, from Nazi affinity for Wagner's operas, and the royal patronage of Shakespeare's troupe The King's Men, what creative individual, group or initiative can survive without marketplace concerns and influences, direct or indirect?

John Dewey (1934) argued in favour of a refocus on 'process' in the so-called 'product' versus 'process' divide; today's debates about these different agendas—if true at all—are argued in a far more instrumentalised fashion. Currently creativity certainly has a greater acceleration inscience, math, and IT education, than in the arts. Why is this? Here I am arguing, like Salehi, that "in an information society, a new economy, the idea of creativity has become a fetishized cultural commodity" (Salehi, 2008, p. 86). This new commodity is in turn evolving its own new aesthetic (see Chapter Nine). But a consideration of aesthetics is always tied to recognisability, the familiar, 'morality' (in some historic periods) and sameness to some degree, otherwise it is unrecognisable as beauty (as Schiller and many others have argued), despite its cultural situatedness. Creativity, on the other hand, is about newness, difference, amorality (un-ethics) and the gaze (Jeanes and De Cock, 2005). What can this tell us then for the relationship between aesthetics and creativity—are they best 'frenemies' or star-crossed lovers?

With the acceleration of knowledge (or idea) productivity, the shelf-life of creativity's market value is diminishing; in other words, a good idea only lasts a moment. Almost anything becomes creativity if it is new or—in neoliberal market discourses—'innovative'. In fact, what used to be considered creative was not so linked with newness—or was it? Isn't Brecht's 'making the familiar strange' the same notion? Or the sense of artworks or artists approaches being 'fresh'? Anyone who has worked in the US film industry or in television development knows that this industry has been seeking the 'next new thing' since its beginning. What's different now is that this search is not tied to aesthetic value, but market value: the contemporary creativity discourse threatens us that, without creativity, our survival is unassured, as well as that of our students. This leads us (unfortunately) back once again to Foucault and his notions of power and governmentality. Deleuze (not Foucault, but drawing on him) (1990) "suggests another kind of power which is on the way to becoming hegemonic: control of communication" (p. 87).

In *Discipline and Punish* (1979) Foucault shows how the penal system and its control mechanisms spill out into society by making that society become increasingly disciplinary and us, as subjects, increasingly docile. Control takes over from direct discipline, and "control societies operate not by confining people but 'through continuous control and instant communication'" (Deleuze, 1990, p. 11). As Deleuze reminds us, in a society of control all old problems are reborn, and "the society of control will not come to be through spaces of enclosure . . . nor through the schools. We must now observe the new capitalists" (Deleuze, 2001, p. 105).

"For the virtual to become actual it must *create* its own terms of actualisation; with no preformed order this is a process of creative evolution" (Jeanes & De Cock, 2005, p. 4). Of course, for Deleuze, philosophy is the ultimate creative enterprise (unlike scholarship, which he calls 'functional'). I am arguing here that, in Deleuzian terms, the turn toward creativity in the current time might be not only a capitalist turn or a turn toward the market, but a philosophical turn as well. Where Deleuze sees philosophers as creators of knowledge, artists see themselves as creators too—even once they become researchers. The following 'researcher monologue' accompanies the two short videos that follow, in which I position myself as researcher/collaborator alongside my co-creator-participants.

An Ethics of Researcher as Subject

>Something got started, from day one
>
>From the day they brought me home,
>
>From the first neighbour who visited
>
>From the first relative who told me 'you're lucky you know,
>
>Not everyone gets a family.'
>
>They told us: 'a lot of those kids got left up in that orphanage you know.
>
>You should be lucky.
>
>You should say thank you.'
>
>Now I'm not OPPOSED to the idea.
>
>Saying thanks is nice, being grateful is a good way to go through life you know, but   Well, I'm a bit orncry that way.
>
>I don't like to be TOLD how to feel.
>
>And no one likes to be told they could have been left behind.
>
>So, I'm talkin' about a pattern here that started a long time ago—a long time before I met Adiba, who you'll meet—and Achak, who you'll love.
>
>I'm not what they call—GRATEFUL, you know, by nature.
>
>But I work at it.
>
>I've thought about gratitude since they brought me home at six-months old.

CHAPTER 4

Adoptees are raised that way, like refugees we're TRAINED that way.

Some people are raised to feel ENTITLED to it all, and some people are raised to feel

Lucky:

Like we scraped through by the skin of our teeth.

Like we had a near miss, before we even got started,

Like we sit on a razor's edge

Like we can be DROPPED

At a moment's notice.

That's what talkin' about gratitude with a kid makes them feel.

What it made ME feel like anyway.

When I turned 8, Mrs Rescott made me give my PARENTS a present for adopting me, to say thank you, never I WANT.

I should learn to GIVE, she said, not receive.

Well it's hard to argue with that, isn't it?

And then when I found my birthfamily they told me I should be GRATEFUL that I had a family at all.

Really?

Ok.

And then when my birthmother wouldn't meet me, she said 'you're a ghost, don't tempt fate, don't push too hard, pick your battles, don't be ungrateful.'

Uh-huh.

I sat on her porch in San Jose for 6 hours that Sunday I found her, but she just never opened that door.

I sat there thinkin'.

I said through the closed curtains 'hey Dorothy, YOU should be grateful I don't start screamin' your past back up into your present'.

And she said 'go away or I'll call the cops' and I said

What you gonna tell them, your daughter's sitting on your stoop?

Is it a crime to find your family?

Well now that you mention it—

So gratitude is a funny thing. It's like pregnant—

You either got it or you aint'. Not like sorta grateful, sorta lucky.

But playwrights don't write plays about grateful people—I can't think of one example. We write plays about hunger. Wounds. Healing. Failing. Redemption.

Now research on the other hand—it's all filled up with people talkin' about gratitude and possibility. Usually other peoples'. Usually the participants'.

Education too—we never talk about the teacher's gratitude or possibility, just the student's.

So when I started calling my community arts projects 'research projects', I really didn't have any interest in the gratitude angle, the us-and-them angle—

too many bad associations.

and when I started teaching I wasn't too interested in the 'empower' thing, feeling sorry for students or trying to help anyone.

I never wanted anyone's help and doubt anyone else does either.

I just thought we could work together toward dreams, hopes, challenges.

My friend Rebecca told me that the best moment of her whole 15-year journey out of South Sudan and Ethiopia and Kenya and Australia into a new life that didn't involve running—the best moment of her whole refugee time was when some Red Cross folks just came down off the truck and walked the last little way to the camp *with* her and her three babies—and I understood that.

I think that's what everyone wants, just someone to walk with.

And that's what I think research should be, and teaching should be, and adoption and the arts. Just walking together. So.

It's easy for me to understand why my refugee-background friends are sick to death of 'grateful' and research and 'possibility'. The 'grateful refugee' is the only character available on this TV.

Refugees *have* to achieve to not piss people off.

Adoptees live in diasporas, like refugees.

We have to be emotionally fulfilled, we can't still be empty—not after being saved, it's an insult. No looking back, no second guesses, just out with the old, in with the new.

But I want to make collaborative arts-based research like ethnocinema that lets us *all* be more 'ourselves', where the only transformation might be in the rich and messy relationships that should be the centre of this work. The following two short videos are examples of the observable differences between what I've written (Harris 2012a; 2012b) about as 'ethical' and 'aesthetic' organising principles in arts-based research. Adiba's 'beautiful' aesthetic video has gained a lot more airplay, and represents what I consider an example of the 'product' focus, or arts-based research that has aesthetics as a primary motivating principle. While we can argue theoretically that the product/process binary is limiting and unnecessary, as researchers we must also admit that not all things are possible, and as teachers that we can't be all things to all students. Adiba's clip is an example of a less-collaborative process in which the filmmaker filmed and Adiba performed as the participant.

http://www.creativeresearchhub.com/#!sailing-into-uni-film-clips/ct99

Compare this with Achol's video *Singing into Language* (Harris, 2012a) which is what I still consider my first attempt to commit to an 'ethical' approach to collaborative arts-based research; our shared ethnocinematic video that constitutes a rigorously and mutually collaborative 'process' example.

http://www.youtube.com/watch?v=WvQ-ybWhol0

These are examples of two ways of using film in arts-based research that have significantly different motivations, methods and applications. I share them to stimulate dialogue about the demands of using video in arts-based research, an area in which many researchers are increasingly using video and other 'aesthetic research tools' for non-arts-based purposes. Is Adiba's clip a piece of film-based research, or is it a promotional video for a university? (It has been called both of those by academic audience members.) Is there a difference, or should there be? Achol's video and the other films and book about them (see Harris, 2012), schematise my ethic of mutual collaboration and co-creation over product-oriented aesthetics.

I wanted the young women in my study to help create these films no matter what. I wanted them to film me, themselves, all of it. I didn't care if they looked attractive (which is what they wanted). I didn't want them to. Not because I didn't want 'beautiful films' of 'beautiful subjects', but because I thought to have that would mean we would have to sacrifice the girls having control—a major priority for me in this study. I would have to use a film crew, a professional editor, lights. I wanted to use the camera as a tool for sharing, not documenting. But now only a few short years later I wonder if that was too narrow, too binary a choice, a framing of the research relationship when the method is film-based.

One participant, Nyadol, who is now a good friend, didn't really want to learn how to use a video camera, and wasn't interested in filming me (see her film *Still Waiting* at http://www.youtube.com/watch?v=rIqwNA8-AE4). In hindsight, I have wondered if this may have contributed to the more polished aesthetic of her film, because our roles were clearer and simpler. She was happy to be interviewed and filmed, but did not want to reciprocate. She did, however, watch the rushes and offer editorial input, including cuts and additions. This can be considered collaboration, to be sure, but the 'tools of the data gathering' were never fully/firmly in her hands; by choice. Is the choice the most crucial part here? Maybe her choosing *not* to is equivalent to or stronger than the value of the others co-shooting, sometimes ambivalently?

This has led me to ask myself important methodological questions such as:

- Are aesthetic considerations always necessary in arts-based research? If so, might they cloud and obscure other issues, content, obligations? Ethical responsibilities?
- If we are required to make 'beautiful things', where is the place for process, trial and error?
- What is sacrificed for beauty? For market? For commodification?

I am a little ambivalent about Adiba's video, and I don't show this clip often. But it made her mother cry. It made her family crowd around and laugh, cry, celebrate. And they were excited to send it home, they were proud, and as a researcher this is very gratifying. But still I ask:

- What were they celebrating?
- What is the ethics of this clip for Adiba, and for her family?
- As creatively-oriented researchers in neoliberal times, do we have a responsibility to the end product?

My ongoing relationship with Achol is currently much deeper than my friendship with Adiba, and I believe this is because of the ethnocinematic approach we used, including significantly more time spent together, the mutuality of it and the pedagogical component of both. Achol, Nyadol and I have always agreed that this kind of research relationship is what may create social change, more likely than the product. But does it have to be one or the other? How can we know if we are making research that has positive aesthetic outcomes as well as good process?

There is no denying that this 'moment' is performative—public, immediate—and visual. Denzin (2003) says this performative (seventh) moment, "enacts the feminist, communitarian ethic", is "subversive", characterised by an "anti-aesthetic" (p. 122), and is interdisciplinary so that "in these texts ethics, aesthetics, political praxis, and epistemology are joined" (p. 123). I would argue that it is *not* characterised by an anti-aesthetic at all—that indeed, with the rise of social media and global flows, the aesthetic is even *more predominant*, but changed by its immediacy. Yet aesthetics remains inextricable from what we think of as 'good' product. Whether this can coexist with Denzin's 'political praxis' or not remains to be seen.

Ethics, Aesthetics, Or a Doctrine of Creativity

Osborne calls a resistance to this pervasive or compulsive productivity discourse around creativity a 'philistinism' in which "this is a kind of ethics, or countervailing power against the threat of the doctrine of creativity" (in Salehi, p. 89). Ethics most often attends to the approach, the process (unless, like for Wagner, you have the misfortune to be taken up by Nazis). In research terms, ethics means the researcher's

CHAPTER 4

obligation to ensure the safety, caution and care of the participants, but also of the institution. In artistic terms it can mean, for example, not stealing someone else's work (plagiarism), defined differently to creative 'borrowing' (derivation). But perhaps a set of rules for creative research (or creativity in general) can go too far toward the safety end of the safety-risk continuum, stultifying both the process and the products that result. Can creative research assist in helping to "liberate us from the potentially moronic consequences of the doctrine of creativity" (Osborne, 2003, p. 507)? Potentially yes, if it can be used to remember the relationship between creativity and diversity.

Ethnocinematic and other video-based research like the examples shared here raise the question of whether Deleuze's notion of creativity can be present without attention to aesthetics, or whether questions of aesthetics is separable from creativity at all. Whether in research or other contexts, aesthetics continues to be central to any creative activity, even those remote from explicit artmaking. Researchers then must ask whether aesthetic consideration is indeed necessary in arts-based research (like ethnocinema) or whether they may inherently cloud and obscure other—sometimes more important—research considerations, such as content, ethical responsibilities to 'do no harm', and the social change agenda of much educational research. For if researchers are required to make research products that attend to aesthetics when using arts-based methods, what is their relationship to/in/with process?

A Deleuzian lens on the capitalist and cultural implications of creativity can be found in his notion of 'differentiation' which "offers a way of understanding the cultural changes effected by creativity" (Hickey Moody, 2013, p. 129). Creativity is always culturally situated, as I have argued throughout this chapter, and of which Deleuze reminds us. The Deleuzian notion that we misperceive that things are static rather than becoming is akin to the creative 'product' (static) versus 'process' (becoming) argument. This tension, I argue, is the same as the tension imbuing the pedagogy and curriculum of creativity in schools.

If, then, creativity is being increasingly decoupled from arts and recoupled with innovation and productivity, we may also question what is lost in the pursuit of creative economies; that is, in market-defined and market-driven creative productivity. As I have argued earlier in this book, any investigation into creativity today will offer a schematic of some kind for 'improving' creativity in the classroom or workplace. While a good deal of this book is devoted to arguing why such lists are doomed to failure, they are nevertheless ubiquitous and offer readers a starting point. In this spirit I offer my own list of skills and attributes central to creative research and creative pedagogy, as a provocation and potentially a place of beginning for those who wish to conduct collaborative research in arts-based ways:

Attributes and strategies:
- **Lead by example**, modelling ongoing research into our own areas of endeavour; just as pre-service teachers think they have more to learn from those in classrooms

who are 'doing the teaching', creativity should be taught by those who are still 'doing creativity'.
- **Help students** 'obtain the tools to find their own way', 'find their own voice', and "enable students to develop their own personal aesthetic direction, critical abilities, and independent thought" (Salehi, 2008, p. 257).
- **Let go and allow becoming**—a process (Salehi, 2008).
- A willingness to allow chaos—the 'creating space', which is often anathema to schools and teachers/teaching—but central to learning (strangely enough).
- **Feel the love**: "Intrinsic motivation as a personal characteristic that contributes to creativity" (Collins and Amabile, 1999, p 300).
- **Love the process**: Cezanne said "my method is to love working" (Jeanes & De Cock, 2005, p. 12).

Skills:

- Provide best practice examples
- Show how to self-research for further info
- Schedule collaborative sessions
- Encourage a wide range of opinions/input
- Encourage productive/intelligent risk-taking
- Learn to 'defend' work and its meaning/place
- Then, secondarily, develop critical skills to differentiate the superior from the mundane
- Develop the tools of self-awareness
- Find or create problems, don't solve them. Put another way, "creators can be distinguished as much by their ability to find and pose new problems as by the capacity to solve problems posed by someone else" (Policastro & Gardner, 1999, p. 220).
- "The explanation of creation thus has to be sought in the *process* of production itself; the power of the paintings lies in their *painting*" (Jeanes & De Cock, p. 12).

This is a starting point only and should not be interpreted as prescriptive. I want to remain mindful that in any categorising or schematising activity in creativity, arts or aesthetic education, it is a beginning which stimulates further development, not a foreclosure. Certainly within a new creativity, most importantly we can remember that identifying pedagogies of creative or artistic skills is not the same as teaching creativity. While admitting that in arts education, and in creativity studies too, foundational skills must always be taught/learnt first, Salehi notes that this is not enough, as "although it is commonly said that art is learned through hard work, it seems more accurate to say that hard work brings greater technical skill, not increased creativity" (p. 276).

Over a decade ago, Ripple in *Teaching Creativity* (1999) noted a creative 'turn', as I do, but for him it was a turn away from quantitative psychometric testing to more qualitative case study and narrative approaches which "construct nomothetic nets with accompanying generalized principles" (1999, p. 633). In response Salehi noted, "he suggests that this shift is a return to a more elitist, aristocratic approach to creativity, away from a democratic one ... it is a revival of the view of creativity as a rare phenomenon that cannot be deliberately improved upon" (Salehi, p. 280). My articulation of a 21st-century creative turn suggests something different: now, nearly 15 years after the turn into a new century, it seems clear that any turn in creativity is not a *re*turn, but a steady march toward the reproducible, the accessible and the instrumentalised. The timeless question 'can creativity be taught?'—as Salehi notes—is not about to be solved now, but we can address the compatibility or contrast between our schools and universities, and the skills and capacities that seem to constitute this changing definition of creativity in the 21st century.

CONCLUSION

If, as Salehi claims, "creation is more possible' (p. 10) in a Deleuzian rhizomatic of 'multiplicity and ephemerality ... forgetting, fragmenting, and diversifying" (p. 10), then what possibilities do schools, and indeed educational research, have to offer creativity as they move more steadfastly into neoliberal standardisation? Can education claim to offer a new way of 'doing' creativity, one in which chaos is not needed, and multiplicity is not wanted? Is articulating an ethics of creativity more possible than an aesthetics of creativity, or harder?

Willis reminds us that "all consumption is cultural to some extent (and therefore to do with meaning, and therefore to do with social representation)" (1999, p. 164). This chapter argues that the creativity explosion or turn is in fact a turn toward creative productivity and consumption, and that such a turn not only forecloses some possibilities but opens others. Within an ethical framework, creativity processes can return to the improvisational within such insatiable contexts of rapid consumption; and articulating an ethics of creative processes does not exclude aesthetic considerations too.

As teachers, if the pedagogy of creativity that we seem to be chasing is a matter of 'lines of flight', might we have to accept that creativity "is fundamentally unrelated to artistic knowledge ... [that] creativity is not about knowledge, but self-awareness, and ... has nothing to do with solutions" (Salehi, 2008, p. 286)? This may be bad news for standardised testing and teaching. This is the nexus of tension between 20th-century definitions of creativity in which the ethics of 'doing' art and 'being' creative were clearer, and 21st-century definitions in which "creative thinking has become a 'timely' thinking, and therefore almost an 'un-thinking' ... [and] is also limited, in a very uncreative manner, to our current perceptions of what creativity is, and how we can be creative" (Jeanes & De Cock, 2005, p. 9). For Foucault, "the notion of creativity as a process of personal and perpetual crisis," is one of "knowing that concepts aren't 'finished', of knowing one hasn't succeeded, of being thrown back into the open sea" (in Jeanes & De Cock, 2005, p. 11). Yet here we still are, suffering in the chasm between knowing such self-evident truths and an ethics of bringing

ETHICS 'VERSUS' AESTHETICS

more of this capacity for discomfort, this un-thinking back into classrooms. It is, in the end, a question of pedagogical and creative ethics.

But what *is* a 21st-century understanding of aesthetics or aesthetics-in-education, and what does it have to do with ethics? Almost nothing, if we are to believe scholars like Salehi who suggest, "the modernist [20th-century] conception appears to describe creativity as an individual trait, as an extraordinary ability . . . yet the post-modern conception sees creativity as ordinary" (p. 288). If this is so, we would seem to be in a period in which the 'ethics' of creativity appear to say that aesthetic concerns rule; a talking back to postmodern concerns with criticality and the 'inaesthetic' ability of art to disrupt, or what Denzin called an 'anti-aesthetic'. Today's emerging aesthetic seems to suggest that everyone can be creative as long as it is profitable, a principle that is almost always in conflict with Deleuze's notion of becoming. Yet examples remain of Deleuze's articulation—creativity in the service of process, disruption and becoming—as the next chapter will show.

REFERENCES

Albert, R. S., & Runco, M. A. (1999). A history of research on creativity. In R. J. Sternberg (Ed.), *Handbook of creativity* (pp 16–35). New York, NY: Cambridge University Press.
Amabile, T. M. (2011). *The social psychology of creativity.* London, UK: Springer.
Boden, M. A. (1999). Computational model of creativity. In R. J. Sternberg (Ed.), *Handbook of creativity* (pp. 351–373). New York, NY: Cambridge University Press.
Carrington, S. B., & Iyer, R. (2011). Service-learning within higher education: rhizomatic interconnections between university and the real world. *Australian Journal of Teacher Education, 36*(6), 1–14.
Collins, M. A., & Amabile, T. (1999). Motivation and creativity. In R. Sternberg (Ed.), *Handbook of creativity* (pp. 298–311). New York/Cambridge, NY: Cambridge University Press.
Colman, A. M. (2006). *A dictionary of psychology* (2nd ed.). New York, NY: Oxford University Press.
Cormier, D. (2008). *Rhizomatic education : Community as curriculum.* Retrieved from http://davecormier.com/edblog/2008/06/03/rhizomatic-education-community-as-curriculum/
Cormier, D. (1999a). Definitions of creativity. In M. A. Runco & S. Pritzker (Eds.), *Encyclopedia of creativity* (pp 511–524). San Diego, CA: Academic Press.
Csikszentmihalyi, M. (1999). Implications of a systems perspective for the study of creativity. In R. Sternberg (Ed.), *Handbook of creativity* (pp. 312–335). New York, NY: Cambridge University Press.
Csikszentmihalyi, M. (1990). *Flow.* New York, NY: HarperCollins.
Csikszentmihalyi, M. (1988). Motivation and creativity: Toward a synthesis of structural and energistic approaches to cognition. *New Ideas in Psychology, 6,* 159–176.
Deleuze, G., & Guattari, F. (1987). In B Massumi (Trans.), *A thousand plateaus: Capitalism and schizophrenia.* Minneapolis, MN: University of Minnesota Press
Deleuze, G., & Guattari, F. (1983). *Anti-Oedipus: Capitalism and schitzophrenia.* Minneapolis, MN: University of Minnesota Press.
Deleuze, G. (2001). What is the creative act? In S. Lotringer and S. Cohen (Eds.), *French theory in America* (pp 99–110). New York and London, NY: Routledge.
Deleuze, G. (1994). In P. Patton (Trans.), *Difference and repetition.* New York, NY: Columbia University Press. (Original work published 1968).
Deleuze, G. (1992). Mediators. In J. Crary & S. Kwinter (Eds.), *Zone 6: Incorporations* (pp 280–295). New York: Zone Books.
Deleuze, G. (1990). In M. Joughin (Trans.), *Control and becoming: Gilles Deleuze in conversation with Antonio Negri.* Retrieved from http://www.generation-online.org/p/fpdeleuze3.htm
Denzin, N. K. (2003). *Performance ethnography: Critical pedagogy and the politics of culture.* Thousand Oaks, CA: Sage.

CHAPTER 4

Dewey, J. (1934/2005). *Art as experience*. New York, NY: Perigree Books/Penguin.
Foucault, M. (1979). In A. Sheridan (Trans.), *Discipline and punish: The birth of the prison*. New York, NY: Vintage Books.
Gardner, H., Csikszentmihalyi, M., & William, D. (2001). *Good work: When excellence and ethics meet*. New York, NY: Perseus Books.
Glowacka, D., & Boos, S. (Eds). (2002). *Between ethics and aesthetics: Crossing the boundaries*. Albany, NY: State University of New York Press.
Gruber, H. E., & Wallace, D. B. (1999). The case study method and evolving systems approach for understanding unique creative people at work. In R. J. Sternberg (Ed.), *Handbook of creativity* (pp. 93–116). New York, NY: Cambridge University Press.
Harris, A. (2012a). *Ethnocinema: Intercultural arts education*. The Netherlands: Springer SBM.
Harris, A. (2012b). (All the) Single Ladies: diasporic women are doing it for themselves. *Australian Feminist Studies, 27*(72), 157–170.
Harris, A., & A. Lemon. (2012). Bodies that shatter: Creativity, culture and the new pedagogical imaginary. *Pedagogy, Culture and Society, 20*(3), 413–433.
Hickey-Moody, A. (2013). *Youth, arts and education: Reassembling subjectivity through affect*. Abingdon and New York, NY: Routledge.
Jagodzinski, J., & Wallin, J. (2013). *Arts-based research: A critique and a proposal*. Rotterdam: Sense.
Jeanes, E. L. (2006). Resisting creativity, creating the new: A Deleuzian perspective on creativity. *Creativity and Innovation Management, 15*(2), 127–134.
Jeanes, E. L., & De Cock, C. (2005). *Making the familiar strange: A Deleuzian perspective on creativity*. Retrieved from University of Exeter: http://www.iacat.com/Revista/recrearte/recrearte03/familiar_strange.pdf
Magyari-Beck, I. (1999). Creatology. In M. A. Runco & S. Pritzker (Eds.), *Encyclopedia of creativity* (pp. 433–441). San Diego, CA: Academic Press.
Martindale, C. (1999). Biological bases of creativity. In R. J. Sternberg (Ed.), *Handbook of creativity* (pp. 137–153). New York, NY: Cambridge University Press.
Mayer, R. E. (1999). Fifty years of creativity research. In R. J. Sternberg (Ed.), *Handbook of creativity* (pp. 449–461). New York, NY: Cambridge University Press.
McNabb, R. (1999). Making all the right moves: Foucault, journals, and the authorization of discourse. *Journal of Scholarly Publishing, 31*(1), 20–41.
Osborne, T. (2003) Against 'creativity': A Philistine Rant, *Economy and Society, 32*(4), 507–525.
Policastro, E., & Gardner, H. (1999). From case studies to robust generalizations: an approach to the study of creativity. In R. Sternberg (Ed.), *Handbook of creativity* (pp. 312–335). New York, NY: Cambridge University Press.
Ripple, R. E. (1999). Teaching creativity. In M. A. Runco & S. Pritzker (Eds.), *Encyclopedia of creativity* (pp. 629–638). San Diego, CA: Academic Press.
Robinson, K. (2006). *How schools kill creativity*. Retrieved from TED Talk 2006: http://www.ted.com/talks/ken_robinson_says_schools_kill_creativity.html
Salehi, S. (2008). *Teaching contingencies: Deleuze, creativity discourses, and art*. Unpublished doctoral thesis, Ontario, Canada: Queen's University. Retrieved from http://qspace.library.queensu.ca/handle/1974/1209
Sawyer, R. K. (2003). Emergence in creativity and development. In K. Sawyer, V. John-Steiner, S. Moran, S. Sternberg, D. H. Feldman, J. Wakamura, & M. Csikszetmihalyi (Eds.), *Creativity and development* (pp. 12–60). Oxford, UK: Oxford University Press.
Schiller, F. (1965). In R. Snell (Trans.), *On the aesthetic education of man*. New York, NY: Ungar.
Sternberg, R. J. (1999). *Handbook of creativity*. New York/Cambridge, NY: Cambridge University Press.
Stokes, P. D. (1999). Novelty. In M. A. Runco & S. Prizker (Eds.), *Encyclopedia of creativity* (pp. 297–304). San Diego, CA: Academic Press.
Weis, L., Fine, M., & Dimitriadis, G. (2009). Towards a critical theory of method in shifting times. In M. W. Apple, W. Au, & L. A. Gandin (Eds.), *The routledge international handbook of critical education* (pp. 437–448). Hoboken, NJ: Routledge.

Williams, J. (2000). Deleuze's ontology and creativity: Becoming in architecture. *The Warwick Journal of Philosophy, 9*, 200–219. Retrieved from http://web.warwick.ac.uk/philosophy/pli_journal/pdfs/williams_pli_9.pdf

Willis, P. (1999). Labor power, culture, and the cultural commodity. In M. Castells, R. Flecha, P. Freire, H. A. Giroux, D. Macedo & P. Willis, (Eds.), *Critical education in the new information age* (pp. 139–169). Lanhan, MD: Rowman & Littlefield.

Zhang, J., Scardamalia, M., Reeve, R., & Messina, R. (2009). Designs for collective cognitive responsibility in knowledge-building communities. *Journal of the Learning Sciences, 18*(1), 7–44.

Zhang, J. (2009). Towards a creative social web for learners and teachers. *Educational Researcher, 38*(4), 274–279.

CHAPTER 5

AESTHETIC POLITICS AND CREATIVE PATHWAYS

Figure 9. Culture Shack logo (2010).

INTRODUCTION

This chapter argues the value of arts-based research-as-pedagogy as demonstrated through two case studies: the *SAILing into Uni!* and *Culture Shack* projects in Melbourne, Australia. Here I draw on Massumi (2011) to help contextualise creative research methods in order to explore alternative pathways into tertiary and further study for refugee-background and culturally diverse young people. This chapter

CHAPTER 5

argues that creative research offers new possibilities for collaborative learning in both formal education and research relationships. As education is a key factor in successful integration for those from refugee and emerging communities (UNHCR 2007, cited in Matthews, 2008), self-reliance and creative problem-solving can be enhanced through creative collaborative research based in local communities, which increases participation and retention in higher education. These two case studies demonstrate some ways of effectively incorporating diverse knowledges in order to collectively address these issues.

Stanford University's Tina Seelig (2012) and others like her are interested in both the neurological underpinnings of creativity, as well as the ways in which we train ourselves in or out of creative confidence. She believes, for example, that by recognising creativity as an "endless renewable resource" (p 75) we begin to see each day as filled with creative acts (sentence-making, relationship-building) and it follows that we begin to expand our capacity for creative success. This is one strength of using creative approaches to education and research, as demonstrated by the two case studies featured in this chapter. According to Seelig, we look at creativity in much too narrow a way.

Sinker (2012) and others have argued convincingly of the intrinsically collaborative nature of multimedia and other collaborative arts work with youth, both in and outside of schools. It seems that—more than being just a necessary evil—the collaborative nature of multimedia production makes it attractive to young people. Yet more than anything, Sinker's insights remind us of the slippery nature of creativity and art, and of the interrelationships between the work of art, communication, counter-information, and acts of resistance.

This chapter draws on two parallel case studies, both of which explore the potential of youth-driven arts-based public pedagogies: *Culture Shack*, which uses the 'tiered and peered' knowledge transfer model by combining the creative pedagogies of artists, researchers, teacher-educators, pre-service teachers and young people in the collaboration (Harris, 2013a); and *SAILing into Uni!*, a video-based pathways consultation in which Sudanese and Afghani young people speak out and respond to the ways in which higher education can be exclusive even when it doesn't mean to be.

In this chapter I will draw on both Massumi and Herbert as critical lenses in helping to understand the words and perspectives of the young people in these two case studies. For Massumi, interactive art is intrinsically affective, and for Herbert (used further in Chapter Eight) such work is intrinsically an exchange, a listening that invites the Other in each of us to engage with the centre.

Aesthetics and Creative Research

Massumi (2011) tells us that "what is central to interactive art is not so much the aesthetic form in which a work presents itself... but the behaviour the work triggers in the viewer" (p. 39), and creative research is similar. He borrows from Rancière in telling us that a "'politics of aesthetics' does not only have to do with 'distributions of the sensible'" (p. 39), but "more intensely, more inventively, and more powerfully, it has to do with distributions between the sensible and the nonsensuous: the double aesthetic-political economy of experience" (Massumi 2011, p. 170). Such distinctions are crucial to understanding the culturally co-constitutive role of creativity, not only in research and arts practice but also at the school level. This interrelationship between the political and the artistic, he argues, applies to "all domains" and the "aesthetically political criteria relevant to all techniques of existence in whatever domain add up to an aesthetic *criterion of politicality* at the core of the speculative pragmatist approach" (2011, p. 170).

In staking such a political claim for aesthetics in contemporary times, Massumi re-links aesthetics to new artforms, importantly including new media. For him, form equals aesthetics, "not a popular position in new media art [where] there is a widespread attitude that aesthetic categories belong to the past" (p. 40). He has noted how contemporary media practitioners and researchers consistently distinguish between participatory creativity and traditional or 'real' art focused on form and aesthetics. He rejects this by exploding preconceptions that "form is ever fixed, that there is any such thing as a stable form" (2011, p. 40) even in so-called traditional artforms. He claims:

> The idea that there is such a thing as fixed form is actually as much an assumption about perception as it is an assumption about art . . . how do you speak of form when there is a kind of openness of outcome that you see in a lot of new media art, where participant response determines what exactly happens . . . when the artwork proliferates, or when it disseminates?" (Massumi, 2011, p. 40).

Like Massumi, I pursue a flexibly aesthetic component in all research I undertake, and theorise the aesthetic and collaborative aspects of arts-based research as the core of its contemporaneity and its power. The two case studies to follow focus on what Massumi calls the 'aesthetic politics' of any event or interaction—in this case research relationships—and in the following methodology section I will detail both the aesthetic and political aspects of the two projects and how they demonstrate parallel capabilities and conduits for engagement.

Similarly, Herbert can help us understand the ways in which the creative elements of these research projects can be considered 'creative listening', itself a political act. A tension in using creative approaches to research and to pedagogy is the intersubjectivity implied in such collaborative and representational forms. The self/other divide is a site of ambivalence for teachers, students and (co)researchers who want to meet but not merge with the other. The potential for committing an act of "metaphysical violence" (Levinas in Herbert, 2010, p. 120) by erasing or merging one's own experience or perspective with different ones encountered through creative research is omnipresent and balanced by the potential for empathic engagement through this same activism/activity. Herbert cautions that if we are to truly learn from "the other in the way Levinas indicates, the subject must be involved

CHAPTER 5

(as opposed to the ego), not only as a weaver of narratives, but also as a listener" (p. 120). These case studies exemplify some efforts in that direction.

CASE STUDY #1

'Sailing Into Uni!' and the Intersection of Health Promotion, Education and Creative Arts

Http://www.creativeresearchhub.com/#!sailing-into-uni-film-clips/ct99

Throughout 2012, I co-conducted a study that joined health promotion and public education using video[1]. The project—*SAILing into Uni!*—focused on the educational experiences of Afghani- and Sudanese-Australian young people, and their thoughts about attending university. The title derives from a partner organisation, the Sudanese Australian Integrated Learning (SAIL) program, a 12-year-old community organisation that supports a range of needs and aspirations of Sudanese communities, particularly concerning education.

Participants were sourced from an open call for participation, which attracted a diverse range of youth including those attending university courses, community college (TAFE) courses, those still in high school, and those no longer attending. In total, five participants made film clips and over 60 focus group participants watched the clips and responded to questions about their efficacy.

The purpose of the creation of video clips was twofold: each participant would create two short clips (of approximately two minutes each). One was aimed 'outward', at the world at large, at fellow cultural community members, and at dominant culture members who might not see many representations of refugee-background students excelling in Australian schools. The other clip was created to 'talk back' to universities, and articulate to the participants' advice on what can be improved in education pathways for those from refugee backgrounds. Of the resulting clips, the goal was to place the 'public' clips online (on community organisation, tutoring group and community health facility websites) and as public service announcements on television. The 'speaking back' clips were pitched for presentation to university staff and administrators who might want to hear directly from those for whom they are developing pathways into their institutions. In both cases, the clips created seemed to be successful when measured by community responses to them, participant satisfaction rates, and health, youth and community sector responses; they were, however, unsuccessful in gaining the attention of their target mainstream audiences. This section will detail the context for this project, and some reasons why it may not have gained the mainstream support it sought.

It has been well established that there is a strong correlation between education and health, as well as between education and wellbeing. Early research showed that education and income had a positive correlation, which in turn had a positive effect on health status (Antonovsky, 1967). Later studies discovered not only a positive relationship between education and income, but also confirmed a more direct correlation between

100

education and health (Cowell, 2006; Rosenzweig, 1995; Taubman & Rosen, 1982). Research shows that education enhances the earning potential and aspirational activities (both work and leisure) associated with good health, including social connectedness and proactive health maintenance (Fayissa, Danyal & Butler, 2011).

As first highlighted by Grossman (1972) and more recently by others (including Cutler & Lleras-Muney, 2006; Ding et al., 2006; Gan & Gong, 2007), health and education may interact in three interrelated ways: education may determine health; one or more other factors may determine both health and education simultaneously; and health may determine education (Suhrcke & de Paz Nieves, 2011). Most agree that education impacts positively on health, and particularly engagement with participatory educational strategies (including creative and arts-based pedagogies). Furthermore, researchers continue to argue that education enhances the individual's capacity to make better-informed decisions about their own behaviours, as well as more generally about good long-term health overall (Kenkel, 1991; Currie & Hyson, 1999; Lleras-Muney 2005).

Education and health are two central determinants of human capital. Their economic value lies in the effects they have on productivity: both education and health impact individuals' capacities to be 'productive'. Education and health have a considerable impact on individual wellbeing as well. In addition, global ranking of nation-states remains linked to a large extent to the educational attainment and health status of its population.

Research shows that 'happiness' or life satisfaction is positively determined by health, a stable job and a satisfying family life. Disease and illness, unemployment, divorce and criminal behaviour are strong determinants of depression and negative attitudes toward life. Many of the aspects that make people unhappy are more prevalent among the less-educated than among the higher-educated. Unemployment rates are generally much higher among workers with less education than among the higher-educated, and lower-educated people experience more health problems and generally suffer from shorter life expectancies and higher rates of mortality through preventable illness than their higher-educated counterparts.

Education contributes significantly to lowering rates of unemployment and poor health and educational engagement contributes to lessening criminal behaviour (Groot & Maassen van den Brink, 2006). Research has demonstrated measurable benefits, both for individuals and for society, amongst those with higher levels of education beyond the compulsory years (to Year 10 in Australia). Three key areas contribute to the social capital of higher education and its positive effects on health promotion: self, context and behaviour. For each of these determinants, the creative aspects of these two case studies has the potential to play a significant part.

Self

An individual has the ability to shape his or her beliefs and psycho-social capabilities. This is related to the role of education, as learning and development

CHAPTER 5

impact on oneself and therefore health behaviours (Groot & Maassen van den Brink, 2006). For those involved in projects like *Culture Shack* and *SAILing into Uni!,* the chance to see peers who may more closely look and sound like oneself can provide welcome and more readily-identifiable role models when considering further education. In addition, as affirmed by Herbert (2010), the positive affective power of having cultural and gendered role models available cannot be underestimated. For those (like these project participants) from migrant and refugee backgrounds, having readily-accessible testimonies of success from those who may have survived similar life experiences can be doubly powerful in changing negative self-talk and increasing personal aspirations.

Context

Context describes factors including environment, social interactions and social capital. The environments in which people study and work can impact their health due to multiple factors, including physical structures and human interactions. Peers and social networks are a very important element of context. These networks can be formed in any location and may hold authority over individuals, shaping and influencing their beliefs, ideas, values and norms in ways that can impact on healthy behaviours and lifestyle choices (Groot & Maassen van den Brink, 2006). Socioeconomic status plays a further role in social capital and can impact on education pathways, options and aspirations, which are closely tied to health promotion and wellbeing. Research has shown that collaborative creative projects conducted in a range of learning sites can contribute considerably to establishing networks and healthy contexts for enhancing aspiration, motivation and academic success (Stevenson & Deasy, 2005; O'Brien & Donelan, 2006).

Behaviours

Often the behaviours of individuals and the choices they make can exacerbate risks of educational disengagement and poor health. Lifestyle choices such as smoking, excessive alcohol and drug use, and many others may place one at harm of living a shorter and less satisfying life. Research evidence shows that levels of education inform patterns of risky behaviours (Groot & Maassen van den Brink, 2006). Social cohesion and belonging—both of which are enhanced by creative approaches to pedagogy and also to research—positively impact a sustainable healthy lifestyle as well as individual choices, development and overall community wellbeing (Dryden-Peterson & Giles, 2011).

Further and higher education form the culmination of a lifelong educational continuum beginning in early childhood, in which learning and achievement patterns are quickly established (Dryden-Peterson & Giles, 2011). For some, these patterns are negative or turn into negative patterns long before secondary schooling. Creative approaches that occur outside of schools can sometimes offer forms of engagement that are non-threatening and offer relief from old patterns of failure and disappointment (O'Brien & Donelan, 2006). Further, the promise of access to higher education has been shown to enhance motivation and academic resilience in children and young people throughout upper primary and secondary school years (Chaffin, 2010), and the possibility of that ongoing educational opportunity can be newly imagined for 'first in family' attenders through imaginative and creative approaches, such as those applied in the two case studies profiled here.

Those from refugee backgrounds are perfectly placed to provide hope and inspiration for others entering higher education, including 'first in family' attenders. Like the four young women featured in the *SAILing into Uni!* public service announcements, young people from refugee backgrounds who watched their clips affirmed the power of positive role models. Post-secondary school education has the potential to give displaced populations a greater voice (Dryden-Peterson & Giles, 2011) in global discourses and in local communities. The 1951 Refugee Convention recognises the fundamental rights of refugees to access education, earn a living and seek justice when fleeing with a 'well-founded fear' of persecution from their homelands (UNHCR, 2002). Since the enactment of the Convention, more than two-thirds of refugees have been denied basic human rights worldwide. Accessing further and higher education is one factor that powerfully enables people from refugee backgrounds to contribute productively to both their host countries and countries of origin, improving not only their own lives but their broader communities as well.

Many migrant and refugee-background men and women miss out on the opportunity to pursue the kind of education that will cultivate the skills, knowledge and thinking capabilities needed to provide a better life. Among refugee-background students who have completed secondary school there is an almost universal desire to attend university (Women's Refugee Commission, 2009), yet many are still advised by study and career counsellors to opt for other, more 'achievable' possibilities (Harris, 2012; Earnest et al., 2010). In addition, many are not provided with the support they feel they need once they do arrive at university, and retention is not high. For their families, they represent the chance for more sustainable economic livelihoods and the kinds of stable and satisfying lives they themselves were denied; for their countries of origin, they promise the possibility of more stable political and social leadership. Yet many are denied opportunities to pursue the kind of education that would help them to cultivate the skills, knowledge and critical thinking capacities required to live up to these hopes and expectations. Even when prerequisites for higher education have been met, other barriers to accessing these opportunities are faced. These include cost, documentation such as birth certificates or exam results, recognition of learning certificates from other countries, and many more. In addition, research continues to show that the enrolment numbers of students from refugee and migrant backgrounds in higher education remain low (Dryden-Peterson & Giles, 2011), and further research continues to be needed to address low retention numbers in a range of further and higher education contexts. Both case studies here were conceptualised to address these dual concerns of access and retention. Better support

CHAPTER 5

at the university level must incorporate the perspectives of the students themselves, and *SAILing into Uni!* incorporates such voices.

Some Voices from the Community

ADIBA (Afghani-Australian):

You need to be able to say 'I fell but I got up and I didn't get hurt.' You need to be able to pull through. Because it is hard and you will fail, you might fail, you're gonna fail!

ANNE: *Everyone does.*

ADIBA: *Yeah. But you can't accept that failure as the be-all and end-all. It's not—no, not at all. Um, and if you fail you can you have another go. And you have another go. And you do it until you are confident that you've passed.*

DONA (Sudanese-Australian):

Maybe encourage them and just talk to them more and more. Because I think, I think that there's a lot of distractions around. That's the reason most Sudanese don't go to university. Just talk to them. And go through the pathways, because I'm pretty sure most Sudanese, they have no idea what the pathways are, not at all. I don't know, a fun program that will engage people to come, instead of boring ones.

CATHY (Sudanese-Australian):

I always think that I would do high school and become a mum and a housewife cuz that's what my mother did, and that's what all my family did. Because you didn't have that support to actually go to uni. If there's someone who'll believe in you, someone who will show you directions or . . . That's the thing: we Sudanese don't understand Australia, all these systems we don't know. So then we don't know where to turn or what to do next. So if I have someone telling me 'this will be good for you, and this is a good start for your career', it's like 'Oh wow, I'll do that'. And then you just keep climbing with that support. But when there's no support, you just have nowhere to turn.

It's the pathway! If they know the pathway which to take and they can take that to get to where they want. I kept failing the exam, which was the only pathway I knew. So finding that friend that says 'you might try this, you might benefit from it'. It's not a direct pathway but it will help you, did make me get there.

I saw with my sisters last week from their high school, they offered them all these booklets from uni, like 'read this' she's like 'I want to do childcare'. And then all she get was all these booklets. And she went to me 'I don't know what to do with these booklets. I'm reading them but there's nothing telling me what to do.' I went to those Open Days. I went to every uni (even Ballarat), and they didn't tell me anything. It's like well 'You can do this for 3 years and this is the benefit you get out of it, and we'll encourage you to apply.' I'm like 'Well that sounds good. But if I can't get in once I finish my Year 12, what other way can I do to actually get there?'

. . . This is what you get from high school, 'ah you finish year 12'. You get an ENTER score and go to uni. So when you fail and you hear the name TAFE, it just disappoints you. So they prepare that. TAFE is a pathway to get you into the degree you wanna do. They say TAFE is . . . you fail and that's where you gotta go.

*What people need to be thinking about? What can we do to help those kids get into uni? You want us to apply and you want us to get that education, but open—***show us the pathways.***

Chapell & Faltis (2013) share a commitment to a reformation of pedagogy and curriculum through the arts and creative engagement. It is no accident that so many activist texts and projects addressing educational and social inequities are centred in the arts or creative collaboration, due to the egalitarian nature of the artmaking process which is so often not dependent upon (any specific) language. Importantly, they too reject a deficit-based view of non-dominant cultural group students and choose to celebrate an "asset-based stance about language and culture in the lives of communities" (2013, p. xix), recognising the interconnectedness of learning, culture, creativity and relationships. The following two case studies hold these values at their core.

CASE STUDY #2

Culture Shack and the Politics of Aesthetics

Http://www.creativeresearchhub.com/#!the-creative-turn---data-assets/cxoe

Culture Shack resonates within a significant body of international research that argues the academic and equity benefits of creative pedagogies. While community-based arts programs have been run often and well (O'Toole & O'Mara, 2007; O'Brien & Donelan, 2006), both in Australian and international contexts (Grossman & Sonn, 2010; Dimitriadis, Cole & Costello, 2009; Bodilly, Augustine & Zakaras, 2008), programmatic innovations to establish formal arts-based pathways from vocational to tertiary study have not been so visible. As educators increasingly seek creative modes for teaching and learning, *Culture Shack's* innovative peered and tiered model for community-based learning, and the ways in which digital technologies can support such collaborative learning communities, suggests one powerful possibility.

Briefly, the *Culture Shack* pilot program ran throughout 2011, with two main branches of activity: an educational pathway plotting component (year-long) and community-delivered arts workshops delivered as an intensive over a two-week school holiday period in April 2011. The pilot included over 100 participants in all, including industry, artist, teacher, academic and youth participants. Three streams of creative workshops were offered: drama, animation and hip hop. The average participant number per day was 16, with 24 participants in all over the two weeks. The ages of the youth participants ranged from 14-24 years. The youth participants were more than 90 per cent female and, while all self-identified as Australian, were primarily from the cultural backgrounds of Samoan, Vietnamese, Chinese and Sudanese. The facilitators/teacher-researchers ranged in age from early-20s to mid-60s and were drawn from Canada, the United States and Australia; from cultural backgrounds self-identified as Anglo-Australian, Vietnamese-Australian, Anglo-American, Greek-Australian, American-Australian, Indigenous Australian, Sudanese-Australian, and Caribbean-Canadian. For more on the program and its methodology, see Harris (2011; 2012; 2013a; 2013b) and Harris & Lemon (2012). This chapter will explore the ways in which aesthetics were central to trust-building and youth engagement in the research relationship.

Central to the success of the *Culture Shack* program was freedom of choice in the alignment of cultural, aesthetic and pedagogical relationships. According to project participant

> JACKIE: *I've met a lot of people here who are very interested in our culture, so they've asked us questions and of course they're interested in the Samoan lifestyle . . . and I've learnt about New York, from Brett! . . . [Brett Reynolds, the playwright workshop leader from New York's Young Playwrights' Inc].*
>
> NILES: *Anyone else?*
>
> JACKIE: *Patrick. He's our bus driver and dance coach. He's chick-a-bom bom. So, uh, yeah. Patrick he, gave us, he told us his family history, like he's Australian. You know how people say what are you, Australian? well . . . not really Australian, like where did he come from? So he has a bit of Irish and stuff, so we learnt about his culture, like . . . he has one! (focus group interview, 2010).*

The coming together of such a cross-section of collaborators was at the heart of this pedagogical-creative work. Student teachers commented on the ways in which this community-based learning program allowed them to get to know these students in far deeper and more egalitarian ways than they had in their practicum schools; the scholars noted the richness of the 'two-way' intercultural pedagogy that was going on; the artists felt the program was enriched by sharing artistic space with educators and academics; the community arts facilities loved the buzz of having the spaces filled so intensively with such an intergenerational and intercultural collaborative team. This 'peered and tiered learning model' (Harris, 2013a) can work across sectors and levels of continuing education (including TAFE, university and secondary schools).

Samoan youth participant Jackie, who loved the professional engagement around drama and playwriting, ended up enrolled in an Arts Management course at a highly-regarded local university, despite thinking at the time of *Culture Shack* (two years prior) that she would not go on to university. When I re-interviewed her recently, she said this:

JACKIE: *Culture Shack definitely left a lasting impact in my life. I've chosen the Arts degree beside my Management degree because I've always had a spot for performing arts in my heart, and although it may not be my major focus at university, all that I've learnt during Shack—especially the drama class—has helped me in teaching my church youth different skits and plays and song performances for our occasional church functions. All the things Brett and Anne taught me during drama enabled me to confidently act out my role as youth leader. Creative arts has a great capacity in improving education because it is useful in all aspects of workplaces, educations, and all other professions. Creative arts enable all educators to think outside the box and view things from all perspectives. Creative arts enables us to be creative with our lives. Culture Shack and like programs definitely build community through collaboration. It brings people from different cultures together to share and learn of each other's cultural heritage. In addition to all other creative arts subjects being taught at these programs, the way these different cultures respond and perceive these learning objectives also gives a much richer perspective on creative arts and its importance to everyday life.*

Good teaching is when the teacher believes and has great passion in what they teach. Through their passion, they teach in ways that has the learner believe and generate their own passion in what they're learning. That I believe is great teaching. A good relationship between a teacher and learner is very important because that's how a teacher is more willing to teach and the learner is more willing to learn. Creative arts is very important because it's a very important aspect in life. I believe it influences our perceptions and enables us to think through many different perspectives.

As a youth leader, I'm pressured to teach performances from the bible while appealing to the Samoan tradition also. It's hard because I was raised in New Zealand and Melbourne and the Samoan tradition was a part-time sort of thing that I learn while I'm at home and I'm at school most of the time learning . . . 'non-Samoan' stuff. Creative arts subjects at school—whether it was creative writing, drama, music, art, or creative drawing, these subjects enabled me to think, act or write creatively. My experiences with these subjects generated my creativity that I now use with everything I do—and with regards to my youth, I was able to produce skits, dances, plays and musical performances using my creativity, and I was able to put the bible, Samoan tradition, and a modernised aspect in all our performances that my church members loved.

CHAPTER 5

> *My whole youth group used their creativity as well as mine to put together wonderful performances that enabled us to feel the spirituality and love in our services to God.*

For Jackie and many other youth participants of this program, creativity is intertwined with relationships, be they spiritual, cultural and/or pedagogical. For us, this was one major 'win' of the *Culture Shack* program: to be able to share in multiple ways, multiple directions, with multiple learnings at once. Such interdisciplinarity is growing in schools and research too. But it was also tied for Jackie (and others) to a new kind of aesthetic—one that incorporates 'modernised aspects' in performance with more traditional ones, combining what Benjamin described as the work's aura with its reproductive or commodity value. For Jackie, these are not mutually exclusive objectives.

While a critical discourse of arts education and research approaches is growing, Bolin and Blandy (2003) point out the urgent need to think more broadly about our research alliances and escape the shackles of siloed practice and research approaches. They encourage a critical approach that promotes "the investigation and appreciation of the broadest possible range of objects, artifacts, spaces, expressions and experience" (p. 246), based in both critical cultural studies and the "proliferation of images challenging the hegemony of text and spoken word" (p. 246); something that many arts-based research programs—like both *Culture Shack* and *SAILing into Uni!*—do.

Real Power of Creative Pedagogies?

Chappell and Faltis' (2013) new book is "intended for school and community-based educators interested in reforming pedagogy (curriculum and instruction) for emergent bilingual youth through an arts-based lens" (p. xvii), which is also a central aim of this book—particularly this chapter. While the young participants you have met here have not claimed to be activists working toward educational change, their abilities, politics, experiences and relationships are creating that change. As the twenty-first century progresses, we see more—and more powerful—student voices from this perspective. This is not to deny the very real overriding material conditions of these students' lives: for example, Jackie is taking a hiatus from her university degree because her family cannot afford to send both her and her sister at the same time.

Many of the youth participants in these two case studies speak more than two languages and represent the intersection of more than two cultures. Their lived experiences represent ways forward for education that occurs both inside and outside of schools, but also for the future of intersectional arts and a new aesthetic imaginary for the latter twenty-first century. Their lives, their artwork and, hopefully, eventually their educational trajectories will reflect what Chappell and Faltis call the "intimate connections among the arts, narrative, and resistance for addressing social (in)justices in school and community contexts" (p. xix), something much creative educational research—and this book—also aspires to do. Cahnmann-Taylor tells us:

As an educator, the arts help you move from cultural and linguistic ways of teaching (a culture of teaching that is relatively unexamined) to culturally and linguistically responsive teaching—an approach to teaching that honors knowing about students' languages, cultural practices and knowledge, that encourages students to express their voices, experiences and styles, and that facilitates students' own empowerment through critical, creative expressions. Arts-based experiences from this perspective encourage reflection *(why does this matter to me?)*, critical thinking *(whose perspectives are told and who benefits from the message in artworks?)*, and action *(how can artistic processes change the status quo?)*, taking seriously the "points of view and cultural and linguistic experiences of children and youth who have been systematically left out of the curriculum" (2013, p. 26, emphasis in original).

What does it mean, we might ask, to be left out of the curriculum? Both *SAILing into Uni!* and *Culture Shack* address this issue through different approaches, but both use arts-based methods. By creating public service announcements, refugee-background young people from Afghanistan and South Sudan (and elsewhere) can speak back directly and indirectly to institutions, dominant cultures, teachers and peers who are already assimilating stereotyped images of 'at-risk learners', of failed students, of an already overburdened education system that doesn't know what to do with students with interrupted schooling (Iqbal et al, 2012). They are able to act as their own voiced, imaged and agentic reminders to the public around them that in fact they are succeeding, they are ambitious, and they are celebrating their educational successes, even when we are not. They remind us of what we don't see in our own exclusionary practices, and they demand more support both curricularly and pedagogically. For the participants of *Culture Shack*, the embodied experience of learning about creativity and creatively learning in collaborative relationships meant education could become a two-way street. It could encompass a multitude of learnings, even when curriculum documents do not. And at the heart of both projects is a recognition of relationship as knowing, of what Pelias (2004) calls a 'methodology of the heart', in which research demands, rather than runs from, emotional engagement.

What Way Forward?

Massumi asks us to respond to the question "what is to be done?" (2011, p. 171) in a more rhizomatic way, rather than seeking a predetermined answer. In creative terms, aesthetic terms, or research/pedagogical terms, answers to the question should, he argues, be concerned with the "intensity with which a process lives itself out" (p. 171) rather than meeting a "prefixed frame of correct judgment applied to it from without" (p. 171). Such intensities continue to challenge traditional schooling, whether in secondary or university contexts. He suggests that all creative endeavour (including interactive) should re-orient itself toward a central concern with an "'intensity of feeling' as part of a 'creative advance' into . . . 'an aesthetic fact' [as] . . . the ultimate

CHAPTER 5

criterion for all process" (p. 171). Can such an 'intensity of feeling' ever become part of 'good pedagogy' or even 'good research', when validity and measurement remain at the heart of both? Interactive art—which is not necessarily digital art, although the discourse has shifted it there—demands this kind of two-way relationship in order to jointly construct a shared aesthetic. It is this negotiation of aesthetic, I argue, that changes behaviour and ultimately promises to change paradigms. For Massumi, "interactive art needs behavior on both sides of the classical dichotomy of object and viewer . . . traditional artworks . . . do not change as a result of the behaviour they inspire in their audiences. It's a one way traffic, there's no exchange" (p. 39).

These research projects—and indeed this book—are concerned with exploding these modes of 'one way traffic' in creative research and educational relationships. Moreover, they are concerned with increasing the ways in which participants can become creative co-participants and co-researchers with their academic and education partners. These higher levels of co-participation do not mean that aesthetics must suffer or be disregarded altogether. As Massumi tells us, interactive art—like interactive research—cannot be so "without a form that is 'interesting', and therefore in some way aesthetic" (p. 39). But being interactive alone does not make it art, nor does it necessarily make it aesthetic.

I opened the chapter with Seelig's rather free-wheeling call to identify the creative moments in our everyday objects and lives, because her approach to this potentially feel-good pop-psychology of creativity avoids some pitfalls that others succumb to, namely, that everything is potentially creative, if only we regard it so. I have written extensively about the dumbing-down effect of this approach to creativity, yet Seelig's approach is compelling, especially so for educators. She keeps the focus squarely on imagination and its relationship to memory. Informed by a keenly-sorted and downloadable memory, our imagination—she claims—is an endlessly renewable resource (something investors love to hear). Yet she differs from other creativity theorists who claim that the heart of imagination and creativity (and innovation for that matter) is to regain a kind of naïve or child's mind which forgets easily and sees forever anew. What I find compelling in Seelig's argument is her sustainability approach; she uses all that she has upstairs, and sees it all as grist for the mill. To me, this is good pedagogy. If teachers approach students with a great excitement about inviting *all* aspects (or assets) of themselves as learners into the learning process, then those possibilities are truly limitless, be they creative, scholarly or something altogether different.

In the two projects described in these case studies, the youth participants contributed to scripting new ways of learning, new ways of accessing learning institutions and opportunities, and new ways of telling the world about their educational successes and capabilities. As research that uses creative methods and creative collaboration as a methodology, they are examples of the ways in which research can serve many functions simultaneously, rather than choosing between 'applied' or 'theoretical', arts-based or educational. By incorporating community and culturally diverse knowledges in research designs, based in educational experiences, projects like these can open new areas of creative, aesthetic and educational innovation. For expanding discourses of aesthetics—now almost wholly absent from education research discourses—they provide much room to grow. In the following chapter, I will address the uneasy relationship between aesthetics and innovation in education discourses, and the very central role of aesthetics in creating a new educational imaginary.

NOTES

[1] With thanks to my two research partners from Monash University, Dr Belinda Crockett and Ruth Klein.

REFERENCES

Antonovsky, A. (1967). Social class, life expectation and overall mortality. *The Milbank Memorial Fund Quarterly, 45*, 31–37.
Bolin, P. E., & Blandy, D. (2003). Beyond visual culture: Seven statement of support for material culture studies in art education. *Studies in Art Education: A journal of Issues and Research, 44*(3), 246–263.
Bodilly, S. J., Augustine, C. H., & Zakaras, L. (2008). *Revitalizing arts education through community-wide coordination.* Santa Monica, CA: RAND Corp.
Cahnmann-Taylor, M. (2013). Arts artifact three: Pinewood estates trailer park. In (Eds.) S. V. Chappell & C. J. Faltis (Eds.), *The arts and emergent bilingual youth: Building culturally responsive, critical, and creative education in school and community contexts* (pp. 24–26). New York, NY: Routledge.
Chaffin, J. (2010). Framing paper 1: Education and opportunity: Post-primary and income growth. Retrieved from June 15, 2013, http://toolkit.ineesite.org/toolkit/INEEcms/uploads/1105/Youth%20 Framing_Paper_1_Final.pdf
Chappell, S. V., & Faltis, C. J. (Eds). (2013). *The arts and emergent bilingual youth: Building culturally responsive, critical, and creative education in school and community contexts.* New York, NY: Routledge.
Cowell, A. (2006). The relationship between education and health behavior: Some empirical evidence. *Health Economics, 15*, 124–146.
Currie, J., & Hyson, R. (1999). Is the impact of health shocks cushioned by socioeconomic status? The case of low birthweight. *American Economic Review, 89*, 245–250.
Cutler, D.M, & Lleras-Muney, A. (2006). *Education and health: Evaluating theories and evidence* (Working Paper No. 12352). The National Bureau of Economic Research.
Dimitriadis, G., Cole, E., & Costello, A. (2009) The social field(s) of arts education today: living vulnerability in neo-liberal times. *Discourse: Studies in the Cultural Politics of Education, 30*(4), 361–379.
Ding, W., Lehrer, S. F., Rosenquist, N. J., & Audrain-McGovern, J. (2006). *The impact of poor health on education: New evidence using genetic markers* (Working Paper No. 12304). The National Bureau of Economic Research.
Dryden-Peterson, S., & Giles, W. (2011). Introduction: Higher Education for Refugees. *Refuge Journal, 27*(2), 3–9.
Earnest, J., Joyce, A., de Mori, G., & Silvagni, G. (2010). Are universities responding to the needs of students from refugee backgrounds? *Australian Journal of Education, 54*(2) 155–174.
Fayissa, B., Danyal, S., & Butler, J. S. (2011). *The impact of education on health status: Evidence from longitudinal survey data.* Department of Economics and Finance Working Paper Series.
Gan, L., & Gong, G. (2007). *Estimating interdependence between health and education in a dynamic model* (Working Paper No. 12830). The National Bureau of Economic Research.
Groot, W., & Massen van den Brink, H. (2006). *What does education do to our health? Measuring the effects of education on health and civic engagement: Proceedings of the Copenhagen Symposium.* Retrieved from June 17, 2013, http://www.oecd.org/education/country-studies/ measuringtheeffectsofeducationonhealthandcivicengagement.htm

Grossman, M. (1972). On concept of health capital and the demand for health. *Journal of Political Economu, 80*(2), 223–225.
Grossman, M., & Sonn, C. (2010). Literature Review. *New moves: Understanding the impacts of the song room programs for young people from refugee backgrounds* (pp. 23–50). Melbourne, VIC: The Song Room.
Harris, A. (2013a). Peered and tiered learning: Action research as creative cultural pedagogy. *Educational Action Research, 21*(3), 412–428.
Harris, A. (2013b). Alphabet rap: hip hop and the re-coolification of creative pedagogies as research. *New Scholar: An international journal of the humanities, creative arts and social sciences (ejournal), 2*(1), 121–135.
Harris, A. (2012). *Ethnocinema: Intercultural arts education*. The Netherlands: Springer SBM.
Harris, A., & Lemon, A. (2012). Bodies that shatter: creativity, culture and the new pedagogical imaginary. *Pedagogy, Culture and Society, 20*(3), 413–433.
Harris, A. (2011). Culture Shack and the art of intercultural learning. *UNESCO Observatory refereed e-journal, multidisciplinary research in the arts*.
Herbert, A. (2010). *The pedagogy of creativity*. Abingdon: Routledge.
Iqbal, N., Joyce, A., Russo, A., & Earnest, J. (2012). *Resettlement experiences of Aghan Hazara female adolescents: A case study*. Melbourne, Australia: International Journal of Population Research.
Kenkel, D. (1991). Health behavior, health knowledge and schooling. *Journal of Political Economy, 99*(2).
Lleras-Muney, A. (2005). The relationship between education and adult mortality in the United States. *Review of Economic Studies, 72*, 189–221.
Massumi, B. (2011). *Semblance and event: Activist philosophy and the occurrent arts*. Boston, MA: MIT Press.
Matthews, J. (2008). Schooling and settlement: refugee education in Australia. In *International Studies in Sociology of Education, 18*(1), 31–45.
O'Brien, A., & Donelan, K. (2006). Risky business: An Australian study of the use of the creative arts as an intervention activity for marginalized young people. *Journal of Psychology and Educational Sciences, 1*(2), 54–66.
O'Toole, J., & O'Mara, J. (2007). Proteus, the giant at the door: Drama and theater in the curriculum. In L. Bresler (Ed.), *International handbook of research in arts education* (pp. 203–218). Dortrecht: Springer.
Pelias, R. J. (2004). *A methodology of the heart: Evoking academic and daily life*. Walnut Creek, CA: Alta Mira Press.
Rosenzweig, M. (1995). Why are there returns to schooling? *American Economic Review, 85*, 153–158.
Seelig, T. (2012). *In genius: A crash course on creativity*. London, UK: Hay House Publishing.
Sinker, R. (2012). Making multimedia: Evaluating young people's creative multimedia production. In J. Sefton-Green & R. Sinker (Eds.), *Evaluating creativity: Making and learning by young people* (pp. 186–214). London, UK: Routledge.
Stevenson, L. M., & Deasy, R. J. (2005). *Third space: When learning matters*. Washington, DC: Arts Education Partnership.
Suhrcke, M., & de Paz Nieves, C. (2011). The impact of health and health behaviours on educational outcomes in high-income countries: a review of the evidence. *World Health Organization*. Retrieved from http://www.euro.who.int/en/what-we-publish/abstracts/impact-of-health-and-health-behaviours-on-educational-outcomes-in-high-income-countries-the-a-review-of-the-evidence
Taubman, P., & Rosen, S. (1982). Healthiness, education, and marital status. In V. Fuchs (Ed.), *Economic aspects of health* (pp. 121–142). Chicago, IL: University of Chicago Press.
United Nations High Commissioner for Refugees. (UNHCR). (2002). *Statistical yearbook: Refugees, Asylum-Seekers and other persons of concern- trend in displacement, protection and solutions*. Geneva.
Women's Refugee Commission. (2009). *Living in Limbo: Iraqi young women and men in Jordan*. New York, NY: Women's Refugee Commission.

CHAPTER 6

AESTHETICS AND INNOVATION

Figure 10. Youthworx crate man, Melbourne (2013).

INTRODUCTION

It might seem ridiculous to begin a chapter on aesthetics by asserting that perhaps (outside of fine arts) aesthetics has become fairly remote from most peoples' interests, apart from philosophers. It may have little to do with 21st century education at the secondary level, if standardised curricula are any measure to go by, yet this is beginning to change. Both in educational discourses and research endeavour (not just arts based research, either), aesthetics is making a comeback. Whether or not this return is linked to the rise-and-rise of creativity, philosophy and cultural theory may still be the clearest counter-voice to the persistent discourse of productivity and commodification both inside and outside education. Adorno famously addressed aesthetics and commodification, including a concern with the hegemonising affects of capitalism on the process and cultural role of creativity. Indeed, he deeply underscored the ways in which aesthetics is always informed by the market, and the "abstractness of the new is bound up with the commodity character of art" (1997, p. 30). One could argue that the accelerated commodification of art is now resulting in the commodification of creativity (the act) itself. How Adorno may assist us in understanding the current creative turn is a rich area for further enquiry, but for the purposes of this chapter, I draw instead on Rancière and his attention to the political nature of both aesthetics and art production.

CHAPTER 6

Rancière (2009; 2006) has repeatedly defined aesthetics as both inseparable from politics and also from production. His work has defined aesthetics as referring to:

> the distribution of the sensible that determines a mode of articulation between forms of action, production, perception, and thought. This general definition extends aesthetics beyond the strict realm of art to include the conceptual coordinates and modes of visibility operative in the political domain (2006, p. 82).

Salehi asserts that "being effective in aesthetics is unlike being effective in business" (2008, p. 30), and education is increasingly the domain of business. In the second half of the twentieth century, creativity research emerged from aesthetics researchers, largely in philosophy and postmodernism. Today that nexus is also undergoing a kind of 'turn', a parallel shift to the one happening in creativity discourses. As Chapter Eight will show, it is largely aligned now with the creative industries, and economics and industry research. This reframing is having a considerable impact on not only the appearance and use-functional role of creativity in contemporary (global) culture, but its content as well. What this means in practical terms is that creativity is increasingly decoupled from aesthetics, and recoupled with innovation and commodity discourses, in what I am articulating here as a creative turn. In this chapter I continue my unpicking of the multiple threads in the creativity-innovation-aesthetics-education tangle, by examining the ways in which aesthetics has become politically inert or unimportant to popular imaginaries of creative culture. It is not perceived as central to considerations of creativity and the role of creativity in global flows and global markets, and therefore has been abandoned in favour of 'innovation'.

Yet there is some overlap between innovation and aesthetics. Salehi (2008) makes clear that from the second half of the last century, novelty and usefulness have become the most defining characteristics of accepted notions of creativity. Aesthetics, however, cannot be studied against criteria of effectiveness as easily as creativity or innovation and this, as the dominant measure, relegates aesthetics to the margins. Salehi argues that "creativity has an ethical element because a new idea cannot have a negative connotation and be considered effective and relevant to the field" (p. 30). I would argue that this ethical consideration is in itself already a neoliberal framing of creativity and that here creativity is more aligned with aesthetics—more than Salehi admits. New creative ideas are exactly what he cautions against: today's creativity is *only* acceptable if it has limited newness, and very limited or no negativity. I would argue that aesthetics—rather than creativity—are what remain of an ethically-infused aspect of creativity, which can have negative connotations or be unfamiliar to the field. Ascendant creativity—or creative industries—on the other hand, must not be dangerous, threatening, critical or negative of cultural ethics, or—when it is—must be neutralised quickly to harvest its maximum market potential (think video games, one of the leading edges of the 'creative industries', which are regularly criticised for both their negativity and newness, danger and uncontainability). In 21st-century creative economies, both process and product innovations must remain consumable to the largest market share, thus countering the political critical potential of aesthetic and ideological artmaking.

Reclaiming aesthetics (or its well-hidden intimate liaison with creativity) can be seen as romanticising an irrelevant or outdated (read 'unprofitable') aspect of creative cultural production. Within a purely market-driven framing of creative industries, Caves (2000) offers some clear explanations for the persistent if schizophrenic extremes of mega-successes or down-and-outs in the creative industries, unlike so many other industries. He troubles the cultural flows that make cutting-edge art works into mainstream (financial) success stories, using the example of Elvis Presley and his colonisation of rhythm and blues into modern rock and roll. There was nothing particularly innovative about the music that Elvis was recreating (yes *re*creating) from the southern Black music that he consumed, but rather his whiteness made it possible for him to fill a crossover roll into mass consumption of an aesthetic form (the 'rockabilly' version of Black-birthed rhythm and blues) that was already long-established. He simply rode the wave. While Caves claims that "the answer is not clear" whether this was the "result of a shift in tastes or a stylistic innovation" (p. 201), it seems perfectly clear to me—the 'dangerousness' of Black music became packageable and reproducible to the wider white audience through the aesthetic of a white body and white-to-white performance. While the 'dangerousness' of its proximity to Blackness might have appeared to remain dangerous to a mainstream, largely white, middle class, it was already cleansed of its embeddedness in Black culture, which provided both its reason for being and its apparent dangerousness. This need of mass marketing to sanitise the dangerous newness that these audiences/markets crave, and which bring them to the work in the first place, constitutes a kind of aesthetic of its own in relation to mass production—or a kind of anti-aesthetic.

This insatiable demand for recognisable but unfamiliar goods can be understood as the difference between an aesthetic shift and a "shift in demand" (Caves, 2000, p. 202). Caves tells us that "it is not quite—but almost—appropriate to say that innovation in creative activities need involve nothing more than consumers changing their minds about what they like" (2000, p. 202). But what—beneath a superficial economic reading of demand—can explain this consumer shift? Popular economics discourses tell us on a daily basis that demand is not an independently-developing market: suppliers aggressively develop 'demand' in their markets, in essence creating un-organic markets where there were previously none or few (think, for example, of the long lineage of i-products). Capitalism's continual and rapid expansion requires this cultivation of markets, and creative industries, I argue, is currently in the throes of just such a repackaging exercise.

Whether or not innovation is a market version of creativity, they share a focus on newness. The kind of newness, however, is what this chapter questions. Aesthetics and arts scholars are most frequently concerned with the ways in which the arts can use a product (artistic creation) metaphorically to represent a *zeitgeist* that is otherwise or was previously inarticulable. Market or creative industries innovation relies—like in the Elvis example—on a form of that product already being familiar

CHAPTER 6

and desirable. Readers may find this to be splitting hairs—they are both relying, then, on striking a chord with an already-present feeling, idea or practice, otherwise they would not resonate at all and would disappear. Indeed, history is littered with both industrial and artistic innovations that have been ahead of their time and were not taken up by the general public (electric cars as an example have unbelievably been around for nearly 200 years and are largely still not taken up despite compelling reasons in their favour). Yet, here I'm arguing that this difference between being marketable (innovation in industry, even creative industries), and being ideologically or political representative (artistically innovative), are wildly divergent things. While they may at times look the same—in fact, the cross-over from artistic innovation to market innovation can often be instantaneous if the timing is right for a given idea, object or style (think Obama's iconic representation by Shepard Fairey; Arnon, 2008). Nevertheless, considerations of artistic innovation almost never get talked about today as 'aesthetic innovations', although Fairey's iconic image of Obama can certainly be considered just that. I am arguing in this chapter that there is a need to differentiate between aesthetic understandings of innovation and industrial (even creative) ones. In this chapter, I will return aesthetics to the spotlight for a brief moment, and consider the beautiful difference of aesthetic innovation, and why we still need it.

This chapter will consider why aesthetics seems to be sidelined with philosophy in the margins of popular discourse, while innovation is taking centre stage as creativity's core definitional term of 'useful'. Aesthetics doesn't speak to utility (necessarily), while innovation seems inseparable from it. In this chapter I turn to Rancière to help examine the current seemingly estranged relationship between aesthetics and industry, and what this means for the relationship between creativity and aesthetics. With this problematisation of aesthetics and industry, I then turn to education and interrogate some possibilities as to why aesthetics is almost completely absent from educational discourses (except in fine arts education), while innovation is gaining traction. Combined as the educational 'dream team' of creativity and innovation, aesthetics has been sent to the margins, and this chapter suggests some reasons why this might not be the most effective way forward.

The Performativity of Aesthetics

Žižek tells us that the second great breakthrough of Rancière is "the assertion of the aesthetic dimension as *inherent* in any radical emancipatory politics" (2006, p. 76), and shows us the ways in which considerations of the aesthetic aspect of arts is not separate from political performativity, nor has it ever been. The hint at education's aspirational nature runs parallel to his emancipatory politics, and aesthetics can simultaneously serve both masters (and has in bygone times). Žižek tells us, "the aesthetic metaphor in which a particular element stands for the Universal, is enacted in the properly political short-circuit in which a particular demand stands for the universal gesture of rejecting the power that be" (2006, p. 76).

Rancière combines art history with labour history to interrogate the battles fought over the ways in which we project an image of society, including what is permissible to say or to show. His work can be usefully employed to see more deeply the present dialectic between aesthetics and creative industries. He identifies an ethical regime of art in which all artistic images are measured for their utility to society. Utility, as you'll remember, is the catch phrase of creative industries, but this is far from the craft labour that has been fought over by Rancière and those before him in aesthetics versus politics debates. Like Benjamin, for Rancière utility is a matter of labour, and the production of art, including 'the mechanical arts'. His notion of aesthetic hierarchies is being repeated in the form of the digital divide in current creative arts versus creative industries debates. Digital media today could well represent what Rancière might think of as the apolitical apex of art-as-activism. The political potential of art is certainly nowhere to be seen in contemporary creative industries, which perhaps is exactly what the state likes about them, and why they are willing—indeed falling all over themselves—to fund them.

For arts philosophers like Rancière, "the channels for political subjectivization are not those of imaginary identification but those of 'literary' disincorporation" (p. 40). Disincorporation perhaps, but any new aesthetic imaginary must itself recognise the permeability of the digital ethnoscape, and digitised worlds as sites of engagement of both the political (think Wikileaks, Syria, Pussy Riot) and the apolitical (think memes). Harder perhaps is the task of separating the creative from the 'non-creative' or reproductive.

Part of the work of the shift away from nation-state identities and toward global flows and global elites is a re-schooling of populations to consider ourselves as part of new 'imagined communities' that go beyond—or allow us to relinquish—nation-based ones. In this sense, the push toward a discourse of global creative industries in which profitable creativity allows us to reinvent and re-align ourselves to new allies, is simultaneously functional for abandoning previous ideological loyalties in which art seemed to promise some higher compensation than financial rewards.

Redfield (2003) reminds us that:

> Anderson's great Benjaminian argument in *Imagined Communities* derives the possibility of this imaginative act out of developments in reproductive and communicational technologies. The modernity of the nation is that of the Gutenberg revolution: as language becomes mechanically reproducible in Walter Benjamin's sense and print-capitalism begins to create markets, the fundamentally anonymous community of the nation-state becomes imaginable (p. 50).

Even ten years ago when Redfield was writing, he commented that as "a commodity that expires within twenty-four hours or less, the newspaper summons its reader to a 'mass ceremony' predicated on the simultaneous participation of uncountable other readers, elsewhere" (p. 50), and now, of course, digital media including Twitter have already superseded this immediacy with no expectation of slowing, only accelerating. Redfield examines Anderson in depth here, particularly the positioning

CHAPTER 6

of what he calls the "state's aesthetic-educational apparatus . . . as an 'imagined community' (p. 14). In this chapter I too argue that the state is still a functional and powerful entity, expressed through its dispersed mechanisms, including education. But unlike Redfield, I disagree with Anderson that this aesthetic imaginary is a conscious one, but rather argue that it is—currently through its development of a creative industries discourse—unconsciously commodifying previous sites of both aesthetic and intellectual activism or resistance; namely, in formal educational structures. Raunig (2013), more recently argues the opposite—that universities still contain radical potential for fighting this commodification. Yet my previous analysis of the spread of creativity discourses that hinge on commodification would suggest otherwise. First, let's look at Raunig's take on things.

Raunig (2013) argues that universities may still be the last bastion for intellectual, political and creative resistance, but surely a majority would disagree, arguing that universities have already been commodified and capitalised out of their political capabilities. Nevertheless, Raunig argues that a Deleuzian notion of modulation can offer us ways forward in positioning university labour as sites of new creative imaginaries. Raunig strikes a romantic tone, however, in presupposing that universities and other forms of institutionalised education can function as autonomous bodies for knowledge production. His argument against universities as new 'factories' of knowledge is increasingly problematic as neoliberalism spreads from standardised discourses at the secondary school level into tertiary education systems. Productivity reigns as MOOCs, online learning and digital course delivery expand rapidly.

But aesthetics is on the move, however begrudgingly in education. It is " now propelled into the ambient field of image production and circulation . . . 'the imagination is today a staging ground for action, and not only escape'" (Appadurai, 1996, p. 7 in Papastergiadis, 2012, p. 226). Here I am seeking to move beyond an industries versus aesthetics binary—itself a political (and false) construct/ distinction.

It is possible that "aesthetics and politics are two forms of an underlying imaginary process" (Papastergiadis, 2012, p. 227) in which art and aesthetics with their focus on the "anti-globalization movement and new artistic collectives have sought to re-route information flows and widen the legal and political frameworks from a state-centric perspective of citizenship to the articulation of a political agenda" (Raunig, 2002 in Papastergiadis, 2012, p. 228). Arts education, with its focus on process and slowness and risk, may represent this anti-globalisation or anti-industrialisation of creativity.

Redfield (2003) counters that, "of the many relics of the romantic era that continue to shape our (post)modernity, the nation-state surely ranks among the most significant" (p. 45). Raunig draws on two Deleuzian notions for a consideration of aesthetics: concatenation and transversality, both of which provide ways to consider time and space in relation to aesthetics. Papastergiadis tells us how Raunig and Deleuze can thus be leveraged for a more nuanced understanding of the art/ politics divide or what he calls Raunig's "crossover between artistic and activist communication techniques" (2012, p. 228). But what do these debates have to do with the flows of creativity and its commodification in education and industry? Is it primarily a political question with aesthetic nuance, or a question of capital nuanced with cosmopolitanism? This, according to Papastergiadis, is representative of the "persisting tension between utopian ideals and precarious realities" (p. 229) which characterises this age. He suggests that in Raunig's Deleuzian approach lies a functional opportunity for "the adoption of an evaluative standpoint that recognizes ephemerality and intensity as a virtue" (p. 229), both temporary and situational. Perhaps, strangely, this model can offer a similarly temporary possibility for education systems in which the old is no longer working but the new is yet to emerge. Both Rancière and Raunig here can assist us in disentangling the dual definitions of commodified creativity and arts education, drawing from the failed binary of political versus the artistic.

Figure 11. Melbourne graffiti, #4 (2013).

Creativity and Innovation in Education: Useful or Just Assessable?

I hope I have successfully argued by now that creativity is not the same as innovation. As many busily engaged in definitional work around creativity have reiterated, creativity across all its flashpoint sectors today certainly centres around something like originality, subjective terms like value, and a sense of newness which many call innovation. And while much about creativity is innovative, innovation can certainly be present without creativity. So why the conflation of creativity and innovation in educational discourses? These days, the two are practically interchangeable in the same ways in which creativity and creative industries are often used interchangeably. However, to finish this chapter on the important differences between aesthetics, creativity and innovation, I'd like to close out with a few thoughts on what innovation is and what it is not.

CHAPTER 6

Innovation is not curriculum. The economist Paul Stoneman (2010) looks at the intersection between business, aesthetics and the commodification of creativity, and works hard to remind readers of "the importance of aesthetics (as compared to functionality) in product demand" (p. 35). This he calls 'soft innovation' and defines as innovation that which primarily impacts upon aesthetic or intellectual appeal rather than functional performance; in other words, innovation of form rather than function. Can the same observation be made of creative arts in education versus creative industries in education? I argue here that the changes that have occurred in educational curricula and discourses over the past five years are aesthetic innovations rather than functional ones. They are changes of form, constructed toward re-imagining the skills of creativity as labour market skills of innovation; in the hope that the creative mind, once trained (still in factory-like schools, mind you), will miraculously produce marketplace innovations that will somehow carry ailing national economies forward into a glorious new century. The very fact that this new vision of a creative imaginary is being framed in nation-based discourses should be our first clue that something is not right. Global elites and cosmopolitan mediascapes will increasingly meet in creatively innovative spaces using dynamic new approaches that well may be creative, and even indeed aesthetically innovative. Yet for most of the workforce employed to ensure the means of production of these reproducible new aesthetic imaginaries, innovation will never be on the cards. My argument, rather, is that innovation has begun colonising educational policies and discourses for the same reason that creative industries is more attractive than creativity: it is measurable, quantifiable, and—most importantly in contemporary education—assessable.

What then can be said about innovation as an assessable form of creativity in education? If "without creativity, it would be difficult indeed to distinguish humans from apes" (Csikszentmihalyi, 1996, p. 2), we need creativity as much as it needs us. Innovation, on the other hand, seems to me as finite in its expansion as capitalism surely must be. For Kimbell & Stables (2008), innovation and standardised assessments in education are almost mutually exclusive. Innovation requires creative approaches at the very least, and often a healthy dose of teamwork, both anathema to league tables and standardised tests. While Australia's incoming national curriculum includes innovation liberally throughout, here I am arguing that it is framed in such a way as to equate creativity with a necessary productivity inherent in innovation. If something is innovative, it is useful, and not all creativity is 'useful'. This pervasive definition (promulgated widely by Robinson and others) is neoliberalism at its best, and carries an inherent market value to the notion of usefulness. In their review of design pedagogy and its assessment, Kimbell and Stables identified this tension between "innovation and creativity [as] central to many of the design programmes" but asked "do students go with a risky exciting idea (and invite failure) or do they identify the rules of the game, play safe and guarantee an outcome?" (p. 165). Contemporary education across the globe, I argue, is moving steadily in the direction of the innovation end of this tension continuum.

Csikszentmihalyi (1996) suggests that creativity is a preliminary step on the road to innovation. Creativity, in this sense, does not have to have value or be useful. It can simply be an original thought or the ability to invent. Innovation, on the other hand requires that "a creative person . . . convince the field that he or she has made a valuable innovation" (1996, p. 41). This definition doesn't hold its market use-value as the measure of its value or its measure as innovation, however. For Csikszentmihalyi and others concerned with the affect and flow of creativity, systems of measure are more about the social role of creativity and the arts than industrial innovation. Why then does education seem to remain so confused? Is it impossible for education and its practices to hold both industrial and artistic/aesthetic values of creativity at the same time? Surely this is already true for some forms of science and mathematics education, including the distinction between 'pure maths' and 'pure science' versus applied or industrial competencies in these disciplines. This is why there are two 'streams' in most high schools, one for each area of study. It is understood too in teacher education that there remains a need for so-called 'pure research' as well as applied research that is more closely tied to procedural and social change. Why then can't education contain multiple approaches to creative arts that recognise the benefits and need for both industrial creativity and its more 'purely' artistically-minded sister? Norman (2004) makes this very point in arguing that "the emotional side of design may be more critical to a product's success than its practical elements" (p. 5).

Kay Stables (2004) draws on both Kimbell and Csikszentmihalyi in coupling creativity and innovation for the purposes of looking at assessment within education (in a British context). She rightly recognises that this conflation of creativity and innovation in education is most frequently found in design, a discipline in which the usefulness of decoupling the terms can also most clearly be seen. While Stables (and Kimbell) have written mostly about the 'gridlocked' design and technology curriculum, here I argue that the general curriculum—particularly in those nations under national standardised curricula—is universally gridlocked. Indeed, this is one primary reason why opponents continue to argue that there is no room for creative arts, only the more generalised 'creativity and innovation'. Assessment, or its impossibility some argue, is the other main 'evidence' most often suggested for the inappropriateness of creative arts in modern curricula.

Like Stables, I argue here that current approaches to curriculum development and implementation are "gridlocked in ritual, convention and constructed realities of what is and isn't possible" (2004, p. 161). Despite the seeming contradiction that universally creativity and innovation are now seen as somehow 'scientifically' measurable and core to any 21st-century program of teaching and learning, the creative arts are seen as unassessable and too 'soft' for direct inclusion in already overstuffed curricular programming. Stables calls this contradictory but insatiable search for magic creativity and innovation strategies the 'holy grail' of contemporary education research, and I agree. That she wrote these words nearly a decade ago in the United Kingdom, and that their resonance continues to echo around the world in increasing subject areas and educational contexts, itself should be cause for alarm.

CHAPTER 6

In addition, the debate she identifies in design and technology education, which is also now pervading all curriculum debates in Australia and elsewhere, is whether the focus should be on education as a tool of social development and contribution (i.e., educating the 'whole student' as a lifelong learner), or as a tool for developing the skills necessary for workplace success (although this continues to be problematic in its own way, confronting as we are rapidly transitioning work cultures which may look completely unfamiliar in a few short years).

Perhaps at the heart of the anxiety about what is not known for future education and workplace success is the notion of unknowability versus assessment. These contrary impulses have created the kind of bipolar standardised curricula that now pervade most western nations. On the one hand, Robinson, Florida and others concerned with creative futures continue to remind us that we have no idea what even the near future may look like or require from its actors if they are to successfully navigate new systems; on the other hand, our anxiety about competing in these unknowable futures has driven education and other sectors toward increasingly programmatic, schematised measures for assessing effectiveness and ditching products, processes and individuals who do not make the grade.

Stables and others continue to draw on Eisner who cautioned long ago against overly relying on traditional (quantitative) measures of effectiveness when dealing with creativity and imagination. What we know now that we perhaps did not quite believe when first introduced to us by Eisner is our great need for what imagination and creativity can bring us, and how crucial it now is in the short (and long) term: "imagination gives us the images of the possible that provide a platform for seeing the actual, and by seeing the actual freshly, we can do something about creating what lies beyond it" (Eisner, 2002, p 4). Stables draws on definitions of play and fantasy to underline the value of creativity and imagination in classrooms, and I don't disagree. However these are the kinds of arguments repeatedly made by primary or early childhood educators and education scholars, and the capacity for introducing or even advocating for these qualities and activities in high schools is being exponentially reduced. In fact, most advocates of both arts education and creativity as aligned with arts or aesthetics draw from or comment upon primary or early childhood contexts. Another distinction between this great body of literature and that of the emerging creative industries is the context: creative industries (as a field of enquiry) is set mainly within the tertiary sector and only occasionally draws down into its secondary feeder concerns and contexts. For the most part, these discourses represent separate operational sites, as well as ideologies.

But what of creativity and assessibility? It returns us again and again to innovation as the in-between representative, the way in which creativity discourse is increasingly "operating in the economic and political field" (Craft et al, 2001, p. 1). Assessment follows, with theorists in the UK suggesting that "greater emphasis should be put on formative assessment in schools, i.e., assessment that is intended to improve the day-to-day quality of teaching and learning" (Joubert, 2001,

p. 27). Further diluting the teaching of creativity, Joubert documents how the UK addressed the creativity gap by introducing "a professional development programme for secondary teachers on higher-order thinking skills, although not creativity *per se*" and how this response fell "short of a full commitment to the promotion of creativity across the whole of education" (p. 28). She identifies the need for the "teaching profession itself to promote creativity in schools [so that] hopefully the policy will eventually catch up with the practice" (p. 32). This kind of 'in spite of' approach requires that teachers "apply the same creative attributes that they are aiming to encourage and foster in their pupils: persistence, perseverance, resilience in the face of adversity and the belief that there is more than one possible way of doing things" (p. 32). Now, a decade later, the incoming Australian curriculum and persistent standardised curricula in both the UK and USA work against this multiplicity of ways of doing.

One suggestion for a changed assessment structure includes "question and answer routines, project work and regular and sometimes informal self, peer and tutor assessment activities" (Gale, 2001, p. 106). Unfortunately these variations from standards seem to be more possible or at least more in evidence in lower-performing schools, where principals and their teachers are already admitting through performance that the same curriculum may not be targeted for them. In his introduction to Craft's book, Ken Robinson reminds us once again that "education has more than economic purposes: it must enable people to adapt positively to rapid social change and to have lives with meaning and purpose" and he praises the arguments there that seek to prove how "educating for creativity is not confined to particular activities or people; that creativity flourishes under certain conditions and, in this sense, it can be taught" (Robinson, 2001, p. ix). What we still don't seem to know, or to be able to communicate about very effectively, is why the conditions that are so easily identifiable as optimal to creativity are still not being established and nurtured in schools, a knowledge gap this book has gone some way toward addressing.

CONCLUSION

There are notable differences between creative teaching, creative learning and innovation. Craft et al. (2001) long ago noted these in the UK context, as did Eisner and others in the US. However in Australia, where we are just on the incoming wave of a national curriculum, it seems that the debate about creative pedagogies, creative learning or arts-based educational content has been hijacked by an emergent creative industries discourse. Such a focus could have productive curricular and theoretical implications for secondary and primary education contexts, but to date these debates are almost completely separate.

In this chapter, I have argued that there may be less contradiction between educational standardisation and a discourse of creativity than is first apparent. As Ranciere suggests, aesthetics in inherently political in ways that innovation

CHAPTER 6

necessarily cannot be, due to its ties to the market. As such, a close examination of the creative turn can suggest not only a new political understanding of commodification and innovation, but a new aesthetic imaginary as well. Further, I have argued that this move toward a creativity discourse may represent a kind of colonisation of creativity, a commodification of creativity re-scripted as a conflation of creativity and innovation. I have reminded readers of an important distinction, however, in some ways in which innovation is distinct from creativity, including in its market-focus, its ever-economic contextualisation and use-value, and the ways in which, in market-driven educational contexts, an overriding imperative for the assessment of creative pedagogies and 'standards' of creative learning may be strangely compatible goals.

Returning to Appadurai (see Chapters One, Two, Seven and Eight for more) reminds us that aesthetics/industrial and innovation/creativity binaries—like global flows—are both disjunctive and uneven,

> are not wholly indeterminable or unpredictable, and that we can discern the asymmetrical shape of the world's 'power-geometry'. Globalization *is*—it exists for those who are in its pathways and may stand to gain or lose by it; globalization *is not*—it does not count for those who have fallen out of its circuit and to whom little or nothing flows" (in Glowacka & Boos, 2002, p. 207).

So, too, with our considerations or consternations about aesthetics and innovation. In order to argue for the value of one's innovation, the arguer must be in conversation with the field. Increasingly, those who are setting the creativity conversation are aligned with notions of innovation and market value. That is why, in this chapter, I have tried to untangle some distinct threads in the weave of creativity discourses, especially as its framing in (secondary) schools as creativity and innovation serves less the needs of aesthetics and more the needs of the workplace.

Both Benjamin and Anderson help us understand the contemporary aesthetic-educational system as an example of the nation-state's imagined community, yet aesthetics in the service of commodity culture remains a very different beast to the aesthetics of art and design. Appadurai insists that we "must avoid 'the kind of illusion of order that we . . . impose on a world that is so transparently volatile" (in Glowacka & Boos, 2002, p. 206) and yet this illusion of order is exactly what standardised assessment in rhizomatic times seems to be. Perhaps educators are grasping at straws; perhaps we harken back to simpler times with our desperate grasp of creativity discourses but, either way, the fragmentation is clear and the cracks are beginning to show. Surely the 'disjunctive global flows' of which Appadurai speaks are pushing us toward developing new theories of cultural and creative generation that work better than the ones from which we are emerging. In the next chapter, the case study of *Teaching Diversities* allows us to examine some ways in which a re-application of Benjamin's interrogation of works of art in the age of mechanical reproduction might point one way forward.

REFERENCES

Adorno, T. W. (1997). *Aesthetic theory.* London/New York, UK/NY: Bloomsbury Academic.
Arnon, B. (2008). *How the Obama "Hope" poster reached a tipping point and became a cultural phenomenon: An interview with the artist Shepard Fairey.* Retrieved from October 13, 2008, from Huff Post Politics: http://www.huffingtonpost.com/ben-arnon/how-the-obama-hope-poster_b_133874.html
Caves, R. E. (2000). *Creative industries: Contracts between art and commerce.* Boston, MA: Harvard University Press.
Craft, A., Jeffrey, B., & Leibling, M. (Eds). (2001). *Creativity in education.* London/New York, UK/NY: Continuum.
Csikszentmihalyi, M. (1996). *Creativity: Flow and the psychology of discovery and invention.* New York, NY: Harper Collins.
Eisner, E. (2002). *The arts and the creation of mind.* New Haven/London: Yale University Press.
Gale, K. (2001). Teacher education within post-compulsory education and training: a call for a creative approach. In A. Craft, B. Jeffrey, & M. Leibling (Eds.), *Creativity in education* (pp. 103–115). London/New York, UK/NY: Continuum.
Glowacka, D., & Boos, S. (2002). *Between ethics and aesthetics: Crossing the boundaries.* Albany, NY: State University of New York Press.
Joubert, M. M. (2001). The art of creative teaching: NACCCE and beyond. In A. Craft, B. Jeffrey & M. Leibling (Eds), *Creativity in education* (pp. 17–34). London/New York, UK/NY: Continuum.
Kimbell, R., & Stables, K. (2008). *Researching design learning: Issues and findings from two decades of research and development.* Rotterdam: Springer.
Norman, D. A. (2004). *Emotional design.* New York, NY: Perseus Books.
Papastergiadis, N. (2012). Aesthetic cosmopolitanism. In G. Delanty (Ed.), *Routledge handbook of cosmopolitanism studies* (pp. 220–232). Abingdon/NY: Routledge.
Rancière, J. (2009). *The aesthetic unconscious.* Cambridge/Malden: Polity Press.
Rancière, J. (2006). *The politics of aesthetics.* London /New York, UK/NY: Continuum.
Raunig, G. (2013). *Factories of knowledge, industries of creativity.* MIT Press.
Raunig, G. (2002). A war machine against the empire: On the precarious nomadism of the publix theatre caravan. Retrieved from http://eipcp.net/transversal/0902/raunig/en
Redfield, M. (2003). *The politics of aesthetics: Nationalism, gender, romanticism.* Stanford: Stanford University Press.
Salehi, S. (2008). *Teaching contingencies: Deleuze, creativity discourses, and art.* Unpublished doctoral thesis, Ontario, Canada: Queen's University. Retrieved from http://qspace.library.queensu.ca/handle/1974/1209
Stoneman, P. (2010). *Soft innovation: Economics, product aesthetics, and the creative industries.* Oxford/New York, NY: Oxford University Press.
Stables, K. (2004). The elusive keys of imagination and play: Unlocking creativity and innovation in design and technology education. *The Journal of Design and Technology Education, 9*(3), 161–171.
Zizek, S. (2006). Afterword: The lesson of rancière. In *The politics of aesthetics* (pp. 67–79). London / New York, UK/NY: Continuum.

CHAPTER 7

ANIMATING CULTURE OR

Where has all the Magic Gone?

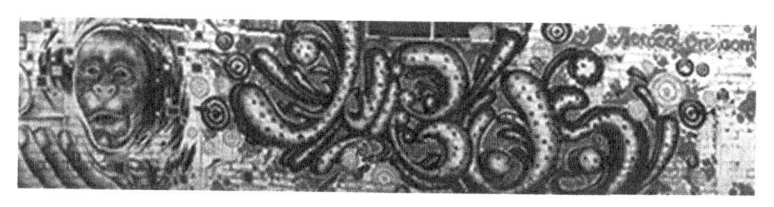

Figure 12. *Melbourne graffiti, #5 (2013).*

... the work of art in prehistoric times when, by the absolute emphasis on its cult value, it was, first and foremost, an instrument of magic. Only later did it come to be recognized as a work of art. (Benjamin, 1973, p. 219).

The public is an examiner, but an absent-minded one. (Benjamin, 1973, p. 234)

INTRODUCTION

This chapter draws heavily on Walter Benjamin's and Marshall McLuhan's notions about the constitutive cultural function of technological innovation in art. To set up this discussion, I turn briefly to Dillard and Okpalaoka (2011) and Rooney (2005) to problematise the difficulties and dangers of naming 'difference' in an age of increasing sameness and visuality. Together, they form a useful matrix for interpreting three diverse animation projects that each address the intersection of cultural, sexual and gender diversities for the young people who made them. These projects are: the *Teaching Diversities* community consultation and its animation outcome *CALDPlay*; a series of short animations in different styles called *Love Stories*; and one collaborative ten-minute composite animation, *In My Shoes*; an outcome of the *Animate Change* queer multicultural youth program run by a Melbourne community organisation. Both Benjamin and McLuhan offer, I argue, some strategies for helping us think about the ways in which creative projects using digital technology do or do not answer a promise to democratise creativity, modes of creative expression and the opportunities for dissemination of those works, particularly for marginalised community members.

In 1936 as Benjamin wrote *The Work of Art in the Age of Mechanical Reproduction*, he argued that the ritual value of art was waning and being replaced by exhibition

CHAPTER 7

value (and production impetus) which was growing. In this chapter I argue that these two values have in fact merged, creating a 21st-century moment in which the exhibition value *is* the cult value, and in which this 'cult of exhibition' has become the economic ritual driving the production of so many works of art.

In this chapter I use my historical moment in the midst of a creative turn and the 'prognostic value' of Benjamin's essay to better understand some implications of digital culture and social media for creativity and aesthetics. But one cannot consider Benjamin's attention to the mechanically reproductive turn of the twentieth century without keeping one eye on McLuhan's fascination with the digital turn. Like Benjamin, McLuhan was concerned with the ways in which new forms of creating represented a significant shift in the way a society saw itself—in McLuhan's case, through digital media and the internet. In this chapter, I combine Benjamin with McLuhan's focus on the ways in which this phenomenon can be seen most clearly in the online world and its tools, including animation, facebook, Photoshop, mobile phones and video-sharing platforms such as YouTube and Vimeo. Together, they can help signpost the current creative turn as one stretch of a long and familiar road.

Contextualised against the work of cyberculture theorists such as Leung (2005) and Berry, Martin & Yue (2003), this chapter frames creative digital technology use as not merely a tool but a contested, emerging, negotiated space in which young people shape cultural, aesthetic and educational transits of being and becoming, radically altering arts-based digital learning as 21st-century global pedagogies. Such global pedagogies are both digitally and culturally diverse.

Queer scholars and activists have cautioned that in working with "gay, lesbian and bisexual students from culturally diverse backgrounds, multicultural and inclusive education policies and programmes need to develop a greater awareness of socioculturally constructed boundaries and borderlines" (Pallotta-Chiarolli, 1999, p. 289), a goal that seems to still have a long way to go. The inability of educators to incorporate multiple diversities, such as sexual, gender and cultural identities, into school communities and policies is still omnipresent. The *Teaching Diversities* community consultation and its accompanying animation project *CALDPlay* was conducted in 2011, in response to this ongoing gap. Others have written about these difficult intersections for students and youth in Australian, New Zealand and Pacific contexts (see, for example, Smith, 2006; Riggs, 2006; Vassilacopoulos & Nicolacopoulos, 2004; Quinlivan & Town, 1999) and elsewhere, but the central concerns are largely the same: in/visibility, naming/terminology, identities/fluidities. Some might find it surprising that Russell & Truong documented the "first available national-level data on US adolescents" on school experiences of "sexual minority racial/ethnic minority youth" (p. 114) as recently as 2009. They too note concerns about language and the ways in which it falls short, and the ways in which it must remain context-specific (for them, e.g., they use 'sexual minority' to correlate with cultural and ethnic minority students).

This chapter will firstly establish Benjamin's articulation of an artistic 20th-century 'turn' particular to photography and film. I will draw from McLuhan's writings thirty years later in order to position Benjamin's turn as one of many along a continuum of relations between creativity/artworks and cultural transits throughout history. After establishing some ways of thinking about our current creative adaptations, I will turn to the case study of *Teaching Diversities/CALDPlay* as an example of what both McLuhan and Benjamin urge us to embrace and to let go of through mechanised artworks. Lastly, after a consideration of whether arts products and processes have ever truly been (or can be) outside of culture, which includes industrial and economic flows, I urge readers to consider the relationship between aesthetics, difference and commodification—and how that might be apparent in today's increasingly homogenised global creative culture.

Queer Works of Art in a New Age

As Marx critiqued capitalist modes of production, Benjamin critiqued the limits of mechanical modes of *re*production while photography and film were still in their infancy. Just 30 years later, McLuhan sought to define the advent of digital technology by coining the now ubiquitous "the medium is the message" (1964), and expertly walked the line between popular and theoretical in order to assist a changing society to understand itself and the transition.

Benjamin reminds us that "the transformation of the superstructure... takes place far more slowly than that of the substructure" (1973, p. 212) and I suggest that this is what is happening now in digital re/production. We are, 14 years after the turn of the century, in the midst of this creative but also industrial turn. I have described in earlier chapters how the creative and the industrial are currently intersecting, and how this new coupling may be moving us away from previous concepts and practices of art, art education and, to some extent, aesthetics. Yet for further insights into the nature of this 'turn', and the effect it is having more broadly in the culture, we turn to Benjamin more closely.

Benjamin borrowed from Marx's material aesthetics in accusing creativity and genius of being "outmoded concepts" (p. 212); nevertheless, he tells us, they are still useful for what he calls a 'politics of art'. Benjamin's focus on reproduction is today superseded by that of digital creative production itself, and the accompanying politics of digital art are changing too (Capistrano, 2013). It is beyond the scope of this chapter to undertake an in-depth investigation into the creative or even aesthetic implications of this new mode of production, but we can agree that the productive ability of digital arts—especially online digital arts—is its most innovative if not transformative difference.

Like Chambers & O'Rourke (2009) do by 'mashing up' Rancière and queer theory, here I'm staging a kind of invented collision between queer youth and digital creativity, hoping—as they do—that this encounter will "add up to much more than exercises in comparison/contrast or trumping efforts... seek[ing] to transform both fields of thought" (p. 1). Benjamin's Marxist analysis can illuminate aspects of the human and creative capital implicated in the development of digital technology.

CHAPTER 7

As Rancière helps us think about subjects as subversive, subjective and positioned (2009, p. 1), Benjamin too focuses on the 'in-between' potential of technology. In this chapter I argue that animation and online worlds might offer new positionalities, new relationalities, and even new subjectivities for young queers who still find non-commodified creativity a radical act.

Two years before Benjamin published his famous essay, Dewey published *Art as Experience* (1934) in which he explored more deeply than in any of his later works the connection between aesthetics and the mystical. While I won't be so simplistic as to suggest that he was foreshadowing the confusion over definitions of creativity, art and innovation that are the central concern of this book, he did understand that the modern era would be characterised by a separation, alienation or a decoupling of the connection between art and spirituality that had existed for so long before. The popular appeal of Dewey's search for a connection between art, spirituality and education is one primary reason why his work is still read today—by educationalists if not philosophers. Yet the coexistence in time and space of Dewey and Benjamin between the wars may have something to tell us about the shared aspects of their visions.

Benjamin and Dewey both spend considerable time linking authenticity in a work of art with its situatedness "in time and space, its unique existence at the place where it happens to be" (Benjamin, 1973, p. 214). What he calls 'aura' is the invisible connection between the product and its specific context. In arts, creativity and poststructuralist concerns have shifted toward less essentialising aspects of capital, from aura and authenticity to embodiment and performativity. Benjamin claims that "that which withers in the age of mechanical reproduction is the aura of the work of art" (p. 215). He calls film's "destructive, cathartic aspect" the "liquidation of the traditional value of the cultural heritage" (p. 215). Yet in this book I have argued that it has rather been liquidated by Appadurai's 21st-century 'tournaments of value' and its embodiment as emerging creative industries.

The twenty-first century has yet to catch up with this latest turn, but neither Benjamin nor McLuhan wasted time on the kinds of public 'what is real art?' debates that currently plague some creativity discourses and sometimes arts education: "Earlier much futile thought had been devoted to the question of whether photography is an art . . . the primary question—whether the very invention of photography had not transformed the entire nature of art—was not raised" (Benjamin, 1973, p. 221). From both Benjamin and McLuhan we are encouraged to see further links here, beyond false binaries like totemic versus economic value. Although McLuhan later articulated it more clearly, Benjamin too understood that "the manner in which human sense perception is organised" is related to "the medium in which it is accomplished", a relationship "determined not only by nature but by historical circumstances as well" (p. 216). Aesthetics (and its relationship to Benjaminian 'aura') are no longer of significant interest to creativity educators, funders, or to policymakers singularly driven by capital. While there is a considerable body of work on aesthetics, it is increasingly from the disciplines of philosophy and fine art, exemplified by the split between creative industries and aesthetics discourses. Benjamin may have been ahead of his time in talking in the 1930s about the "decay of the aura" (p. 216) but what of the aura today?

Cult Value Versus Exhibition Value: Everyone's 15 Minutes of Fame?

> Every day the urge grows stronger to get hold of an object at very close range by way of its likeness, its reproduction (Benjamin, 1973, p. 217).

The last aesthetic turn occurred nearly 100 years ago, and was recognised by Benjamin. The current creative turn marks a kind of liberation from embodiment as Benjamin's marked liberation from aura. He recognised that the rise of photography, which corresponded "simultaneously with the rise of socialism", was un-coincidental and that, in such a climate, "art sensed the approaching crisis which has become evident a century later" (p. 218). Despite the power of hindsight which has proven Benjamin's observations to be laser-accurate, his turn (like ours) has precipitated inconsequential arguments about 'pure art' versus the 'social function of art' (p. 218). Benjamin and McLuhan have both reminded us that, "with the different methods of technical reproduction of a work of art, its fitness for exhibition increased to such an extent that the quantitative shift between its two poles turned into a qualitative transformation of its nature" (Benjamin, 1973, p. 219). Similarly, here I want to avoid any arguments about pure art versus creative industries, as these are always empty and history proves them not the point of interest: they are an inevitability but nothing more. Rather, here I am interrogating the ways in which the digital impact on aesthetics and creativity has transcended or reproduced previous inequities in making and accessing art, which I have also explored elsewhere (Harris & O'Mara, 2013).

Benjamin claims that of the two values of works of art (cult and exhibition value), mechanical reproduction hastened a waning of the cult value, leaving nothing more than its exhibition value. An argument can be made that this pattern has now, nearly 80 years on, only accelerated to the point where little (neither creative industries nor commercial art) is made with consideration for its ritual value, with the possible exception of fringe arts or arts education. However, this is not the case. Rather, what now predominates is a merging of the two values, in that the ritual (or cult value) *is* its exhibition value. That is all it has, and exhibition has itself become the cult or the ritual. "Uniqueness and permanence are as closely linked in the latter as are transitoriness and reproducibility in the former" (p. 217), Benjamin tells us, and contemporary art—especially digital art—provides limitless examples. He goes further, claiming that the

> ritualized basis, however remote, is still recognizable as secularized ritual even in the most profane forms of the cult of beauty. The secular cult of beauty, developed during the Renaissance and prevailing for three centuries, clearly showed that ritualistic basis in its decline and the first deep crisis which befell it (pp. 217-218).

CHAPTER 7

If Benjamin's era marked the beginning of reproducible art and the decline of a Renaissance cult of beauty, our era cannot be so easily classified. Countless examples in both online art (think laser arts, digital stories, online imagebanks) and commodified 'art' (think all Apple products) scream the power of aesthetics in contemporary culture. The 21st-century turn does not mark a decline in aesthetics but rather a shift in aesthetics based on its 'transitoriness'. What Benjamin saw as secular/religious cults defined by aesthetics or ritual values has been replaced by other cultural practices, in ways that parallel organised aesthetics. In other words, it's not that aesthetics is not there, but rather that it is becoming rapidly undefinable, redefinable, or infinitely definable. Unlike religion and its own accelerating turn toward conservatism, both creativity and aesthetics are characterised by speed, reproducibility and sameness, rather than aesthetic or affective impact.

Benjamin notes his 'turn' in both content *and* form (like McLuhan) as a difficult one, saying "cult value does not give way without resistance" (p. 219) and today we see the same resistance between creative industries and creative art—or the shift from manual or even mechanical arts to digital ones. Creative industries is overwhelmingly dominated by digital (or digitally reproducible) arts, but beyond their digital form it is characterised by works and 'work' (labour) which can be characterised as profitable and transferable, exportable—what I define in Chapter Eight as a shift from human capital to creative capital. Digital media serve the ever-expansive (virtual) marketplace, so in some sense this turn may also be characterised as a shift from the affective or embodied to what Deleuze and others have identified as the possibility of the disembodied 'inauthentic' simulacra (Deleuze, 1968).

Contemporary culture—like Benjamin's in his day—benefits and suffers from the "spell of the personality, the phony spell of a commodity" (p. 224). Under the 'new creativity' discourse, in the absence of a working definition of creativity, of innovation, or of art versus entertainment, everything becomes creative, everyone can be creative. This suits the market just fine. If it is undefinable, it is marketable: it means it can be commodified in limitless ways to suit diverse consumers. The flip side of the democratisation of creativity via online media and rapid technological advances (even more rapid than Benjamin's mechanical reproduction) is that everyone believes they are creative, everyone is an artist, and everyone wants their 15 minutes of fame—to which they have access at home and online. As Benjamin noted of the close of the 19th century: "with the increasing extension of the press, which kept placing new political, religious, scientific, professional, and local organs before the readers, an increasing number of readers became writers" (p. 225) and the reader-writer ratio changed forever. Or perhaps the self-image of the writer changed: everyone became an expert. What began with the democratisation of newspapers in the 'letters to the editor' section has now, through blogs, Twitter and image-based media like Instagram, become complete as the fulfilment of everyone's fantasy that they are instantaneously a writer or a journalist. Or, as Benjamin tells us below, that they are because they think they are, and the web provides authenticity (or at least legitimacy) in the reader-as-writer transformation.

"Thus," Benjamin tells us,

> the distinction between author and public is about to lose its basic character . . . At any moment the reader is ready to turn into a writer. As expert, which he had to become willy-nilly in an extremely specialized work process, even if only in some minor respect, the reader gains access to authorship (p. 225).

Our efforts to even distinguish between reality and illusion have ceased to some degree, and arguments like Benjamin's, that "under these circumstances the film industry is trying hard to spur the interest of the masses through illusion-promoting spectacles and dubious speculations" (p. 226), are useless: today the forms of digital representation are everywhere and everything; more specifically, they are every*one*.

Yet a filmmaking colleague recently argued to me that not everyone is creative, and that the firm distinction between 'art and creativity is that art disturbs', and 'everything else is mere entertainment.' Benjamin agreed, at least in his discussion of Dadaism, by noting how "one requirement was foremost: to outrage the public" (p. 231). I disagree. By this reasoning, the moment at which a Banksy stencil moves from the street into the gallery it ceases being art; a proposition with which my friend agreed. Or the moment that a critical mass began to love (consume) Jackson Pollock paintings they suddenly and mysteriously morphed from being art to entertainment? Yes, he confirmed. 'It's all a continuum,' he claimed. 'Then everything is on the creativity or art continuum?' I asked. 'And the genesis of a new release of the iPhone is the same as an experimental theatre piece in Williamsburg Brooklyn?' Alas, art is not so easy to define perhaps, but does it matter? Like Benjamin, let's wonder about the useful questions and the not-so-useful. Yet even Benjamin recognised that "the greater the decrease in the social significance of an art form, the sharper the distinction between criticism and enjoyment by the public. The conventional is uncritically enjoyed, and the truly new is criticized with aversion" (p. 227). So perhaps my friend is right, and it has always been so. Maybe, unlike the proliferation and evolution of digital media, art never changes.

The Commodification of Difference

But before I turn to the case study of *CALDPlay*, let's return to the issue of aesthetics and its relationship to diversity in social media and the arts. Rooney (2005) and others have noted how 'difference' can be commodified in ways that tie it to aesthetics. Is it possible—contrary to Benjamin's point that mechanical reproduction breeds sameness— that digital reproduction can in fact commodify difference? Rooney points to art *as* difference as a confusing mixed message between the media industry and increasing nationalism and xenophobia. If, as she reflects with irony, "the ubiquitous commodification of differences coexists with the continuing alignment, in the USA and elsewhere, of difference with threat, specifically disloyalty, even with treason and terror" (p. 407), how can artists argue safely for activist art, or even art that doesn't represent (or indeed advance) a hegemonic mainstream?

133

CHAPTER 7

It's hard to avoid commodification, even the grassroots kind online. I remember standing at the front window of New York's iconic lefty St Mark's Bookstore, staring at a slew of slick Routledge publications on the Occupy movement by early 2012, certainly a commodification of sorts. One recent example at this writing is the overthrow of Egypt's president Mohamed Morsi advertised online as "Watch it here live-streamed!" while dozens died in the protests that brought him down. Truly, the convergence of Benjamin's cult and exhibition value is upon us. Yet Rooney stresses that these choices we supposedly celebrate are marketised choices, aimed at consumerism dressed as freedom. They are social inclusion that can be embraced "only insofar as it is not *seen* to impose any change or to impose any change on *you*" (p. 408).

Cultural 'acceptance' of sexual and cultural diversities (in families, communities or nations) sometimes works in the same way. Many presume that western families and values are more accepting of sexual and gender variance but research shows that religion—more than nationality or culture—has the biggest impact on families' responses to queers 'coming out' (Harris, 2011; Pallotta-Chiarolli, 1999). Difference is accommodated as long as there is no discomfort, and yet, as queers have long asserted, accommodation or tolerance is not acceptance, valuing or integration. This, essentially, is the argument being asserted by the 'anti-gay marriage' critics—not that it shouldn't become legal, but that it will not ensure the kinds of equality that its proponents imagine it will—and the resources it consumes in its pursuit could perhaps be more usefully applied elsewhere.

Criticality is a key for both transcultural collaboration and for understanding the potential of digital technology for addressing difference. Despite the foregrounding of cultural diversity in the participant group and facilitators of the project, the participants of *Teaching Diversities* felt differently about whether their identities, values and creative potential were represented in either the process or the product of a small animation project like this one. While some recognised the community-building value of working together on a shared project around an intersectional identity space that they all (maybe) shared, others felt they were left out of the discussion by more dominant members of the group. In two out of the three animation projects (none of whom had animators who identified as LGBTI or Q), participants felt it was significant that the animators didn't understand their queerness, yet the pace of the projects propelled them on. Like Rooney's call to critically engage both 'difference' and 'differences' through commodity culture and representations, these community-based multicultural queer youth animation projects demonstrated the difficulty of remaining inclusive across multiple communities, especially when creating digital artworks on short timelines.

Benjamin claims that in film, the "critical and the receptive attitudes of the public coincide" because "individual reactions are predetermined by the mass audience response they are about to produce" (p. 228); certainly one of the key considerations of the *CALDPlay* animation project. While McLuhan is known most widely for his notion that the 'medium is the message', Benjamin took it one step further by suggesting that the medium not only changes the content but also the reception, which is the third inextricable axis of the tripartite relationship between maker-made-audience.

If Benjamin links criticality to the ways in which the ever-accelerating consumption of artworks renders us increasingly uncritical, McLuhan—later in this chapter—stresses that these patterns of consumption can function as a cultural mirror. For *CALDPlay* and other youth animation projects, this chapter interrogates the notion that digital technology can both provide opportunities for creative transcultural collaboration and dissemination, and also replicate patterns of exclusion—certainly acting as a cultural mirror in both welcome and challenging ways. First let's turn to the case study itself: the community consultation *Teaching Diversities* and its animation outcome, the *CALDPlay* video.

WHAT'S IN A NAME? A CASE STUDY

'Lani', Sri Lankan queer female, 26: *My Sri Lankan family and community . . . can invite my partner to family functions, they're ok with that as long as they never call them my partner. It's the friend! And they are fine with me being gay as long as I never talk about it and never try and use it as an identity . . . . I came out to my dad when I was fifteen and he was like 'Yeah, I know.' I got up all this courage to tell him, but he didn't even put the paper down, like 'yeah, duh, very gay' . . . . I think with my cultural community even if they know that I'm gay, I feel like I'm still not being really truthful. I don't think I'm gay in the way they think I'm gay.*

The QPOCalypse

The *Teaching Diversities* community consultation and animation project entitled *CALDPlay* struggled at its core with this tension of naming and in/visibility. Throughout 2011, the project team reached out to culturally and linguistically diverse communities in order to address what appeared to be some homophobia in cultural communities, and also pervasive racism in LGBTIQ communities. The intersection of cultural, religious, gender and sexual diversities seemed to present a recurring tension and this research project sought to address this through a community-based approach which included creative collaboration. Yet it was plagued from the beginning by these very intersections and the problem of finding language that was sufficient to address them.

Dillard and Okpalaoka (2011) trouble notions of names, naming and clear categories in diasporic peoples worldwide, and the ways in which dichotomised categories can reduce rather than expand consciousness and consciousness-raising movements. For them, when speaking of Black feminism, "these arguments over naming Black feminism are not simply about the act of naming: they are also about defining and constructing the boundaries and possibilities for relationships

CHAPTER 7

across Black feminisms, across racial, ethnic, and national differences, as well as advocating for fundamental *human* rights" (p. 154).

Others have written about the links between digital technology—particularly the internet—and the emergence and visibility of queer communities and identities in previously 'unplugged' or remote places (Leung, 2006; Berry, Martin & Yue, 2003), as well as the co-location around these links of freedom/constraint and visibility/fetishisation. I have written previously (2013) about the difficulty too of names, naming and identities at the intersections of culture, identity and the arts. This case study—known alternately as *Teaching Diversities* and then *CALDPlay* (Harris, 2011)—exemplifies some of the ways in which Appadurai and McLuhan's understandings of new scapes in the online world can present new sites of contestation, even within the process of collaborative creative (digital) arts.

For some of the 34 participants in the *Teaching Diversities* project, the crucial difference between their own ways of seeing, doing and being versus 'western', 'white' or 'Anglo' ways of being is echoed by Dillard and Okpalaoka's assertion that "in contrast to the Western tendency to dichotomize the material and the spiritual, male and female . . . the African spiritual concept of communal well-being is more highly valued than the individualism that marks Western feminist thought" (p. 154). But it is important to remember that 'culturally diverse' does not always equate to identities of colour, any more than queer always equates to gay, lesbian or otherwise non-heterosexual. Most know this, but language remains cumbersome and contestable—like varying definitions of creativity, among other things—and it's this unwieldiness that invites reductions and subsumptions.

But of course it can also be other things, like covert or overt racism, sexism or westernism. Dillard and Okpalaoka (2011) remind us that "hooks (1994) welcomed these contestations in naming, perspectives, positions, and language, seeing these confrontations as less about naming and more about how these 'differences [mean] that we must change ideas about how we learn'" (p. 113). Much of the *Teaching Diversities* community feedback also stressed the need to learn differently: in cultural, religious and sexual communities as well as the 'wider' dominant culture at large. The project struggled both internally and inter-communally with hooks' admonishment: "rather than fearing conflict [in naming], we have to find ways to use it as a catalyst for new thinking, for growth" (cited in Dillard and Okpalaoka, 2011, p. 154).

Newer publications feature discussions of QPOCs—Queer People of Colour—an acronym favoured by several (though not all) of the participants of the *CALDPlay* animation project and those interviewed in the *Teaching Diversities* consultation. While QPOC as an identity was asserted in our research team as an age-, class- and politically-aligned label (young, working class, left-leaning politic), there were several younger 'culturally diverse' working class people who did not identify with it. For example, our youngest participant in the animation project (15-years old) was a Greek-Australian female who did not identify with the label, and was upset by the unremarked transition from the term 'CALD' or 'culturally diverse' used in the community consultation to the QPOC term used by the smaller group who did the animation project. Though identifying as 'non-Anglo', she did identify as European and working class and rejected a conflation with 'QPOC'. Others, including the Ethiopian recent arrival who had flown from a neighbouring city to participate, did not identify as QPOC. Once the group explained to him what it meant, he felt it was a 'political' term that represented a more radical orientation than his. He also questioned the sense of a project which espoused the values of 'teaching diversities' if the pervasive feeling amongst the QPOC group was one of oppression and anger toward whites, and whether they would be in a position to teach about their own culture, or rather more comfortably to protect it. Some also expressed a resistance to working with white collaborators on a project of this kind, preferring instead the safety or comfort of cultural/racial groups, whilst others felt that intercultural collaboration would have to be involved for true education and bridging across the gap.

Others have written about these issues before. Some queer people of colour are "really an invisible group in our community at large" (Mawji, 2004, p. 100), and "many people often think to themselves that people of color couldn't possibly have diverse sexual orientations because they're already Black or South Asian or East Asian" (p. 100). A consistent area of focus is the need for QPOC visibility, including positive visibility, in which "we as queer people of color, do take up space and we do act as role models" (p. 100). Russell & Truong (2009) clarify that any chosen terminology must come from the participant group—as did *Teaching Diversities'*— but not how to resolve whether, when and how these self-identifiers conflict within a participant group. They acknowledge that "we do argue that their reported feelings place them in the *sexual minority* among their peers" (p. 114), highlighting the tensions between a range of identifiers, identities and labels within queer cultural groups.

Most participants rejected a 'hierarchy of oppressions' and its concomitant sense of competition between, rather than intersectionality of, identities. 'Lani', for example, highlights in her story the slippage between brownness and sexuality, in fluctuating ways:

> *I think for a long time, I definitely chose my queerness over my non-whiteness. It's only quite recently that I've tried to combine the two and introduce my queer life to my cultural community. I think a lot of the time I do choose one over the other. I wouldn't say I would choose to negate one, but I definitely squash one down a bit more.* (Harris, 2011, p. 32)

As in the previous chapter (Chapter Six) where I drew on Rancière for ways of considering aesthetics and intersubjectivity, Chambers & O'Rourke (2009) have used Rancière to remind readers of the un-identified, un-commodified and un-articulated possibilities still inherent in being queer in an increasingly normative gay politic— one which often elides cultural and religious diversities. In this sense, Rancière is a useful interlocutor for this view of the *Teaching Diversities* project, in that his

CHAPTER 7

work—if not explicitly or comfortably queer—disrupts the fantasy that speech or indeed performativity can neatly encompass any community identity, be it creative, sexualised or gendered. Like Benjamin and McLuhan, Rancière's strategies can help readers consider the ways in which creative projects like this one do or do not fulfil an early promise to democratise creativity, modes of creative expression and the opportunities for dissemination of those works—particularly for marginalised youth, the focus of this chapter.

CASE STUDY OVERVIEW

http://www.creativeresearchhub.com/#!cald-play/cwkh

'Laura', Papua New Guinean, Torres Strait Islander, Scottish genderqueer, 21: *My family has been so intensely Christianised that they just don't believe gay people exist and that you are Satan or something if you are gay . . . . There is no gay movement in Papua New Guinea . . . I feel like we're living in such an internet and video age now, FaceBook and all that social networking is where it's happening . . . .and I really feel for young queer people of colour particularly in remote communities, who don't have access to stuff like we do* (Harris 2011, p. 20).

Is it Possible to 'Teach' Diversities?

The community consultation *Teaching Diversities* was conducted throughout 2011 and involved 34 respondents from non-Anglo backgrounds in interviews and focus groups discussing what it was like to be from a minority cultural, racial or ethnic background and be LGBTI or Q. This project has been documented in detail elsewhere (Harris, 2011; Harris, 2013), but for the purposes of this case study I will draw primarily from the final report (Harris, 2011). At the end of that year, it culminated in a month-long animation project which included seven participants, a multimedia social enterprise in urban Melbourne, Australia, and a four-person research team from a range of cultural, racial, gender and sexual backgrounds. For the purposes of critically analysing this case study, I will also draw on a subsequent animation project that built upon the *Teaching Diversities* study, facilitated by the same sponsoring organisation, called *Animate Change/ In My Shoes* (CMY, 2013; Petrie, 2013). Finally, I will also draw upon a longer animation project, *Love Stories*, conducted throughout 2011-2012 by a local well-established queer youth performance group called YGLAM (2012) also in Melbourne, Australia.

Both *Love Stories* and *In My Shoes* dealt with issues of cultural diversity and coming out, although in *Love Stories* it remained secondary to the issue of loving 'differently' for same-sex attracted youth. A defining difference of *Love Stories* is the long-term collaboration between the ongoing youth performance group and the animator who was brought in as a consultant to help the young people realise their goal for 2012. This performance group has done community-based live performance for over ten years, but desired for the first time to use animation as a tool to tell their stories in a way that was easier to disseminate and might reach larger audience—a limitation of live performance that is of constant consideration in all three case studies discussed here. With this primary goal of wide dissemination, the series of short animations were also pitched more widely in their telling and in a way that could be viewed comfortably in primary school settings. Containing 'soft' components such as cute music, mostly non-identifying stop-motion and drawn animations, and story lines that address 'love' rather than 'sex', they can be read in some ways as a sign of both the neo-conservative queer times in which they were made and the production desire for them to reach as broad an audience as possible. The lengthy collaboration, however, is also immediately clear in the careful and highly-finished products. The group identified that this was primarily a result of the safe and well-established relationship between the group's ongoing facilitator and members, into which only the animator and composer were newly introduced. Yet there were other artistic tensions that recurred in all three projects.

One recurrent issue in all three of these projects was the ways in which creative and organisational teams are comprised. A research assistant in *Teaching Diversities* succinctly recommended that "any intercultural queer arts projects should demand . . . [that] the animators working on the project are educated, aware, invested and responsible about issues to do with racism, cultural diversity and homophobia . . . [and that] preferably, they are queer people of colour themselves" (p. 29). Yet for these projects, the filmmakers who were eventually employed were primarily seen as appropriate due to their culturally diversity rather than sexuality (i.e., when both sexual and cultural diversities were not available, the team hired culturally diverse). In two of the projects, the (non-queer) filmmakers lost the confidence of the participants by expressing ignorance of aspects of LGBTIQ identity. In both cases, they asked the participants to clarify the meaning of various elements of queer terminology. Rather than creating a context of openness or trust in the youth participants, in which they felt empowered to 'educate' the older artist-experts, some of the young people in each project expressed dismay or concern that the project had not been able to source queer artists or that in the case of non-queer artists the artists themselves had not 'done the homework' to self-educate about this queer cultural group. These case studies are useful for reconsidering the opening gambit of this chapter—that the opportunities made possible through online technology, namely, access to unlimited audiences, the means of production, and non-capital-based dissemination—may or may not disrupt established social and cultural capital flows. If the internet and digital technology presents possibilities for democratic artmaking and art-disseminating, what emerged in various ways in all three case studies were the pervasive human limitations of the participants, facilitators and funders.

CHAPTER 7

Figure 13. Film still: CALDplay video (2011).

For the four-person research team that conducted *Teaching Diversities*, we noted the challenges of our own diversities which sometimes seem to enrich, and sometimes to interrupt, the good work that was happening. Spanning three decades, four cultural backgrounds, two genders and three sexual identities, our complications mirrored those of the study and our participant body. The final report enumerated six main emergent themes, and seven principle recommendations. I highlight them below in brief:

Themes

1. *Our own roles:* the impact of our own roles as research team on the full breadth of the study and project.
2. *Lack of participation, but a lot to say:* the difficulty of finding people of colour for both the research team and the participant groups led to use of underground, personal and snowball sampling, which produced a less broad sample than was hoped.
3. *Hyper-visibility:* "a frequently recurring theme was this tension or double-bind of hyper-visibility/invisibility" (Harris, 2011, p. 27). The research assistants noted the ways in which visibility often led to objectification, fetishisation and stereotyping rather than inclusion.
4. *Self-identifying, identity and diversity:* "considerations of labels, language and identity have productively and problematically informed this community consultation from the beginning" (p. 27), as noted by the research assistants, and often culminated in participants and research team members feeling uncomfortable or unwilling to share their views with a dominant culture which had seemed so unwilling to receive, and frequently hostile to, their previous attempts.
5. *Language, always language:* the examples of language as stumbling blocks proliferated the longer the project progressed: from our own lives, from the anecdotes of friends and colleagues, from the participants' focus groups, in the families of those we interviewed, we all experienced 'kick back' against whatever terminology we adopted, even temporarily.

Queer people of colour (QPOC), pansexual, homoromantic, queer, genderqueer, ethnic, culturally diverse, different, non-Anglo, non-European, non-Caucasian, Brown, Yellow, White, Black, culturally-specific terms for non-normative sex and gender identities . . . none served well enough to function as a universal term, even in this short, year-long project. The research team and participants discussed the ubiquity of this problem and its historical recurrence for marginalised communities and identities, but reaffirmed that the opening up, the attempts at bridging, the hopeful revisiting of sometimes long-closed spaces was still desirable, but enough to ignite fires that sometimes burned too hot. What was clear was what we *didn't* like or want—but what we preferred was often just too elusive.
6. *Homophobia as a western notion:* some participants stressed that an apparent increased homophobia or transphobia in non-Anglo families or communities was not the result of cultural diversity but religious conservatism. The study itself revealed that, overwhelmingly, Catholic and other Christian practitioners were more likely than those of other religions or spiritualities to demonstrate marginalising discourses and practices.

Recommendations

1. *Role models* – Culturally diverse young people need role models from our own cultures, but also cultural advocates who are not LGBTQ – cultural diversity in the mainstream helps broaden the minds of all. For parents or families of culturally diverse queers, it helps to hear cultural community members talk of acceptance of sexual and gender diversities, and keeps communication open which may otherwise be closed to culturally diverse queers.
2. *Peer support groups* – participants agreed that often they do not feel safe or open to share in white-dominated queer environments, and that culture-based support groups address this need. In Australia, there are many such groups around but numbers remain low, often compromising anonymity or identities-separation.
3. *Same Sex Attracted Young People (SSAYP) deserve information handouts in our own languages* – many participants discussed the need for "information about sexualities diversities distributed in local languages, but not just translated. The call is for materials to be devised within own communities" (Harris 2011, p. 30).
4. *Address the racism in the LGBTQ community* – pervasive racism continues to divide queer communities and cause people of colour to withdraw. The report identifies the lack of safety felt by 'multi-queers', particularly due to racism on online dating websites, and the 'I can't be racist, I'm gay' syndrome which hampers conversations that attempt to address the problem.
5. *Intergenerational issues* continue to cause pain in all communities, not just culturally diverse ones. Arts education initiatives that can address the age gap would be welcome.

6. *Educate about traditional sexualities diversity.* Queerness is not a western invention. Many participants and others desire greater documentation of the history of LGBTIQ lives and contributions, but terminology is one obstacle to identifying these varied histories. Arts-based initiatives can bring these stories into view in entertaining ways.
7. *Arts are more effective for educating about SSAYP lives* – arts projects can deliver difficult messages in soft or humorous ways. Often, they create collaborative (and sometimes cross-community) relationships along the way that other approaches do not.

Top 10 Arts Projects Recommended By the Participants

A primary driver of the *Teaching Diversities* community consultation was to poll these queer communities of colour on what creative arts strategies would best serve a public education campaign to address 'multi-diversities'. The majority of participants agreed that, in regard to public education campaigns, the older generation (the parents and grandparents of participants, anywhere from 40-85) were 'too far gone'. They recommended strongly that any public education campaign be directed at the younger generation, who were perceived to be more flexible and open. Logistically, this interrupted our goal of dissemination to the widest possible audience. For targeting the 'younger' generation, participants immediately identified the internet; if slightly older, television. More traditional 'public arts' ideas such as exhibitions and live performances were rejected, as the participants felt that older people would never attend and younger people might not feel attracted to these modes of arts or entertainment (although they acknowledged the power of being together in live interaction). They also felt that such localised performances attracted mainly sympathetic audiences, thereby diminishing the potential for real education of those who might need it most.

Therefore, despite the many advantages of other forms of artmaking, the participants recommended a range of approaches that were in many ways surprisingly homogeneous. Their suggestions also seemed to reflect less an imaginary of what 'might be' for multi-diverse people and digital technologies, and more a replication of demonstrated success stories of other international creative initiatives. All three case studies—*CALDPlay, Love Stories* and *In My Shoes*—importantly reflect a post-*It Gets Better* and *Stand Up/ the BeLonG Project* recognition of the power of digital dissemination.

The following were the most popular **arts project recommendations** from the participants for what they considered effective, achievable arts projects with a public education agenda about what they came to refer to as 'multi-queers' (multicultural queers):

1. A *Teaching Diversities* animation, especially using facebook. English language animation is fine as young people learn really quickly, but if targeting older people make sure that there are translations as well, provides anonymity. This was completed as the *CALDPlay* pilot animation (in English only).

2. *Video projects* like the *'It Gets Better'* (USA) and *Stand Up* (Ireland) campaigns.
3. *YouTube film clip parody* of the 'I'm a PC, I'm a MAC' idea, using 'I'm a queer, I'm a straight' or a montage of different people self-identifying across the spectrum.
4. *Slowmation,* slideshow.
5. *Online painting exhibition* (to retain anonymity) or bus shelter visual arts.
6. Chinese, Indian or other group *soap opera* on TV or YouTube.
7. *facebook pages* that provide support networks, advertising of events (including arts and cultural events). Inclusive and simple message.
8. Create *Twitter, tumblr, Instagram feeds,* fluid and moving where people can post.
9. *Private online groups* for people who are in the closet but want to connect with people in their cultural community.
10. *Infomercials,* for screening on television.

Importantly, participants said that they would welcome "anything with humour!" (Harris, 2011, p. 35). In addition to the participants' recommendations for explicit projects, the report is filled with recommendations for best practice approaches to working creatively with marginalised community members (as above). While organisations and individuals rightly wish to innovate their own approaches, a continuing need to build on rather than start over persists. Creative partnerships both inside and outside of schools sometimes suffer from a lack of continuity and short-term project-based cycles driven by funding requirements and limitations. While the *Teaching Diversities* project went to great pains to draw on its precedents in the area of 'multicultural queer' literature (AGMC, 2008), it can be difficult to find or widely circulate these kinds of documents. Arts-based projects that meet multiple diversities still have considerable room for improvement. Yet those like 'Rahim', below, agreed that projects and funding that continue to expand the definitions of cultural, sexual and religious communities are a step in the right direction:

> 'Rahim', Egyptian gay male, 26: . . . *It's been difficult. When I went into the gay community, I made lots of gay friends and cut off my faith background; when I went back to my faith background, I cut off the gay community and I'm now trying to find some way back in the middle. I think there's reasons why that happened, because there's lots of people in the gay community that may not have an appreciation for the great world of religions. And I guess the Muslim community do not have an appreciation for wider sexuality, so I've kept them pretty separate. Sometimes I feel like I'm playing with fire . . . [but] I think there's hope.* (Harris, 2011, p. 8)

Whether it is the difficult business of naming difference (Dillard & Okpalaoka, 2011), or the letting go into the future that McLuhan sees art urging us to do, digital art as it is being made, consumed and disseminated by young people from diverse backgrounds is serving a clearly constitutive cultural function. The *Teaching*

CHAPTER 7

Diversities community project exemplifies some ways in which arts products and processes are never truly outside of culture, including industrial and economic flows. Yet it reminds us too that creativity can remain diverse, even as it becomes increasingly market-driven.

ON THE IMPOSSIBILITY OF POLITICAL ART AND RITUAL PRACTICE

In some ways, the entirety of *Teaching Diversities* (report and *CALDPlay* animation) exemplifies what Rooney calls the "relentless commodification of difference" (2005, p. 406), even in the tangled web of self-commodification. In the midst of a frustrating inability to find language for so much difference, the co-creators of the work at times devolved into fairly stereotyped disagreements. This can be read as identity politics, sure; I argue, however, that these sites of personalised and performed politics of diversity are exactly the coalfaces at which change can and does occur—even messily, even painfully. Arguing from the abstracted theoretical helps form language to articulate the impossible or the unimaginable, but its performance must occur in the chaos of lived experience.

And the acceleration of artmaking in digital media lends itself to this chaotic identity formation, perfect for young people. Sinker (2012) notes how

> making multimedia allows for a form of creative expression which is not usually judged by the same criteria as drawing or writing, but can, nevertheless, display imaginative composition, technical prowess, narrative understanding, a wide range of cultural influences, ironic comment and visual invention.... Young people are very familiar with the constant remaking, remodelling and recycling of visual and aural forms, none of which are judged harshly, simply because they borrow or quote (p. 207).

Drawing mainly on school-based multimedia projects in the 1990s, Sinker cleverly foreshadowed some reasons for the explosion and power of video-based queer projects impacting global youth today, both inside and outside of schools. Consider, for example, the *It Gets Better* campaign, which has had unprecedented circulation, and the 10-year old Irish *BeLonG To's 'Stand Up'* campaign, now in every secondary school (http://www.belongto.org) in the country and referenced by UNESCO. Their very ubiquity equals power, especially to young people who live more fully in these mediascapes and who appreciate perhaps more readily the possibility of unedited global visibility. Even university research ethics processes are changing from an almost-universal aversion to using methods that identified under-aged participants to embracing the potential of non-anonymous video data in a wide range of disciplines. What is ethical in university research contexts has and continues to change rapidly.

Multimedia and creative online anti-homophobia campaigns and LGBT youth advocacy work has the potential to reach the people and places that are most isolated or most resistant, sometimes with increased safety for consumers, participants and practitioners. Even so, the tensions of language, performativity and community continue to plague 'identity' projects of this kind, and in some ways digital technology makes this more apparent and more complex, not less, in its need for speed and 'sound bite' content. Dillard & Okpalaoka state that "the issue of appropriate naming of the struggle" (2011, p. 149) is a long-standing and perhaps unresolvable tension for all margin-dwellers, and has been handled by the masters like "hooks (1994) [who] welcomed these contestations in naming, perspectives, positions, and language, seeing these confrontations as less about naming and more about how these 'differences [mean] that we must change ideas about how we learn'" (p. 113). *Teaching Diversities/CALDPlay*, *Love Stories* and *Animate Change/In My Shoes* are three examples of digital community-based projects with multicultural queer youth who are helping audiences learn differently. Returning now to McLuhan, the three case studies can be read through a critical cultural lens to better understand some common objectives, obstacles and patterns in the projects.

Earlier Turns

McLuhan, like Benjamin, can help us understand the current 'turn' in creativity. In *Understanding Media* (1964) McLuhan gave us the 'medium is the message', and before that still, in *The Gutenberg Galaxy* (1962), he argued that movable type provided the advent or 'turn' toward other ways of cognition and *of being* in culture, much like the creative turn which I am arguing here. For the young participants of all three projects above, the creative possibilities of digital media are providing them with new ways of being in their own and others' cultures, but is it altering their processes of cognition?

Drawing primarily in this chapter on Benjamin and McLuhan, and by tracing back a kind of history of 'creative turns', three emergent common themes become clear: 1) that they have almost always been turns toward the visual (even the printing press/movable type, as argued by McLuhan); 2) these turns have always been cultural in nature, but preceded by artistic, creative or aesthetic turns; and 3) that they almost always announce the advent of new forms of cognition. In this long-view of culture, creativity can be considered both an aesthetic driver but also—always—a cultural one, which includes but is not limited to economic flow. The creative turn is also—perhaps most profoundly—cognitive and intersubjective.

For McLuhan, the 15th-century print culture or the 'technology of typography' foregrounded new ways of thinking (such as individuation, linearity) and backgrounded others (like intersubjectivity and causality). Its three main technological or mechanical advances could typify western culture up to the 20th century, he believed: phonetic alphabet (organised speech), movable type (print) and telegraph (electric dissemination). Just as these mechanical advances allowed the illiterate human to become (through the democratisation of different kinds of information and informational tools) inventor and landowner, the digital revolution may be opening the ways and means to a new kind of creativity such that our moment is typified by a democratisation of 'creativity.' Everyone, now, is creative. Creativity must be instant, public and consumed, for whatever you try must be broadcast and instantly receive a response or—worse yet—silence. The ACT UP cry of 'Silence = Death' for AIDS sufferers has now become true for society at large: creators are welcome to try anything and everything, as long as it is not met with silence or invisibility. If it receives responses or participation (likes, views, reposts) then you are recognised as an artist, a creative presence. The medium has altered the message of creativity, in that it may be no longer about 'disturbing' but rather 'reaching'. Is there a difference in contemporary society between entertainment and art? It is increasingly hard to say.

Perhaps most importantly throughout all McLuhan's writings is the notion that each new technological advance has wide and long-term repercussions for not only the way things get made (the medium), or even the *content* of those things (the message), but indeed for altering the way we think about those and all other things. In a sense, McLuhan telescopes Benjamin's deep analysis of one 20th-century 'turn' into a long-view of history, reminding us that these cycles have been with us since time immemorial. If so, what are the implications for the relationship between creativity and digital technology as at the forefront of 'innovative' creativity in the early 21st century? In this chapter I have argued that the creative turn we are currently experiencing can be read (through Benjamin and McLuhan) as a fundamental shift in the way we think about creativity (creative cognition), brought on by a technological shift (creative medium) which is now awakening the aesthetic potential (message) of digital capability.

If McLuhan believed that digital media would facilitate the establishment of a 'global village', "dissolving borders and replacing individualistic capitalist print culture" (1962, p. 158), Benjamin was concerned with the auratic or artistic value of mechanical reproduction, focusing as he does on what is lost: the 'aura', the 'totemic value', a mythology or fantasy of 'authenticity'. Whereas McLuhan—though writing less than 30 years later—has the mind of a modernist and the mind of a techie: he does not wax lyrical about what is lost, but rather focuses his analyses on the ways in which it has always been so in cycles of change. Because of his remarkable absence of nostalgia—which is not to say he doesn't consider the affect and intersubjectivity at the heart of all change—he is able to see clearly into the future, predicting not only the development but the cultural effects of developments such as the internet and worldwide web. He understood that digital media would retain and extend all previous technologies, and that it would have commercial value.

McLuhan continually encourages readers and thinkers to divorce the so-called moral outrage from the bare facts of what he observes happening. He might, it may be argued, have had the mind of a Creative Industrialist, whereas Benjamin had the mind of an artist. Yet they identify similar aspects of their turns, and aspects that have wide resonance with our own: McLuhan's 'tribal man' is stereotypical but not nostalgic, and his belief that the internet would ultimately return western cultures to a state of tribal collectivism (global village) may have been accurate. Benjamin, on the other hand, mourned the loss of aura, tied as it was to aesthetics, but recognised as did McLuhan that such a loss of aura in art "opens up the possibility of a new, more universal experience of beauty" (McLuhan, 1962, p. 168).

Conclusion

Despite his concerns about the last creative turn, Benjamin surprisingly concluded that "quantity has been transmuted into quality" (1973, p. 232), a claim that many, including McLuhan if he were alive, might find contestable today. For all his nostalgia, Benjamin didn't argue that the loss of aura signalled a lamentable loss of quality, and Brooks might have argued it about deadly theatre. Yet neither did so: rather, Benjamin cautioned us with cool resolve that "the fact that the new mode of participation first appeared in disreputable form must not confuse the spectator" (1973, p. 232). Whether we can with any certainty claim such simple binaries as spectator/artist, as Benjamin did, is in some ways beside the point; more importantly for us is the acknowledgement that we need not be doomed to repeat the anxieties and petty divisions of Benjamin's or McLuhan's time.

What they both in their own words lamented were some artists' "spirited attacks against the superficial aspect" (Benjamin, 1973, p. 232) of reproducible art, a diversion they believed siphoned valuable time from making the most of these inevitable innovations. Arguments (then and now) against 'entertainment' and in favour of so-called 'high art' were (are) framed in discourses of elitism versus banality, a line not so simply drawn now. Today we live in an era of the glorification of banality; the celebration of what my filmmaker friend called the 'art disturbs' versus 'entertainment soothes' divide. Such simplistic binaries echo those equally unhelpful labels stalking multicultural queer young people in the three digital case studies discussed here.

Today's creative turn seems to suggest that now, fewer than ever before have the time or desire for complexity, perhaps especially for art's difficult demands. The difference between so-called high and low art were summarised by Benjamin in recognising this same phenomenon in his own time, that "the masses seek distraction whereas art demands concentration" (p. 232). But Benjamin—like those involved in these projects—was deeply concerned with whether a new form of mechanically reproduced art (in his case film and photography) could stimulate audiences in the same way that 'real' art can. He asks whether a viewer in front of a film concentrates in the same way as they do in front of a painting, and in the same way the young makers of *CALDPlay* and the other animations want to know if their disembodied digital artwork can move others—those like them, and those unlike them. Certainly any possible answer is as fluid and context-specific as any work of art. One person's pacified, unfocused distraction in a film can be the opposite of a film buff's attention to every detail, and reflection on the nature of life itself as represented in the film, superficial or not. Perhaps Benjamin's search for the stimulus of film is as elusive as the current search for a definition of creativity.

The creative collaborators responsible for all three animations drawn on in this chapter remind us that questions about 'intention of creator' and 'audience reception' are age-old binaries, and indeed "a certain oscillation between these two polar modes of reception can be demonstrated for each work of art" (Benjamin, 1973, p. 238).

CHAPTER 7

Yet today's creative turn seems to imply a new aesthetic imaginary in ways that even Benjamin didn't dream of. These ways may be tied to Deleuzian experience aspects—replacing Benjamin's focus on the mystical—yet online digital creativity suggests something further.

The three animations here that perform something of the fluid and multi-identities of their makers might be considered something like a 'queer aesthetics' or an extension of 'what art can be and can do today' (Rancière, 2008) in queer youth contexts. If so, what typifies them? Is the politics of art and aesthetics that so concerns Rancière (and which I examined in more detail in Chapter Six) anything like what is on the digital horizon currently embodied as creative industries and digital art? Chambers and O'Rourke (2009) suggest that for Rancière, "politics is aesthetic (a challenge to dominant social perception) and aesthetics is political (introducing the principle of equality in the practices, representations and perceptions that count as art and aesthetic experience)" (p. 5). These animations suggest something close to this, with humble but rich commentary on the distance between representation and perception, between power and presence.

In this chapter, I have primarily used Benjamin and McLuhan to help readers consider some of the spiralling complexities of three online animation case studies and, more generally, the cultural constitutive function of technological innovation in art. Through Rooney's (2005) attention to the dangers of difference in a post-9/11 context, and a deep untangling of naming in the age of visibility (Dillard and Okpalaoka, 2011) these local digital creative projects take on universal resonance of the fears and aspirations for both a new aesthetic, and a newly-democratic access to creativity in the digital age. The ways in which both Benjamin and McLuhan articulated the influence of mechanical and technological reproduction of arts on social ways of knowing and being are useful to us in understanding today's creative turn toward innovation and commodification, but also for understanding an emerging aesthetic imaginary. I have argued that both offer important strategies for helping us think about the ways in which digital technology does or does not help democratise creativity, modes of creative expression and the opportunities for dissemination of those works in our present moment.

REFERENCES

Appadurai, A. (1991). Global ethnoscapes: notes and queries for a transnational anthropology. In R. G. Fox (Ed.), *Recapturing anthropology: Working in the present* (pp. 191–210). Santa Fe: School of American Research.

Benjamin, W. (1936/1973). The work of art in the age of mechanical reproduction. In *Illuminations* (pp. 211–244). London, UK: HarperCollins.

Berry, C., Martin, F., & Yue, A. (Eds.). (2003). *Mobile cultures: New media in Queer Asia*. Durham, NC: Duke University Press.

Capistrano, D. (2013). *Read a f*cking zine: 50 zines by queer people of color*. Retrieved from http://www.autostraddle.com/50-zines-by-queer-people-of-color-184692/

Centre for Multicultural Youth [CMY] (2013). *In my shoes*. Retrieved from http://www.youtube.com/watch?v=hoWsXJ-kcA4

Chambers, S. A., & O'Rourke, M. (2009). Introduction. *Borderlands e-journal, 8*(2), 1–19.

Deleuze, G. (1968). *Difference and repetition*. New York, NY: Columbia University Press.
Dewey, J. (1934/2005). *Art as experience*. New York, NY: Perigree Books/Penguin.
Dillard, C. B., & Okpalaoka, C. (2011). The sacred and spiritual nature of endarkened transnational feminist praxis in qualitative research. In N. K. Denzin & Y. S. Lincoln (Eds.), *The sage handbook of qualitative research* (4th ed.) (pp. 147–162). Thousand Oaks CA: Sage.
Harris, A. (2013). Animating failure: Digital collaboration at the intersection of sex, race and culture. *Continuum Journal of Media and Culture*, 1–13.
Harris, A. (2011). *Teaching diversities: Same sex attracted young people, CALD communities, and arts based community education*. Carlton: Centre for Multicultural Youth.
Harris, A., & O'Mara, B. (2013). *Intercultural crossings in a digital age: ICT pathways with migrant and refugee-background youth* (Race, Ethnicity and Education).
Hooks, B. (1994). *Teaching to transgress*. New York, NY: Routledge.
Leung, L. (2006). *Virtual ethnicity: Race, resistance and the world wide web*. Hants, UK: Ashgate Publishing Ltd.
Mawji, E. (2004). Queer a Space . . . Woman of Colour coming through! In *Hear me out: true stories of Teens Educating and Confronting Homophobia (TEACH)*. Planned Parenthood of Toronto: Second Story Press.
McLuhan, M. (1964/1994). *Understanding media: The extensions of man*. MIT Press.
McLuhan, M. (1962). *The Gutenberg galaxy: The making of typographic man*. Toronto, CAN: University of Toronto Press.
Pallotta-Chiarolli, M. (1999). Multicultural does not mean multisexual: Social justice and the interweaving of ethnicity and sexuality in Australian schooling. In D. Epstein & J. T. Sears (Eds), *A Dangerous Knowing: Sexuality, pedagogy and popular culture* (pp 283–301). London, UK: Cassell.
Petrie, A. (2013). *Coming out is hard, whatever your background*. Retrieved July 7, 2013, from The Age newspaper: http://www.theage.com.au/victoria/coming-out-is-hard-whatever-your-background-20130706-2pj2e.html
Quinlivan, K., & Town, S. (1999). Queer as fuck? Exploring the potential of Queer Pedagogies in researching school experiences of Lesbian and Gay Youth. In D. Epstein & J. T. Sears (Eds), *A dangerous knowing: Sexuality, pedagogy and popular culture* (pp. 242–256). London, UK: Cassell.
Rancière, J. (2009). *The aesthetic unconscious*. Cambridge/Malden: Polity Press.
Rancière, J. (2008). Aesthetic separation, aesthetic community: scenes from the aesthetic regime of art. *Art & Research*, 2(1), 1–15.
Riggs, D. W. (2006). *Priscilla, (White) queen of the desert: Queer rights/race privilege*. New York, NY: Peter Lang.
Rooney, E. (2005). The predicament of differences without positive terms. *Ethnicities*, 5(3), 406–421.
Russell, S. T., & Truong, N. L. (2009). Adolescent sexual orientation, race and ethnicity, and school environments: a national study of sexual minority youth of color. In K. Kumashiro (Ed.), *Troubling intersections of race and sexuality: Queer students of color and anti-oppressive education* (pp. 113–132). Lanham, Maryland: Rowman & Littlefield.
Sinker, R. (2012). Making multimedia: evaluating young people's creative multimedia production. In J. Sefton-Green & R. Sinker (Eds.), *Evaluating creativity: Making and learning by young people* (pp. 187–215). London, UK: Routledge.
Smith, L. T. (2006). *Decolonizing methodologies: Research and indigenous peoples*. London, UK: Zed Books.
Vassilacopoulos, G., & Nicolacopoulos, T. (2004). Racism, foreigner communities and the onto-pathology of white Australian subjectivity. In A. Moreton-Robinson (Ed.), *Whitening race: Essays in Social and Cultural Criticism* (pp. 25–41). Canberra: Aboriginal Studies Press.
YGLAM. (2012). *Love stories animations project*. Retrieved from http://www.youtube.com/channel/UCAAA6ZaP_hNQ9YM26id2kUg

CHAPTER 8

CREATIVE INDUSTRIES OR CREATIVE IMAGINARIES?

Figure 14. Melbourne graffiti, #6 (2013).

INTRODUCTION

Benedict Anderson, as well as Appadurai who has drawn on him extensively, encourages us to be skeptical of truth-claims (1983/2006). He suggests that the modern notion of nationhood or nation-states was an invention (or imaginary) of disenfranchised power-hungry colonials who wished to reset the rules of the game to their own locality and benefit, rather than accept the values, rules and agendas of governing forces far away. He further suggests that these imagined communities might in fact have been convenient fabrications to begin with, and always only temporarily useful; that in fact they were at the time of his writing in 1983 already well-declined. Their usefulness, he argues, was particular to the twentieth century as an organising principle for localities somewhat arbitrarily linked back to colonial powers resistant to sharing the coffers these colonial outposts helped to engorge. An acceptance of that exchange, he argues, is over but, perhaps more importantly, the nation-state as a central organising unit is also no longer functional.

He makes a famously good case for this, and situates it in non-hegemonic, non-European Asia (especially Vietnam), a regional neighbour of Australia, and his choice highlights both a geo-political and racialised approach to critiquing the notion of community. If Anderson helped Appadurai theorise ethnoscapes made up

CHAPTER 8

of geographically reimagined and reconfigured communities, I argue that neither Anderson nor Appadurai went far enough in stimulating a consideration of other alterities. Gender and race, for example, emerge and re-emerge in new imaginaries, including creative ones. Creative industries versus creative arts and pedagogies are both already showing signs of gendered orientations, and funding and policy implications follow. Indeed, there are other patterns emerging globally, and I will start with the move from community-school creative arts partnerships to a creative industries focus in funding.

In the UK, the Creative Partnerships artist-in-schools model (2002-2011) recently gave way to 'Creative Industry Finance: Arts Council England' as government funding continues to shift toward the creative industries sector. In Australia, the incoming national Australian Curriculum is singularly paired with The Song Room (a national artists-in-schools program) for enhancing resources and delivery of discipline-based creative arts programs, in partnership with teachers in schools. Certainly artists in schools, and community-school arts partnerships continue to thrive in various incarnations in most countries where data is available. Yet media coverage of a recent major British government funding scheme makes it clear that even artists should start thinking like entrepreneurs. And while the trend may be seen most clearly there, in this chapter I will suggest that it is on the rise.

The government is willing to support the development of "creative content" through providing "practical advice and support for creative entrepreneurs wishing to grow their business as a viable commercial enterprise" (Arts Council UK, 2013, n.p.), as long as it has profit potential. Most recently this can be seen as the British government's Skills Development Fund allocated a further 25 million pounds "to help contribute to economic growth" (that's after a six million pound win in late 2012). These investments are strongly geared toward the UK digital content sectors and, we are told, follow "increased production in the creative industries since 2012's announcement of new tax reliefs for high-end TV production, animation and video games companies" (Gov.UK, para 4). No mention here of the quaint-sounding 'creative development' funds of yesteryear for film, theatre and creative writing—all of which artists previously complained were 'development hell' or development ghettos where production went to only the slick few. Now even these are being cut back in favour of more high-end digital products. To untangle the threads of this aspect of the new creative turn, this chapter will draw on Appadurai's imaginary to assist in unpacking the economic and aesthetic 'lines of flight' dominating creative production and marketing today.

Twenty-first century global economic flows are similarly going through a reorganisation of both systems and ideologies. For this reason, I am suggesting that modern education structures and systems are similarly *imagined communities*, organised around manufacturing and a human workforce—or human capital—that is no longer the central organising principle of the global knowledge economy in which we live. In this chapter I will problematise the creative explosion we are now seeing as the new organising principle of not only economies but of a new kind of creative capital. From 1972, Bourdieu identified and clarified his notion of social, cultural, economic and symbolic capital, and with it changed the way we think about the function of education and its role in culture. For Bourdieu, capital plus field equals habitus. Capital, in Bourdieuian terms, can be economic, cultural and social, but in this chapter I explore the possibility for an emergent creative capital as well. Certainly I acknowledge tensions between multiple interpretations of capital, signalling two main branches of Bourdieu's influence. I am not attempting in this chapter to fully unpack the significance of creative capital as it will differently impact those two branches, but rather deploying the notion of creative capital as a flashpoint for further exploration.

The last ten years, can be characterised by the emergence of an age of creative capital, both in ideological terms (note the numerous texts on the topic, and the rapid proliferation of definitions of even creative capital itself), but also in systemic terms (as the rapid change in economics and education demonstrates). The rush to define, understand and harness creative capital is in fact a desire to colonise it for the purposes of profit; in other words, to identify the nature and market value of a notion of creative capital in order to commodify it.

This chapter takes a closer look at the notion of creative industries as the clearest example of this commodification of creativity. To do so, I return to Appadurai's articulation of imaginaries, critiqued against the current 'industries' reframing of creative investment in Australia and the United Kingdom. I deploy Anderson's notion of imagined communities in order to extend his ideas about the ways in which imagined (nation-based) communities are being replaced by 'imagined' creative communities, and discuss the dangers this shift may represent.

Defining Creative Capital and Creative Industries

It may be impossible to define creative capital today without defining it in relation to 'creative industries'. Yet clarifying exactly what is meant by creative industries itself is no more clear-cut than defining creativity itself. Davies and Sigthorssun tell us that "the creative industries is a metaphor, which implies that creative production has been industrialised, set up in factory-like structures and managed along the same principles as the manufacture of any other mass-market goods" (2013, p. ix), in other words as human capital-driven. Yet, "Adorno and Horkheimer's universal conception of the cultural commodity, where 'the mere existence of an industrial form of production lead them to lump together jazz and comic strips, radio and cinema'" (Mattelart & Piemme, 1982, p. 53 in Flew, 2012, p. 62) is an earlier example of the way in which mass production has blurred the lines between aesthetics and commodities. The creative and knowledge economies represent a shift away from human capital to other capital—in other words, it is no longer about the work of people but about a new understanding of creative capital in Bourdieuian terms. "Urbanists have used the term . . . 'creative capital' to refer to the putative economic benefits for arts spending and creative industries for urban

CHAPTER 8

economies" (DiMaggio, 2005, p. 169). If cultural capital has, in the past, been concerned primarily with "aesthetic knowledge or its 'cultural heritage'" (p. 169), creative capital represents a new deployment and understanding of creativity in a 21st-century commodity culture. Yet as undiscovered as this sounds, it remains not so terribly far from Marx's own definitions of capital that prioritised over all else a concern with "human activity and not the distribution of things. Humans are defined by their creative capacities. To be denied of the process creatively to labour, is to be denied our humanity" (Beilharz, 2005, p 10). Yet is it possible that in this new explosion of a so-called creative economy that "mass consumption of mass-produced commodities is not a creative process" (Ritzer, 2005, p. 492) yet might *appear* creative in the sense of being generative; that is, perfectly matched to a commodity culture which has an insatiable need for creating and fulfilling new markets, markets flooded with commodities of sameness? While non-business arts or creative practitioners may be dismayed to think that creativity is indeed being colonised in a new and suffocating way by neoliberal actors and investors, in this book I am taking it as *a priori* and prefer to focus on an examination of the ways in which this might suggest a new aesthetic imaginary.

I am not suggesting that this is a good state of affairs, but rather an inevitability; and one that some arts educators and artists would rather not acknowledge. Yet such an acknowledgement is the only way in which we might all see this current turn in broader historic and cultural terms, and hope to gain some control over the modes in which creativity as an aesthetic enterprise continues to have relevance to contemporary commodified culture, particularly education. As Hartley et al. (2012) tell us:

> The jargon of flexible creativity and innovation must not be allowed to obscure or sidestep difficult questions about creative labour. We need to get beyond this 'pro' versus 'anti' impasse, to rethink the categories of labour and work more fundamentally, while observing carefully the actual changes that are unfolding in the economy as a whole (p. 65).

Educators must become a more significant part of this rethinking—including and especially secondary and primary school teachers, not just those in higher education. It's not hard to find—through a quick literature review of publications since the turn of the (twenty-first) century on the topic of 'creative capital'—the clear message that creative capital (also understood as the value of the creative in the social order of things, or marketplace) is clearly distinct from earlier definitions or alignments with arts, aesthetics and affect, and newly and boldly aligned with venture capital (Ante, 2008), critical urban theory (Kratke, 2012), the creative class and so-called creative occupations (Florida, 2007), creative tourism (Wurzburger et al., 2009) and creative industries, economies and policy (Hartley et al, 2012; Caves, 2000; Henry, 2008; Flew, 2012; Potts, 2011). Creative capital, economists and scholars confidently tell us, has replaced human capital (Florida, 2007).

The number of these texts that seek to define creative capital almost solely in terms of its economic value has proliferated, particularly since 2003. The collective exhalation after the turn of the century, as well as the fear and conservative turns in response to both the terrorist attacks of 2001 and the global financial crisis after them have contributed to this moment. Those seeking to define creativity (and sometimes the arts, and less often aesthetics) in terms of marketplace concerns are gaining traction. I was advised by one leader in the field against ever henceforth using the term 'creative pedagogies' to describe what is done regarding the arts and aesthetics in schools, but rather 'creative industries' because that is where the 'scene' is at now. When I protested that in fact devoting time and value to 'doing creative arts' in high schools was not, as I saw it, an industry and had different terms and concerns, my views were dismissed as out of step. It is worrying when the proliferation of publications and discourses around any area of enquiry inexorably lead back to industrial concerns and capital, implying a dangerous narrowing of the discourse.

In this section I will offer a brief overview of the growth sector of creative industries in Australia and its relationship to the same rise in the UK. In Australia, perhaps the most well-known centre for development, and education of creative industries' research is the ARC Centre for Excellence for Creative Industries and Innovation (CCI) at the Queensland University of Technology (QUT) in Brisbane. It is well-funded, well-published and well-connected, and the wide range of publications by core staff at the centre makes clear some common characteristics of the ways in which creative industries are being framed, researched, funded and disseminated not only in Australia but globally.

The CCI is the only administering organisation for the ARC Centre of Excellence for Creative Industries and Innovation in Australia, which includes a range of projects and sub-institutional partners (they are not, in fact, synonymous but the CCI is the lead institution). In addition to maintaining strong links with the parallel project of creative industries that preceded it in the United Kingdom, the CCI also conducts a large volume and scale of research in Pacific Rim countries, including increasingly in China, a market many in Australia (and elsewhere) are keen to understand better and to 'capture'.

According to *Creative industries, a Strategy for 21st Century Australia*, "The term 'creative industries' describes the generation of creative intellectual property with the potential to be commercialised" (Arts Gov, 2011, p. 4). The focus here on commercialisation is what concerns some involved in creative arts and arts education, by the governmental conflation of all creative activities into ones that should be commercially viable. This report, like many other government strategy documents, place creativity and creative industries at the forefront of 21st century prosperity: "Australia's creative industries are a vital and innovative force in the 21st century [and] the Australian Government recognises their significant contribution to our prosperity and capacity to propel a creative, imaginative nation into the future" (Arts Gov, 2011, p. 23). Like this one, there are an increasing number of government-funded or government-led reports that encourage the convergence of the arts and creative industries. Ironically, the one report which documents a cross-sectoral study, *Arts and Creative Industries* (Australia Council, 2011), was prepared by a member of the Creative Industries Faculty at the Queensland University of Technology, and examines some ways in which the "often polarised sectors of arts and creative industries might be re-thought and approached more productively" (para. 1). Yet the study itself was conducted by a team of Creative industries scholars, at the Centre for Creative industries, using a methodology that interviewed "18 leading practitioners across the creative industries" who discussed their "perceptions of the similarities, differences and connections between the arts and creative industries" (para. 2) but seemingly no 'artists'.

The myopic range of views can be further accounted for by the fact that the two 'co-funders'—the Australia Council for the Arts, and the ARC Centres for Excellence in Creative industries and Innovation at QUT—are both funded by the Australian Government. Not surprisingly, its recommendations were to combine the 'arts' and 'creative industries' sectors, a move that they recommend should be reflected in government policy. Frustration with this kind of 'evidence-based reporting' that (in this case) only polls one side of the 'divide' (in this case creative industries) can be seen in some online reader comments. They challenge the number of sector of the 18 interviewees, the agenda of the commission and execution of the report itself, and one reader who felt that the Australia Council "asked the wrong people to conduct it" (Australia Council, 2011, n.p.). In response, these criticisms are strongly defended by those responsible for its. While the comments there and elsewhere sometimes get side-tracked into bickering about validity, statistics and high versus low art, one thing is clear: there are no singular definitions for either creative industries or arts, but those tapped to frame and define them stand to gain a great deal.

In addition to international links with creative industries per se, the CCI is now leading the well-funded development of links with the Australia Council for the Arts (including the example above) and links across the creative industries/ arts education gap, with a database of web-based resources to support the implementation of the incoming National Arts Curriculum. While these steps may represent a refreshing move toward re-integrating the currently separate agendas of so-called 'arts', 'arts education' and 'creative industries' sectors, such a re-centralising of funding for research, development and international linking may also raise concerns in all three sectors regarding access to funding and hegemonising of creativity discourses in Australia. These are the global flows toward establishing standardised criteria, epistemologies and discursive frameworks for what 'counts' as creativity.

Commodifying Creativity in Industry

Two prominent characteristics of the creative industries as defined in the *Creative Industries* report are it's strategic digital focus and the links between creativity and innovation. While the introduction to this report claims that 'Creative innovation comes from many sources . . . and enriches Australia's cultural capital" (2011, p. 5) it is primarily an economic analysis which follows. Hartley et al. (2012) suggest that "human attention is the scarce resource of the creative industries" (p. 9). Partly they argue that the present creative turn is demanding a "new theory of economic value . . . because attention would replace money" (p. 9). They articulate the turn as being one from a Kantian aesthetics-driven notion of creativity, which is mystical, mysterious and muse-inspired, to a more contemporary notion of creativity and its products and processes as an industry. Their argument importantly proposes a continuation of Enlightenment constructions of creativity or creative thought through to the present, with a refocus rather than a complete break; in other words, a 'turn' rather than a stop and start. They claim that "from a conceptual perspective creativity represents the interplay between *similar differences* and *different similarities* . . . creativity from this perspective is a process of continuing and never-ending differentiation" (p. 66) whether in the arts or the sciences.

Hartley et al. go on to assert that creativity (creativity scholarship anyway) was co-opted by social scientists and psychology long ago, including by the now-standard psychometric tests of Guildford and studies by Sternberg & Lubart (1999). They claim "Creativity however is not a generic term despite attempts by the behavioural sciences to attribute it to the individual. The 'creative industries' concept is undoubtedly more a pragmatic development, breaking away from the narrow usage associated with divergent thinking and performance tests" (p. 67). I would argue, however, that it is only a more pragmatic view in relation to social science, and not in conversation with the long rich history of creative pursuits that were not within academic or other superstructures seeking to quantify and codify them as skills, attributes or products.

Unsurprisingly, Hartley et al.'s approach to an analysis of creativity (within an industrial frame) draws on Mockros & Csikszentmihali (1999) in that, "the root of the creative industries is cultural policy, bureaucratically determined rather than organic and ultimately concerned with outputs that can be counted, compared and evaluated" (p. 67). Bilton tells us that creativity has historically been linked with individualism, and its downside is that it can "disconnect creative thinking and creative people from the contexts and systems which give their innovations and individual talents meaning and value" (2007, p. 3), referencing the cultural embeddedness of all creative outputs (whether and how they are taken up as 'expert', 'genius' or 'significant'—questions that are intrinsic to any creative arts scene or field of endeavour). All fields have measures of value, and industries associated with creativity need not be any different, yet the 'creative industries' per se take the codification a step further in prioritising market value over almost everything else. Even Hartley et al. admit that "the relationship between the creative industries and creativity has become a divisive issue" (2012, p. 67).

Yet the obsessive search for unilateral definitions, practices, conditions and measures of creativity are accelerating, not slowing. "Almost all current definitions of creativity and innovation agree on the importance of three attributes: newness, value and usefulness" (Hartley et al., 2012, p. 67). Robinson said the same as discussed earlier, in defining creativity as "the process of having original ideas that have value" (2008). As the leader in creative industries in Australia, CCI has sought to democratise a definition of creativity that distinctly decouples creative commodities from aesthetic creativity:

> Despite the general celebration of novelty, the creative industries, as defined globally, are made up of practices, occupations, and commodities that are more often routine, frequently standardised and generally derivative. While this critique deflates the sense of wonder associated with aesthetic creativity and acquisition of cultural capital, it also points to the fact that all creative acts are generative: they enable more variations to emerge (Hartley et al., 2012, p. 68).

Yet the argument above can be applied more easily to industrial innovations than to 'creative' acts. Both are generative, but an ability to stimulate further innovation and product generation is the driving concern of creativity as an industry, as opposed to being a by-product of creative arts.

In Europe, a range of nation-based texts are available that discuss creative industries' business models and funding requirements, identifying local differences (see Schneider et al., 2010 and Weckerle, 2008, for example). These texts often articulate differences between nation-state creative industries and their European context (Lazzeretti, 2012; Davies & Sigthorsson, 2013). Yet they all share a strong orientation toward business, creative professions, capital finance opportunities and needs, and marketplace innovation. Australia's Centre of Excellence for Creative Industries and Innovation (CCI) partners closely with Potts (2011) in the UK, who calls his focus 'an evolutionary economics of creative industries' and acknowledges his collaboration on the book and research with QUT institutionally, and Hartley et al. personally, indicating some strong ideological and methodological links emerging in joint research between the two countries. While this particular cross-national collaboration is important (and certainly productive!), it raises the question of how diverse this research into a so-called 'explosion' of creative industries really is. As with many other areas of educational and cultural endeavour, research relationships between Australia and Britain remain strong, but this same cross-pollination is not so apparent between the United States and Australia (although for a still-timely and excellent overview of creative industries in the United States, see Caves, 2000). Importantly, Potts notes that "the momentum to develop a national creative industries policy for the United States is virtually non-existent" (2011, p. 40). And while the momentum for creative industries has certainly had positive spinoffs for creativity in general across Australia and Europe, recent changes within Australia (reflected in the CCI report discussed earlier in the chapter) show the beginnings of a shift toward a merging of creative industries and creative arts endeavour more generally.

One clear example of the way in which the creative industries' concern with commodification is affecting arts disciplines and discourses emerges from the

Design Institute of Australia (DIA), which seeks to optimise the ways in which "design exemplifies the creative industries' concept of commercial applications of creativity" (Flew, 2012, p. 85). Flew notes the convergence of economics and creative arts discourses in that "the study of markets is characteristically the domain of economics, and so it is to economic theories that we turn ... yet what we can take from economics for understanding creative industries markets is less clear-cut than it may first appear" (2012, p. 115). The convergence, he claims, can be characterised by three interrelated statements:

1. Standard economic measures of value, such as willingness of consumers to pay for something, are inadequate ways of assessing cultural value.
2. As a result, the allocation of resources exclusively or primarily through the price mechanism will fail to produce the socially desirable output of cultural goods and services, or distribute these resources in ways that are socially appropriate.
3. Cultural activities therefore require some form of public subsidy, and the role of cultural economists is to determine the appropriate levels and best means of providing these subsidies (p. 115).

Flew notes the ways in which this produces two overlapping but contradictory roles of economics and/in the arts in which "cultural economists see their primary role as being to protect the arts and culture from other economists" (2012, p. 116). Parallel to the project of commodifying creativity will necessarily become that of 'protecting' it from such commodification. He notes that "concerns about how more traditional frameworks for analyzing culture, such as aesthetics, can act to perpetuate social and cultural hierarchies" (p. 3) can contribute to the homogenising of creativity in its process of commodification. Such concerns, he points out, are "increasingly central to school curricula in areas such as English literature, in ways that were inconceivable even 20 years ago" (p. 3). These are not the only troubling patterns emerging from the explosion of creative industries' funding, policy and scholarly attention. The emergent positioning of creative industries in the Australian cultural landscape may be read as a "conceptual framework of global flows [functioning] as gendered cultural pedagogies" (Savage & Hickey-Moody, 2010, p. 289), in which arts education remains a strongly feminised discursive space dominated by notions of 'development' 'empowerment' and 'nurturing', while this emerging creative industries discourse certainly focuses on more masculinsed areas of concern such as profit, market share and productivity. Any potential new aesthetic imaginary, applied as a lens to creativity and commodity culture, will certainly "be [both] pedagogical *and* gendered" (Savage & Hickey-Moody, 2010, p. 289), in its conception and implementation. As noted in the opening of this chapter, such concerns relating to the acceleration of attention on creative industries, and its relationship to both arts and arts education, deserve much more critical attention in current and future research; the establishment of these discourses is a flashpoint only that I offer as a background for my discussion of creative imaginaries.

CHAPTER 8

CREATIVE IMAGINARIES

Social Fact or Social Fiction?

The imagination is now central to all forms of agency, is itself a social fact, and is the key component of the new global order (Appadurai, 1996, p. 31).

Flew, like Appadurai, understands the market value of imagination and creativity. Perhaps more than any other contemporary creativity theorist, Flew has identified the ways in which the current fixation with creative industries can be read against a historiography of capital, industry and Marx's historical materialism, drawing as he does on Adorno and others: "Adorno and Horkheimer presented the gloomy prognosis that the once autonomous sphere of culture—art, aesthetics, music, literature, etc.— had become fully integrated into the dynamics of capitalist domination in the form of the culture industry" (Flew, 2012, p. 62). As Flew and those involved in creative industries discourses are identifying, the cultural study of creativity and sameness by Adorno and others has now become a critical study of the commodification of creativity – based squarely in digital media. But rather than drawing on the sociocultural views of Adorno, here I will explore the ways in which the digital focus of creative industries can shed light on its marketization, by revisiting Benjamin and his theoretic of reproducibility.

Education, perhaps more than any other sector but certainly not alone, is reflective of the industrial need for standardisation as well as its perseverative reiteration of the need for more flexible, creative and innovative thinking and operationalising. For Flew, this is exactly "'the achievement of standardization and mass production, sacrificing whatever involved a distinction between the logic of the work and that of the social system' (Adorno & Horkheimer, 1979, p. 350). What appears as great consumer choice and cultural freedom for the masses is thus their complete integration into the machinery of mass culture" (Flew, p. 62). This is the beginning of a critical interrogation of creativity discourses in which seemingly no distinction is being made between this 'machinery of mass culture' as a kind of reproducible creativity, versus the attention to aesthetics and individuality that pervaded waves of earlier creativity discourses.

Flew further highlights some interesting ways in which earlier interrogations of commodified art could be understood as imbued with a "nostalgia for a cultural experience untainted by technology" in which an earlier critique of aesthetics "under capitalism is underpinned by a distrust of reproducible cultural forms delivered by mass communications technologies" (2012, p. 63)—a kind of healthy distrust of mass communications which is now all but forgotten. What else, however, might creativity be? If creative industries have a power and persistence in the current climate of productivity and commodification, is this then 'all' that creativity might mean to a culture so in need of expansion (even beyond innovation)? For those in education, the question of what creativity might *be* is only half the equation— and inherently linked to the questions *how might it be invited in? And how might it be nurtured?* One discomfort within educational grapplings with the current creative turn is our inability to agree on whether the creativity focus should be on the teaching, the learning, or the space in which it all happens. One approach in the training of pre-service teachers to better facilitate a student-focused creativity has been termed 'creative pedagogies' or creative approaches, and leading that pack is British educationalist Anna Craft.

The notion of creative pedagogies is one way of identifying what teachers can do in their classrooms to facilitate greater creativity in the space, to the benefit of all. As Craft sees it, creative spaces and activities are of course linked, and not contingent upon discipline-specific content or activities. But the gap between a tertiary-centred 'creative industries' focus and the secondary 'creative pedagogies' remains. What is needed to bridge the nurturing of creative approaches in classrooms, with the kind of market-focused, profitable and world-class innovative and creative training in tertiary institutions? Will it be an industry of 'creative industries' which trains a kind of Floridian 'creative class' to comprise a 21st-century global 'creative workforce' which includes digital and economic products?, or will it be a program of 'creative pedagogies' that approaches all endeavour of knowledge-generation more creatively? In one respect these are exciting times precisely because we don't yet know, which extends Anderson's *imagined communities* (addressed in the next sub-section).

These creative communities may not be terribly different from the so-called creative class that creative industries tertiary programs are helping to create and discursively frame, or they may signal a change in teacher education toward creative pedagogical training. Are both approaches adding to the formation of new global, transnational 'imagined creative communities' to drive their agendas, to establish new power bases for themselves or others (as per Anderson)? Do these practitioners or creative workforces have anything at all in common with the 'creative pedagogies' of Craft and others like her? Here I will highlight some intersections between Craft's creative pedagogies and Appadurai's notion of an imaginary—a creative imaginary that does not yet exist. In the following section, I return to Appadurai's use of Anderson's imagined communities to see the ways in which his notion is closer to a 'creative industrial' conception of creativity and less like Craft's widely-recognised work on creative pedagogies. Without critically interrogating this gap, we are missing opportunities for better nurturing both industrial creative skills and more aesthetically-driven ones.

In addition to articulating a creative pedagogical approach, Craft (2005) identified it as a core component of a differentiated twenty-first century, and rightly situates it specifically and distinctly within this time and place: the aspects of creativity being investigated at this point, in the early years of the twenty-first century, are quite distinct from those emphasised in the mid to late twentieth century" (p. 15). She and others (Craft, et al., 2001) have also decoupled 'creative learning' from 'creative teaching' as well as 'co-creating', itself a powerful form of educational engagement. Further, she argues, "in the early years of the twenty-first century, the policy, practice and research discourse has expanded to include the 'middle ground'

161

CHAPTER 8

of Creative Learning" (2005, p. 54). So Craft powerfully situates her analysis within the emerging twenty-first century, yet also firmly roots it in the specificities of British educational programming and discourses, a geo-political positioning that unfortunately goes largely unremarked by her. Craft says that "everything that we do is situated and relational to values and beliefs" (p. x) and yet those of us working and theorising our experiences and empirical evidence in/from non-northern states continually confront the supposed generalisability of northern data versus the 'regional' framing given to our marginally-positioned work. This book attempts to go some way toward bridging that gap.

Despite the growing focus on creative industries, there is a more quietly growing discourse around creativity in schools (as distinct from arts education, which is more focused on doing the 'big five' arts), and yet they hardly overlap. Perhaps it is easier or more accurate to speak of the focus of these two distinct areas of research—a focus *on* rather than *in*—for any vibrant creative industries discourse relies on a development of understanding of creative pedagogies and pedagogical practices in schools and education discourses overall. And as I identified earlier in this book, while discourses of creativity are growing in national curricula, the hours budgeted for arts activities and arts engagement are steadily declining. Could this be another by-product of the ways in which these discourses are blind to aesthetics? Without a doubt the person who has published most widely in recent years on the topic of creative pedagogies and creativity overall in education is Anna Craft. Importantly, she frames key dilemmas for educators and scholars grappling with various understandings of creativity in education today, including new definitions for the educational context, and the differences between learning and teaching creativity. For Craft, creative pedagogies begin with 'naming':

> the name that we give an activity or process acts as a 'frame' for how we then put it into practice. The very fact that we might distinguish between our use of the terms creativity, imagination and innovation could alter how we go about emphasising activities in the classroom. And similarly, the value that we place on the three elements of pedagogy discussed here, i.e., creative teaching, teaching for creativity and creative learning, seem likely to influence the way a classroom is organised and executed (Craft, 2005, p. 24).

She also importantly identifies a new set of criteria at the heart of creative *learning* (as distinct from pedagogical, or teaching, approaches): "Early characterisations of creative learning suggest that it involves learners in using their imagination and experience to develop learning, that it involves them strategically collaborating over tasks, contributing to the classroom pedagogy and to the curriculum" (Craft, 2005, p. 23). Once again Craft, like almost all others writing on the topic, devotes considerable time to defining creativity—defining it against other related terms, like innovation and imagination, and also, in her case, within education. The strong influence of her British context is pivotal but still remains largely unremarked. While some of these North American and European writers acknowledge some context-specific organisations or policies that borrow from or contribute to their definitions or case studies, I have still not found one that recognises or critically problematises how these influences may make their definitions more appropriate to some contexts, and less to others. In other words, none of them at all wonder 'what might an Asia Pacific definition or expression of creativity be?' or 'What might an Australian, Indigenous or Southern states pedagogy look like or require?', beyond one reference in Craft which refers to recent policy "in different parts of the world" (p. 85). Clearly this is an area for further development.

Craft acknowledges transparently that her definition of creativity is drawn from "the committee's definition of creativity" (p. 20), that is, the British National Advisory Committee for Creative and Cultural Education (NACCCE, 1999, p. 29). Her writing extensively addresses the differences between creative teaching and learning (in the education sector), but such linked-up discourses are disappointing if searching for critical treatments of the issue. If the most pervasive definitions of creativity in both the UK and Australia are derived from government-funded reports and/or projects and/or centres driven by a neoliberal growth imperative, what room is there for critical talking-back to standardised approaches to curriculum or even arts funding? And what room is there then for real innovation, the neoliberal companion term to industry-driven creativity?

Starting from a very different point is Herbert (2010), who attempts to link creativity in classrooms with creativity in dreams, using poststructuralist and psychoanalytic theory to help imagine new creative futures in pedagogical practice. Such new futures depend on Lacan's *connaissance* (or 'imaginary knowledge') leading us back to Anderson's communities. Post nation-states communities of creativity might be characterised by just such imaginary knowledge, and secondary schools could be the places where these creative communities begin and grow. This linked self/other knowledge which can be developed through creativity is aligned more closely with Renaissance notions of creativity and aesthetics, but also sounds like good teaching and learning. However, the trickle-down of globalising profit demands and funding structures keeps creativity as an 'imaginary knowledge' orienting principle still a long way off.

Herbert also claims that "pedagogy is an art form, taking shape within teacher-student interaction, or rather within a space emerging from this interaction" (p. 3), a notion I find infinitely compelling—especially in relation to standardised curricula and standardised testing. She notes how difficult it can be to find words for the 'aha!' moments in classrooms, "even if the experience is profound" (p. 3), and how Lacan can assist with this. Stuck in a Benjaminian experience of 'reproducible' education outcomes, teachers can lose hope of ever finding a meandering creative moment to savour.

On this basis, I suggest that creativity is going through a shift that increasingly resembles Appadurai's tournaments of value. In a formulation that echoes an analysis of creative capital today, Appadurai's tournaments are contingent upon "not just status, rank, fame or reputation of actors, but the disposition of the central

163

CHAPTER 8

tokens of value in the society in question" (Appadurai, 1986, p. 21). Certainly Herbert and others' arguments indicate that creativity is going through a similar turn as its dispositional role as a central token is under question if not attack. This current transit is all the harder to address given its ubiquitous but increasingly hollow presence in a range of sectors and discourses. While Appadurai drew on the darker view of contemporary culture evident in Anderson's *Imagined Communities* in his consideration of creative flows, culture and the dying nation-state, Anderson also informed Appadurai's articulation of 'post-national' global flows, ones I have suggested include a new formulation of creativity as capital.

Creative Imaginaries as a Globalising Pedagogy

Appadurai reframes "imagination as a social practice" (1999, p. 34), as both being and becoming, as both *act* and *orientation:*

> . . . no longer mere contemplation (irrelevant for new forms of desire and subjectivity), the imagination has become an organized field of social practices, a form of work (in the sense of both labor and culturally organized practice), and a form of negotiation between sites of agency (individuals) and a globally defined field of possibility (p. 31).

While imagination suggests a beginning or—in his terms—a cohesion, what Appadurai articulated as the 'globally defined field of possibility' of imagination has already now come to realisation as creativity. That is today, less than 20 years after he wrote these words, creativity has emerged as both a social practice, a globally significant and globally defined field of possibility, but also as an affective site of performativity. To think about imagination as a practice of negotiation may have seemed radical when he wrote these words, but it is not today. Appadurai's notion of imagination is something closer to what is being constructed as creativity today. To usefully deploy this frame onto a discourse of creativity, we need only look to his notion of structures of feeling, in which place no longer relies on geography, but on the feeling of a locality or a practice. Is there a difference between the social practice of imagination, and the social practice of creativity? The Appaduraian notion of the imaginary might bridge these two.

The creative industries sector can be seen to represent not so much a *becoming* creative (as in schools, identities, development), but a *doing* of creativity, and includes the erosion of multiple borders; that is, between nation-identified artists, between 'art' and 'craft' and 'business', between artist and worker, between virtual and real, between innovation and commodification. Appadurai has helped us think about diasporic identifications within the ethnoscape/s as engaged in a process of "construction of locality, as a structure of feeling, often in the face of the erosion, dispersal, and implosion of neighborhoods as coherent social formations" (1996, p. 199), and I suggest that creativity is going through such a transit now and losing its locality, its affect and to some extent, its aesthetic. More than anything else, it is losing its relationship to education. The implosion we are confronting is of the 'neighbourhood' of education, a social formation that has outstayed its welcome, and increasingly has no relationship to the creativity, imagination and innovation that will supposedly take us into the unknown future.

Robbins (2003) draws on Appadurai (2000) to consider the power of the imagination not only to control and program, but to imagine a life beyond 'creative forms'. He reminds us that "Appadurai makes it clear that globalization has given the imagination a *larger* role in social life" (p. 203). Imagination, like creativity, holds an ill-defined place in contemporary culture, however, and certainly in education. By most accounts, imagination remains within the realm of thinking or thinking-feeling (Massumi, 2008), while creativity moves us out into doing. If creativity is increasingly, in popular culture terms, about products, imagination is still about thinking and becoming. Paradoxically, in Appaduraian terms education is becoming increasingly both the domain of *doing* (but not creativity)—oriented as it is around outcomes and products—but also less and less about imaginative *becoming*. Programs of study are compacting and while the rhetoric of imagination and creativity permeate curricula, they increasingly see no room to include for the activities of imagination; possibly because they remain ill-defined, possibly because this thinking-time of imagination appears unproductive. Yet schools have been taking advantage of the darker side of governmentality through imagination since the beginning, as Robbins notes: "he [Appadurai] knows that 'it is in and through the imagination that modern citizens are disciplined and controlled—by states, markets, and other powerful interests. But it is also the faculty through which collective patterns of dissent and new designs for collective life emerge" (2003, p. 203). He calls them, after all, "creative forms of social life" (Appadurai, 2000, p. 6 in Robbins, p. 203) and suggests that these are the sites where culture moves forward.

If (as Appadurai claimed) things also have social lives circulating in different regimes of value (1988), then we might expect that the context into which this circulating value is set was always going to accelerate. The rapid expansion of commodity culture, however, cannot last forever. For Appadurai, this cultural context is always infused by ethnohistorical perspectives, a longer view than most educators and certainly most policymakers bring to daily analyses. Appadurai keeps it pretty simple. He tells us that creativity is changing because it is suddenly profitable, reflected in his "new perspective on the circulation of commodities in social life" (1988, p. 3). With his simple claim that "economic exchange creates value" (p. 3), Appadurai opens a keyhole into contemporary creativity studies and helps us better understand the implications of this statement—that creativity, as an exchange commodity, is undergoing a political change, not just an ideological or instrumental one.

If creativity has completely transformed into the newest expansion commodity form of Appadurai's "objects of economic value" (1988, p. 3) this has implications not just for its social role at the current moment, but for its function. Commodities

CHAPTER 8

cannot, by their nature, be innovative, as they must be driven by demand. In order to be demanded by sufficient numbers, they must be recognisable. Appadurai's tournaments of value go some way toward helping understand this cycle but falls short in sufficiently explaining the current creative turn.

Appadurai tells us that, "at the top of many societies, we have the politics of tournaments of value, and of calculated diversions that might lead to new paths of commodity flow" (1988, p, 57). He draws on a number of definitions to explain that economic value (like creativity) is never "an inherent property of objects, but is a judgment made about them by subjects" (p. 3). This is exactly the kind of discourse being promulgated about creativity today—that it must have market value—and those who define creativity and its function and its best uses are jostling to have their definitions taken up broadly, because, as Appadurai and others tell us, commodity value is a subjective and subjectively framed proposition, not an inherent one. He and others have argued effectively though that the circulation value of commodities that was once tied to their supply and demand, creating different "regimes of value in space and time", (p. 4) (i.e., by virtue of their scarcity) is now being replaced in this knowledge economy not by scarcity but by over-supply (that is, by honing editing abilities to sift through all the limitless data now becoming available).

Appadurai draws on Marx again to define the commodity as a socialised thing: "a commodity is a product intended principally for exchange, and . . . such products emerge, by definition, in the institutional, psychological, and economic conditions of capitalism" (1988, p. 6). But he critiques the Marxist understanding of commodities, and that they are "distinguishable from 'products', 'objects', 'goods', 'artifacts' and other sorts of things" (p. 6). He returns us to Marx's writing to better understand the 'social use value' of things. I would argue that today creativity is going through a period of capital(ist) transformation in which its use value is changing; and this indeed has implications for what art and creativity are. While innovation has always been tied to definitions of use-value, arts and creativity have not. He draws on Marx: "every product of labour is, in all states of society, a use-value; but it is only at a definite historical epoch in a society's development that such a product becomes a commodity" (in Appadurai, 1988, p. 8).

Appadurai links back to both Benjamin and Anderson in his urging us to understand the "new role for imagination in social life" (1996, p. 31) by bringing together

> the old ideas of images, especially mechanically produced images (in the Frankfurt School sense), the idea of the imagined community (in Anderson's sense) and the French idea of the imaginary (*imaginaire*) as a constructed landscape of collective aspirations, which is no more and no less real than the collective representation of Emile Durkheim, now mediated through the complex prism of modern media (p. 31).

Here imagination takes on a socially co-constitutive role, part creativity, part pedagogy. Appadurai's notion of imagination as a social practice can also be used to bring pedagogical considerations to the fore, by noting the ways in which "his theory lends itself to a consideration of pedagogy" (Savage and Hickey-Moody, 2010, p. 279). Here I am suggesting a consideration of his 'imagination as social practice' as a global flow of creativity. Such creative global flows are inextricably linked to their emergence as commodities (which creative discourses and practices become globally mobile, consumed, proliferating), and which both draw on and co-constitute multimedia or multi 'scapes'.

Savage and Hickey-Moody articulate these flows as culturally pedagogical in similar ways to creativity-as-commodity: "it is because of these intersections between public, private, people and things that we feel 'cultural globalizing pedagogy' offers an intimate and pervasive expression . . . of informal, unbounded, culturally mediated and subjective learning" (2010, p. 279). In a commodified flow of creativity, pedagogy can once again become unbounded and locally mediated. A positive by-product, if you will, of the commodification of creativity may well be that through its pervasive flows globally, local expressions of creativity might be extended as well. The social life of things that Appadurai argued may now be turning into the social life of virtual practices, be they creative or pedagogical, or both.

Creativity represents a series of increasingly well-documented, well-analysed, but no less mystical products and industries, as well as a network of ideological sites of cultural and commodity practices; increasingly, it can be understood as an emerging globalising pedagogy with its own evolving aesthetic standards. Creativity, too, can be understood as "in motion, insofar as their discourses are forever moving through globalising circuits of popular and corporate cultures, but are also disjunctive in that they are not uniformly disseminated or received" (2010, p. 279). Here they articulate a resistant discourse to Giroux's public pedagogies, and situate their affective multiple publics as cultural pedagogy productively outside of an American context, as I do. Savage and Hickey-Moody offer a productive gender critique of Appadurai's articulation of imagination, and of Giroux's public pedagogies, and in this chapter I have used Appadurai and Anderson to identify some ways in which the creative industries are impacting on creativity in schools, and some flow effects of the positioning and funding of each streams' attendant commodity value.

Conclusion

In this chapter I have tried to disentangle some important aspects of creativity in the contemporary global landscape, namely the ways in which the ascendant creative industries may be functioning—or appearing—as the leading edge of creative arts and arts education. Through a close analysis of the parallel UK/Australian development of funding and research structures, as well as scholarship, in the creative industries, and by noting its almost complete absence from the American cultural landscape, I have raised the question of what function for nation-states and economies this shift toward an industrial conception of creativity might give rise to. I then asked the question

CHAPTER 8

whether this growth industry is the same as creative arts and arts education in its cultural role. Finally, I have considered the possibility that creative industries might be functioning culturally to produce or advance a new creative imaginary, which is aligned with commodity culture more than aesthetics, and in which business people emerge as experts over aesthetic, artistic or pedagogical practitioners. If a 21st-century creative imaginary is thus being defined through industrial discourses, largely built or led by (struggling) nation-state governments, what are the implications for a new aesthetic imaginary in both artistic and educational contexts?

I have drawn on Anderson's imagined communities to problematise the urge to commodify creativity in/through industry, and have critiqued Anderson's assumption of dying nation-states and the shift away from colonial conquest (arguing rather that creative industries represents only a new shift in the colonial project). I have returned to Appadurai's notion of tournaments of value to help understand and problematise the limitations of reframing all creativity as innovation and industrial enterprise. Lastly, I am asking readers to consider a new possibility for creative imaginaries, one tied more closely to aesthetic concerns rather than neoliberal discourses of productivity, innovation, and use-value. I suggest that whether this current 'creative turn' continues its current trajectory toward commodification or delivers us to a new aesthetic imaginary, there are significant implications for creative pedagogies and education for the twenty-first century, both popular/public and formal.

Within these possibilities, I claim that the fluid nature of creative endeavour and pedagogical exploration will ultimately ensure that its biggest 'turn' will become most visible outside of the so-called creative industries, a temporary growth industry in which digital media and exportability characterise an insatiable expectation of economic capital. New elites and underclasses based on 'creative capital' will recognise what Walter Benjamin noted in the last century, and Flew and others have reminded us of:

> While economic capital is associated with possession of goods and services associated with wealth and status, cultural capital revolves around practices of distinction that may be linked to taste and aesthetics, but which operate in a cultural field whose definitional criteria, institutions, rules and practices are highly fluid and contested. At the same time, its patterns of inclusion and exclusion are no less real, and no less keenly felt, than those arising from inequalities of access to economic resources. (2012, p. 115)

In the next chapter I will extend this discussion of imagination and creativity to problematise the intersection of imagination and aesthetics. That is, how does this new imaginary that is replacing our so-called dying nation-states move beyond a simple acceleration of commodification and into a new aesthetic imaginary? This involves a reconceptualisation not only of the marketisation of creativity—which carries with it a set of implications for the ways in which creativity gets produced, and by whom, how, where and how it gets distributed—but importantly, it also carries a new set of aesthetic implications which go deeper and to the very heart of what it means to be creative. And for this 'new aesthetic imaginary' we use McLuhan as a guide back to Benjamin.

REFERENCES

Adorno, T., & Horkheimer, M. (1979). The culture industry: Enlightenment as mass deception. In J. Curran, M. Gurevitch & J. Woollacott (Eds.), *Mass communication and society* (pp. 349–383). London, UK: Verso.
Anderson, B. (1983/2006). *Imagined communities: Reflections on the origin and spread of nationalism*. London/New York, UK/NY: Verso.
Ante, S. E. (2008). *Creative capital: Georges Doriot and the birth of venture capital*. Boston, MA: Harvard Business Press.
Appadurai, A. (2000). Grassroots globalization and the research imagination. *Public Culture, 12*(1), 1–19.
Appadurai, A. (1996). *Modernity at large: Cultural dimensions of globalization*. Minneapolis, MN: University of Minnesota Press.
Appadurai, A. (1988). Commodities and the politics of value. In A. Appadurai (Ed.), *The social life of things: Commodities in cultural perspective* (pp. 3–63). New York, NY: Cambridge University Press.
Appadurai, A. (Ed.) (1986). *Social life of things: Commodities in cultural perspective*. Cambridge, MA: Cambridge University Press.
Arts Council UK. (2013). *Creative industry finance*. Retrieved from http://www.artscouncil.org.uk/funding/apply-for-funding/creative-industry-finance/
Arts Gov / Attorney General's Office. (2011). *Creative industries: A strategy for 21st century Australia*. Retrieved from http://arts.gov.au/sites/default/files/creative-industries/sdip/strategic-digital-industry-plan.pdf
Australia Council. (2011). *Australia should seek new and liberating ways to bring together the arts, popular culture and the creative industries*. Retrieved from Arts and creative industries: http://www.australiacouncil.gov.au/resources/reports_and_publications/subjects/arts_sector/arts_and_creative_industries
Beilharz, P. (2005). Alienation. In G. Ritzer (Ed.), *Encyclopedia of social theory* (Vol. 1) (pp. 9–10). Thousand Oaks, CA: Sage.
Bilton, C. (2007). *Management and creativity: From creative industries to creative management*. Boston, MA: Wiley Blackwell.
Caves, R. E. (2000). *Creative industries: Contracts between art and commerce*. Boston, MA: Harvard University Press.
Craft, A. (2005). *Creativity in schools: Tensions and dilemmas*. Abingdon: Routledge.
Craft, A., Jeffrey, B., & Leibling, M. (Eds). (2001). *Creativity in education*. London/New York, UK/ NY: Continuum.
Davies, R., & Sigthorsson, G. (2012). *Introducing the creative industries: from theory to practice*. Los Angeles, CA: Sage.
DiMaggio, P. (2005). Cultural capital. In G. Ritzer (Ed.), *Encyclopedia of social theory* (Vol 1) (pp. 167–170). Thousand Oaks, CA: Sage.
Flew, T. (2012). *Creative industries: Culture and policy*. London/Thousand Oaks: Sage.
Florida, R. (2007). *The flight of the creative class: The new global competition for talent*. New York, NY: HarperCollins.
Government UK (Department for Culture, Media & Sport). (2013). *Budget 2013: Boost for creative industries sector*. Retrieved March 20, 2013, from https://www.gov.uk/government/news/budget-2013-boost-for-creative-industries-sector
Hartley, J., Potts, J., Cunningham, S., Flew, T., Keane, M., & Banks, J. (2013). *Key concepts in creative industries*. London, UK: Sage.
Herbert, A. (2010). *The pedagogy of creativity*. Abingdon: Routledge.
Kratke, S. (2012). *The creative capital of cities: Interactive knowledge creation and the urbanization economies of innovation*. Malden, MA/Oxford: Wiley Blackwell.

Lazzeretti, L. (Ed). (2012). *Creative industries and innovation in Europe: Concepts, measures and comparative case studies*. Abingdon: Routledge.

Mockros, C., & Csikszentmihalyi, M. (1999). The social construction of creative lives. In A. Montuori & R. Purser (Eds.), *Social creativity* (Vol. 1). NJ: Hampton Press.

NACCCE. (1999). *All our futures: Creativity, culture and education*. London, UK: Department for Education and Employment.

Potts, J. (2011). *Creative industries and economic evolution*. Cheltenham, UK / Northampton, MA: Elgar.

Ritzer, G. (2005). Means of Consumption. In G. Ritzer (Ed.), *Encyclopedia of social theory* (Vol. 1) (pp. 491–499).Thousand Oaks: Sage.

Robinson, K. (2008). *Sir Ken Robinson on the power of the imaginative mind (part one)*. Retrieved from Transcript. Edutopia: http://www.edutopia.org/sir-ken-robinson-creativity-part-one-video

Robbins, B. (2003). Cosmopolitanism, America, and the welfare state. In W. Fluck & T. Claviez (Eds.), *Theories of American culture: Theories of American studies* (pp. 201–224). Tubingen: Gunter Narr Verlag.

Savage, S., & Hickey-Moody, A. (2010). Global flows as gendered cultural pedagogies: Learning gangsta in the 'Durty South'. *Critical Studies in Education, 51*(3), 277–293.

Schneider, F., Haigner, S. D., & Wakolbinger, F. (2010). *The Berlin creative industries: An empirical analysis of future key industries*. Berlin: Gabler Verlag.

Sternberg, R. J., & Lubart, T. I. (1999). The concept of creativity: Prospects and paradigms. In R. J. Sternberg (Ed.), *Handbook of creativity* (pp. 3–15). New York, NY: Cambridge University Press.

Weckerle, C., Gerig, M., & Sondermann, M. (2008). *Creative industries Switzerland: Facts, models, culture*. The Netherlands: Springer.

Wurzburger, R., Aageson, T., Pattakos, A., & Pratt, S. (2009). *Creative tourism: A global conversation*. Santa Fe, NM: Sunstone Press.

CHAPTER 9

OUR CREATIVE CENTURY

Toward a New Aesthetic Imaginary

Figure 15. Melbourne graffiti, #7 (2013).

I have talked a lot about inner and outer worlds, but like all oppositions it is a relative one, a convenience of notation. I have talked about beauty, magic, love: knocking these words with one hand, seeming to reach towards them with the other. And yet the paradox is a simple one. All that we see connected with these words seems deadly: what they imply corresponds to what we need. If we do not understand catharsis, that is because it has become identified with an emotional steam bath. If we do not understand tragedy, it is because it has become confused with Acting The King. We may want magic, but we confuse it with hocus-pocus, and we have hopelessly mixed up love with sex, beauty with aestheticism. But it is only by searching for a new discrimination that we will extend the horizons of the real. Only then could the theatre be useful, for we need a beauty which could convince us: we need desperately to experience magic in so direct a way that our very notion of what is substantial could be changed (Brook, 1968, p. 96).

INTRODUCTION

I have argued throughout this text, through a range of lenses, that creativity is being co-opted and commodified by current neoliberalist discourses and increasingly industrial educational practices. This includes but is not limited to a move toward

CHAPTER 9

quantitative measures of educational efficacy, including the ways in which measures of creativity and innovation are rapidly replacing arts education and educational transformation through embodied or experiential art. As Brook implores us to do above, a fruitful focus for wondering about creativity's potential may be through its evolving aesthetic magic, and in retaining our ability to separate it from the hocus-pocus of current commodity needs.

In this concluding chapter I propose a new aesthetic imaginary which blends the emerging creative 'imaginary' of Appadurai (freshly detailed here), in conversation with Deleuze's ontology of creative becoming from Chapter Three. This productive merging of Deleuze and Appadurai was traced through the three case study chapters, with Brooks and Rancière reminding us of the cultural role of art-as-magic. Finally, synthesising Benjamin's and McLuhan's visions of a reproductive art that includes a politics of aesthetics shows us one possible future for our new aesthetic imaginary of the twenty-first century, and some ways in which it may finally find its way into schools. Any aesthetic is embedded interdependently in its historio-cultural moment and place, and so part of understanding the shift toward a new aesthetic orientation lies in understanding or contextualising it within its co-constitutive historio-cultural moment.

Part of any project to trace this creative turn toward a new aesthetics involves mapping a shift in understandings of aesthetics over the recent past, leading up to today. Throughout this book I have tried to do so, drawing on pivotal texts from the past century from a range of disciplines, including more traditional sources like John Dewey's *Art As Experience* (1934), and less obvious ones like Peter Brook's *Deadly Theatre* (1968). Those like Dewey articulated a 'product' versus 'process' binary which remains unresolvable and in some ways is finally being superseded by a more rhizomatic approach that encompasses both and rejects dichotomised approaches in general. Case studies like New York's *Young Playwrights' Festival* and the *Culture Shack* education pathways program reinforce this move beyond such debates. Yet standardised testing and nationalised curricula seem to indicate an inability to embrace a new 'educational imaginary' in that sector. The *SAILing into Uni!* and *Teaching Diversities* case studies exemplify some ways in which a new educational imaginary is sprouting from outside of schools. Such institutional innovations are calling out for change, and can be seen in new possibilities like MOOCs and Open Access Learning and Publishing as two education-related examples, but institutional change is still slow to come.

This closing chapter articulates a new vision for the ways in which western culture is moving toward a more pragmatic conceptualisation of creativity and its place in emerging global economies. While education and health sectors continue to struggle with the ways in which creativity does or doesn't share intent with arts endeavours and arts identities, new conceptions of creativity and our shared need for its skills and dispositions continues to grow. This chapter suggests some new ways of looking at, nurturing and thinking about creativity as a rhizomatic and increasingly fluid component of our ever-expanding knowledge economy, particularly in relation to market innovation and new institutional and educational structures.

Turn, Turn, Turn

For more than three decades, Eisner (and Dewey before him) has argued the value of attending to process rather than product in creative endeavour in schools, and the ways in which process is also inseparably aligned with aesthetics. Now creative industries experts are doing the same, and while the focus is on industry and productivity, the role of aesthetics has once again emerged to the forefront. From Pixar to Apple to other industry innovators, creativity is increasingly seen as good business as well as beautiful business. Renaissance ideals of the rarefied artist who works apart from the marketplace rough-and-tumble of business and industry are being replaced by the possibility that creative dispositions can co-exist with industry acumen—all pivoting on aesthetic craft. While various authors (both popular and scholarly) have recently attempted to define, codify and schematise creativity (Araya & Peters, 2010; Murphy, Peters & Marginson, 2010; Sefton-Green & Soep, 2007; Florida, 2007; Bamford, 2006), this chapter argues that our insatiable emerging knowledge economy has need for multiple and diverse forms of creative and aesthetic productivity (and process) that are not mutually exclusive. In Chapter Six I claimed that aesthetics had become the domain of philosophers and had been abandoned by educators almost completely. This chapter extends that critique by proposing a new aesthetic imaginary and the as-yet unanswered question of where our current lines of aesthetic flight may be leading. Because while aesthetics have seemingly moved away from education, they are moving rapidly toward industry, but a new kind of industry based on a reproducible aesthetic for a new era.

McLuhan articulated a 'technology of typography' and how it foregrounds certain things (like individuation and linearity) and backgrounds others (like intersubjectivity and causality, or what he calls 'interplay'). Most importantly, he established throughout his work that each new technological innovation has wide and long-term repercussions for not only the way things get made (the medium), or even the *content* of those things (the message), but indeed alters the way we think about those and all other things around us—in other words, it universally alters our perception of self and other. In a sense, McLuhan telescopes Benjamin's deep analysis of one 'turn' into a long-view of history, reminding us that this has been happening at deeper levels than we realise since reflexivity began.

In Chapter Seven, I established productive links between McLuhan and Appadurai and their views of a contemporary mediascape and its cultural implications. In *The Global Village* (McLuhan & Powers, 1989), McLuhan argues that their 'creative turn' is a shift from visual to acoustic space, with the advent of online technology and digital culture, while both he and Appadurai's mediascapes problematise an ability to cognitively keep pace with this new model. McLuhan claims that "Acoustic Space is multisensory" (p. 187), and asserts that modern man is still stuck in 17th-century sequentialism, linearity and left-brain logic—not unlike the claim Robinson makes against modern schools being stuck in outmoded 19th-century industrial models. McLuhan's assertion is even more apparent in our structuring of curricula, which are all highly sequentialised, linear and logic-driven. This way of thinking, he suggests, is not only out of date, but also incompatible with digital technologies, communities and forms of cognition. Critics have noted McLuhan's vague non-definitional use of the term 'media', and in this text I have argued its parallel is the current slippery use of the term creativity. Yet McLuhan returns us to Benjamin's aura with aesthetic and affective implications in many ways beyond what Appadurai's imaginary offers, and equally beyond Benedict Anderson's imagined communities. What then, might a new aesthetic imaginary entail?

McLuhan might have suggested that the current relationship between creativity, aesthetics and innovation must by its nature be altered by current shifts in digital technology. In this book I've argued that the current creative turn is a fundamental shift away from the way we have previously thought about creativity, brought on by the awakening of the aesthetic potential of digital technology. While this may be superficially evident in form, content and even interactivity, Appadurai still asks us to dig deeper in understanding the *perceptual* shift this turn is engendering, and which is still only in its infancy, rather than rest with its embodiment. In the next section I will draw on Anderson to help consider the perceptual implications of this aesthetic expansion.

An Aesthetic Imaginary that Transcends Both the Nation and the 'Scape'

> ... modern consumption seeks to replace the aesthetics of duration with the aesthetics of ephemerality (Appadurai, 1996, p. 85)

What does Appadurai's core notion of the mediascape suggest about aesthetics? His "general theory of global cultural processes" (1996, p. 45) focuses on five "streams or flows along which cultural material may be seen to be moving across national boundaries" (p. 46). As Anderson breaks down the very notion of nationhood and the construction of boundaries established to contain these 'imagined communities' (to Appadurai they are 'imagined worlds'), online digital technology can be seen as central to both ideas. It certainly has come to function as and also represent a channel through which new communities are imagined, as well as the lines along which these flows can travel. Although I would assert that Appadurai's five 'scapes' are interrelated in a way that paints a complete picture when examined together, it can also be useful to disentangle them to throw a temporary light on particular aspects of a cultural analysis. Let's look for the moment more closely at the notion of *mediascape* alone.

Appadurai borrows, sometimes directly and sometimes indirectly, from theorists we have visited earlier in this text, including Benjamin, Anderson, McLuhan and Deleuze. Like them, he knows that what begins as a "mechanical metaphor" of "disjunctive flows" (p. 46) will have to invariably proceed to alter the nature of human interaction. We are seeing that alteration now, and one arena in which it is most transparent is in the commodification of creativity and its implications for new aesthetic horizons.

Creativity, not unlike nationalism, is "an expression of fundamental human needs (for continuity, for affective bonds) in an age of mechanical reproduction" (Redfield, 2003, p. 48) and into our own digital age as well.

Appadurai argues that we can "speak of some of these flows as being, for a priori structural or historical reasons, always prior to and formative of other flows" (p. 47), and this is the context in which I argue that the current creative turn (or disjunctive flow) is a priori formative of an aesthetic flow to follow. They are interrelated, and they are always related to capital. But Appadurai tentatively also argued that "the relationship of these various flows to one another will be radically context-dependent" (p. 47). So how does this context-dependence intersect with the global transnationality of online imaginaries? Like the participants of *Culture Shack*, *Teaching Diversities* and *SAILing into Uni*, transnational youth are increasingly representative of Appadurai's mediascapes burst beyond the ethnoscapes-in-motion that they emerged to represent. They are "terminological kaleidoscopes" (p. 37) and represent both the local and the global simultaneously. Any new aesthetic imaginary is also by its nature a combination of the local and global flows from which it simultaneously emerges.

Anderson uses Benjamin's notion of "a simultaneity of past and future in an instantaneous present" (p. 24), surely a core characteristic of any new aesthetic. They both suggest that our inability to turn our faces to the future, through remaining shackled nostalgically to the past, is our greatest challenge for understanding the possibility and the chaos of the present turn. This is, for Anderson, not only an examination of nationalism, but of humanism itself.

Redfield (2003) deploys Anderson's work to make more explicit links between the persistent function of nation-states and their relationship to aesthetics:

> The state's core mission thus becomes pedagogical: its job is to acculturate its subjects into citizens. The production of a docile citizenry thereby obtains an ethical aura and an aesthetic character, insofar as the artwork—and the domain of aesthetic or 'cultural' experience generally—become imaginable as disinterested spaces in which the subject of aesthetic education achieves a proleptic, formal moment of identification with humanity per se (p. 47).

Further, he suggests "the roots of the association between these two romantic inventions—imagination and nation—run very deep indeed" (p. 47). I extend that premise here by suggesting that creativity too is a romantic invention, which serves the nation now more than ever, and which is not contingent upon aesthetics. Like the ways in which *Imagined Communities* both "opens up and veers away from a critique of aesthetic nationalism" (Redfield, 2003, p. 48), the current creative turn is equally a narrative of contamination and loss. This contemporary commodification of creativity creates new imagined communities, organised around capital-driven but not nation-contingent groupings. It too, allows us to locate the possibility of aesthetic formalization—the engine of modernity's aesthetic narrative—in a 'prior' condition of anonymity, contamination, and loss, a predicament that aesthetic narrative both forecloses and records. Anderson's text suggests that the 'imagined community' of the nation develops in productive tension with the conditions of mechanical reproduction that make it possible, and that imagining the nation entails fantasies about communication and technology, and the production of gendered and irretrievably mournful scenes of pedagogy (Redfield, p. 48).

This inextricable relationship between reproducibility and loss, aesthetics and commodification, extends both Benjamin and Anderson in ways that allow us to think about what a new aesthetic imaginary might entail. If aesthetics is no longer shackled to profitability but rather to ubiquity (the natural extension of reproducibility), the aesthetic transcends anything like mechanisation and becomes self-proliferating (or takes on what Anderson calls "infinite reproducibility" [p. 186]). Imagining new communities—in relation to these new aesthetics—becomes a limitless and simultaneously local/global set of fantasies.

But are we really post-national yet? Cosmopolitanism suggests new forms of thinking about and cohering as globalised communities, and theorists have considered post-national boundaries and ties in a range of disciplines and endeavours. Yet, Anderson's text suggests an inextricable link between aesthetics and any imagined community, particularly ones that require imagination—such as the nation—that cannot be directly experienced or encompassed. The virtual worlds of social media and online exchange represent new extensions of imagined communities, and ones which may demand even finer aesthetic consideration than the nation did. But how does the nation—or by extension online engagement—"*as* 'imagined', inevitably become the object of aesthetic pedagogy" (Redfield, 2003, p. 48)?

Redfield says "the nation, like one's own death, cannot be imagined and can only be imagined; inevitably—if often in banal and prefabricated ways" (p. 50). Creativity too is periodically imagined in such banal and prefabricated ways, and I argue this is one of those times. Aesthetics may be a way forward, and it increasingly functions as an organising principle in online and digital data overload. Until now, the great technological leap has been concerned with presence. Beyond the most basic visuality of online presence, aesthetics have played a supporting role. But as the sheer volume of data available online threatens to drown even the most innovative of creative users, aesthetics may find itself once again front and centre.

If, as Redfield asserts, "Anderson's great Benjaminian argument in *Imagined Communities* derives the possibility of this imaginative act out of developments in reproductive and communicational technologies" (p. 50), our new aesthetic imaginary might newly humanise the anonymity of the early creative explosion of online technology. In the same way that 'print-capitalism' in Benjamin's analysis made possible what Redfield calls the "fundamentally anonymous community of the nation-state" (p. 50) become imaginable, so too the digital/creative revolution makes a new aesthetic become imaginable. Throughout this text I have attempted to advocate that this present moment heralds the advent of a new kind of imagined community based in aesthetics. While Anderson credits print-capitalism with the material production of national consciousness or "nationally imagined community"

(p. 48) for the first time, I am arguing that digital technology and the commodification of creativity is now facilitating a new consciousness embedded in aesthetics as a unifying factor (rather than language), one that transcends (but is not exclusive from) nationality, or the nation-state. This is an extension of what Benjamin calls the "shock experience, the shattering of the aura" (in Redfield, p. 52). But if so, what aura is being shattered by today's Turn; what are the aesthetic implications or responsibilities of a globalisation of creativity?

A return to Appadurai may assist us in proposing our new aesthetic imaginary that draws on but goes beyond his 'scapes'. Firstly, he suggests that contemporary engagements with online technology represent a "cyber-proletarianization" (2000, p. 2), focusing on the structural impact of global flows mediated by digital technology. Until now, globalisation is evolving along a "double apartheid" (p. 3), characterised by a divorce between the first form—western internal or parochial concerns that can be characterised as "Americanization disguised as human rights or as MTV" (p. 2)—and the second form which Appadurai calls that of the poor, or "globalizations from below" (p. 3).

Like the case studies here of *Culture Shack* and *Teaching Diversities*, Appadurai notes the significance of 'globalisations from below', simultaneously embedded in the local and global, a kind of imaginary globalisation "which strives for a democratic and autonomous standing in respect to the various forms by which global power further seeks to extend its dominion" (2001, p. 3). The case study examining the *Young Playwrights' Festival* might represent Appadurai's first form, which is characteristically western, inward-gazing, and concerned to a greater degree with commodity or market concerns than with proletarianisation. The two forms are, as Appadurai suggests, fairly divorced from each other politically and constitutively, yet may represent a kind of democratisation of digital technology (or at least access to online spaces).

These case studies equally illustrate the central role that digital media plays in creating a new aesthetic imaginary as a globalised phenomenon, as it offers consumers the capability to imagine regions and worlds—and indeed to interact with them—in new and powerful ways. That is, due to the activities of migrants, media, capital, tourism, and so forth, the means for imagining never-to-be-encountered strangers, regions, and practices is now itself globally available to the proletariat. This is crucially intertwined with Anderson's notion of the pedagogical role of aesthetics, in ways that creativity has long since abandoned.

In the Australian pedagogical context, Lassig (2009) and others continue to draw from a discourse of creativity increasingly divorced from aesthetics. The scholarship employed includes that of Ken Robinson, Anna Craft, and Sefton-Green and Soep (in or about the UK), the Centre for Creativity and Innovation (in Australia, where Lassig writes from), and Czikszentmihalyi (in the USA). But the emerging discourse of creativity-as-innovation in the Pacific Rim is equally devoid of aesthetic considerations. Is the de-aestheticising of creativity-as-commodity a characteristic of its servitude to capitalism and globalised economics?

CHAPTER 9

Much discussion within education remains distracted by the search for a creativity metric (alternatively for the measurement of levels of creativity, the optimal conditions for nurturing creativity, and for the commodity value of creative outputs), and a globalisation of creativity discourse. Creativity is largely homeless, moving constantly between education disciplines of the 'gifted and talented', science, mathematics and, infrequently, arts education. Creativity studies in education remain entwined with scientific approaches to 'specialness' and academic achievement, rather than aesthetics and process. These widely divergent aspects of creativity keep the focus of its study dispersed, with the commodity-inflected foci far more highly funded. For this reason, the value of the arts, artmaking or aesthetics remains marginal and low-status. Where they overlap, as stated in the introduction to this book and elsewhere throughout, arts education has become informed by 'professional' or outsourced arts practice through creative partnerships models. What role then can educational enquiry into creativity possibly have in a globalised discourse of the commodification of creativity?

TOWARD A NEW AESTHETIC IMAGINARY

Appadurai argues for a "diversion of commodities from their original nexus" (1986, p. 28) which, when considered alongside my previous engagement with Benjamin in Chapter Seven, can tell us much about the additional aesthetic potential of our own digital century. Apart from understanding the mechanics of how aesthetic considerations are affected by changing the mechanics or technologies of how they are produced, it is helpful to return to the culturally constitutive role aesthetics plays in how we see ourselves. For a moment, let us turn to Castronovo for help.

Castronovo notes the political power of aesthetics to revolutionise thinking and social behaviour. He claims that aesthetics philosophers and social movements (including in education) have always been closer than we imagine, but particularly so now. For Castronovo, aesthetics is concerned with form, and form is a cultural construction. Can aesthetics bear a direct impact on social reform? At the turn of the 20th century aesthetics played a considerable role in a new democracy and its global dissemination, a social role that by its nature demanded a "fundamental heteronomy that is an inescapable aspect of aesthetics" (2007, p. 194). In our own turn of the century, the aesthetic turn precipitated by a creative coming-of-age in digital technology suggests a move from the current aesthetic homogeneity to an explosion of aesthetic heterogeneity, which Castronovo calls the ways in which "the universal simply cannot avoid the foreign" (p. 194). It is impossible to separate the aesthetic from other cultural scapes, because of its inherent nature as "traversed by multiple vectors of the specific and the abstract," (2007, p. 185), a kind of being in difference that innately resists homogenisation.

Aesthetics are anything but universal. They are class-, geography- and historically-based, and for this reason, Castronovo is able to demonstrate the relationship between aesthetics and violence, a symptom of difference; as he claims, "aesthetics never escape from the unfamiliar and foreign—even if that contact is primarily negative" (p. 192). Digitality now serves the homogeneity impulse, unifying a kind of sameness aesthetic globally much more easily than any previous era; yet difference continues to emerge. When theories of aesthetics have arisen periodically in attempts to determine and impose supposed universal definitions on (usually under-) classes by bourgeois elites, all hell breaks loose—as history has shown multiple times. The site of this tension in current contexts is surely in the online digital world.

Is there—or has there ever been—a universal or inherent understanding of aesthetics, beauty or creativity? They have always been aligned with cultural values, and these strongly influenced and disseminated by the upper classes. Appadurai sees aesthetics (and imagination) as an escape from the shackles of corporate or political determinism. While he does not see aesthetic sensibilities as individual, the universality of Appadurai's notion is more closely aligned with a Jungian collective unconscious than a McLuhanian global village.

Through a Castronovian lens, a new aesthetic imaginary (or aesthetic imagination as he calls it) "always contains materials that are other to it" (p. 186), and therefore is both itself and its Other. On the web, too often,

> ... it's not just sound that is being turned into a consumable good but the concept of creativity itself. . . . Appadurai could be right about the newly empowered imagination, but at the same time one has to note that the imagination and creativity are being commodified with sales talk (Taylor, 2007, p. 136).

So how is it possible—if indeed it is—to separate this commodified sales talk from creativity itself? And how to separate a new aesthetics from new commodities?

I have not attempted to do so, or to suggest that new media, creative industries, aesthetics and philosophy of art are incompatible enquiries. I have chosen instead to look at the ways in which innovation has become synonymous with creativity, and industry with aesthetics. Questions concerning the new imaginaries into which this turn might take us remain to be answered, but I hope this text goes some way toward untangling threads that are increasingly tightly intertwined. If we take as a starting point the ways in which Benjamin and McLuhan have, before us, attempted to cast light on the cultural implications of the creative and innovative turns of their own times, and apply Appadurai's notions of the imaginary and mediascapes to our own turn, I suggest we might be better able to discern some patterns of a new aesthetics that is emerging in relation to both our history and our current moment. That moment is informed not only by the exciting and sometimes homogenising new developments in economics, education and cultural cognition, but by a history of aesthetics and creativity. Understanding the place of our current turn, and its relation to these many cultural tentacles, may help orient us as the new aesthetic imaginary unfolds.

CHAPTER 9

Conclusion

In Chapter One, I introduced the possibility that creativity is being co-opted and repackaged as 'innovation' in education discourses, and linked to notions of productivity. This discursive refocus comes at the same time as a systematic diminishing of arts education (hours) in standardised curricula across the globe, and an outsourcing of creative arts engagement through 'creative partnership' models to non-teaching artist professionals. The implications for this in both primary and secondary education contexts seem tied to the productivity imperative in 'creative industries' discourses, which seek to irrevocably link productivity to legitimate creative pursuit—in other words, no other arts practice is particularly relevant to governments and the economic 'global village'. At the same time, this 'productive creativity' imperative is increasingly concerned with aesthetics as a part of its commodity value. We have certainly moved on from a more 1970s-era 'process' era in arts education and, despite a democratisation of online publication through social media and other digital dissemination methods (which one might imagine would make aesthetics less of a concern), aesthetics have jumped to the forefront in establishing commodity value for creative products. Seminal examples are the iPhone and most Mac products, known primarily for their aesthetic superiority to other products that do the same thing. So too in creative industries, and creative industries training at the tertiary level, aesthetics are re-emerging as a central concern.

Why then do primary and secondary schools continue to ignore the role of aesthetics in creative skills development? Chapter Three explored some ways in which there is already a change-or-die imperative present in schools. This might be correlated with with the steady turn toward outsourcing creative arts engagement in 'creative partnership' models (widespread in the US and UK, incoming in Australia and elsewhere) as a silent nod toward the 'professionalisation' of arts engagement in schools. Yet aesthetics remain absent from the discourse.

In the case studies examined in Chapters Two, Five and Seven, it is clear that aesthetics in pedagogical community arts projects like these are central to the youth participants when creating arts products, engaging creatively together, or trusting the professional artists with whom they might work. Even in the Young Playwrights Festival reminiscences from nearly three decades ago, the alumni all cited working with theatre professionals and attending to aesthetics collaboratively as a central benefit of that experience in terms of affecting their personal and professional development in the ensuing years.

Yet in Chapter Four and Chapter Six I problematised the relationships between aesthetics and ethics, and aesthetics and innovation—and asked whether as a threesome they are interconnected. This text builds an argument toward identifying an emerging new aesthetic, one that is firmly interconnected with innovation and productivity (or what Benjamin and others have called reproducibility). Here I am arguing that this new aesthetic has a new ethics all its own; that, like other creative turns which are equally (irrevocably) culturally-embedded and culturally-altering, this turn is irrevocably altering our ethical structures as well. Like Benjamin, Rancière and McLuhan on whom I have drawn, I do not limit this aesthetically-affected alteration to ethics only. However, I do claim that this new ethics is not yet recognisable as a permanent shift in culture, and that by looking to our changing aesthetic we can better understand its ethical implications. This book urges schools to change their perceptual and processual focus more quickly than they are doing.

Chapter Eight asked the difficult question of whether the creative industries can deliver a comprehensive new creative imaginary for our rapidly-changing global culture, or whether this new creative imaginary will be limited by them. Industry-related creativity (commodified creativity) is certainly driving creative cultures and discourses today; indeed, even a superficial look at the history of artmaking and patronage confirms that economics has always been inextricable from the industry of art. However, conflating 'creativity' and 'commodity' or 'industry' so directly is new, and offers potential benefits but also potential dangers. One such danger is the narrowing of notions of creativity, the homogenising of art and creative products (if not practices). In Chapter Six I explored some strong signs that already the kinds of creative endeavours that the UK, Australian and US governments are willing to invest in are becoming increasingly homogeneous.

So where to from here? This book returns us to aesthetics in order to understand our current turn and where it may be leading us. A new aesthetic imaginary co-constituted by creative industries imperatives, however, does not mean that we will not continue to yearn for less-commodified processes or products, that in fact the next turn may not be away from commodification itself and back toward what Benjamin called the 'aura' of artworks. In the meantime, this text seeks to help us move forward with eyes wide open, and to integrate this cultural transit better in our training of the next generations who will have to navigate what we are creatively, educationally, and productively establishing today. As Brook reminds all theatre-makers, artists, and educators:

> If our language must correspond with our age, then we must also accept that today roughness is livelier, and holiness deadlier, than at other times. Once, the theatre could begin as magic: magic at the sacred festival, or magic as the footlights came up. Today, it is the other way round. The theatre is hardly wanted and its workers are hardly trusted. So we cannot assume that the audience will assemble devoutly and attentively. It is up to us to capture its attention and compel its belief. To do so we must prove that there will be no trickery, nothing hidden. We must open our empty hands and show that really there is nothing up our sleeves. Only then can we begin (1968, p. 97).

We too must move beyond current educational and even industrial trickery to return to the magic of creating—intellectually, culturally and aesthetically. It is my sincere hope that this book goes some way toward assisting in that process.

REFERENCES

Anderson, B. (2006). *Imagined Communities: Reflections on the origin and spread of nationalism.* London/New York, UK/NY: Verso.
Appadurai, A. (2000). Grassroots globalization and the research imagination. In A. Appadurai (Ed.), *Globalization* (pp. 1–21). Durham, NC: Duke University Press.
Appadurai, A. (1996). *Modernity at large: Cultural dimensions of globalization.* Minneapolis, MN: University of Minnesota Press.
Appadurai, A. (Ed.). (1986). *Social life of things: Commodities in cultural perspective.* Cambridge MA: Cambridge University Press.
Araya, D., & Peters, M. (Eds). (2010). *Education in the creative economy: Knowledge and learning in the age of innovation.* New York, NY: Peter Lang.
Bamford, A. (2006). *The wow factor: Global research compendium on the impacts of arts in education.* New York, NY: Waxman Munster.
Brook, P. (1968). *The empty space.* New York, NY: Atheneum.
Castronovo, R. (2007). *Beautiful democracy: Aesthetics and anarchy in a global era.* London, UK: University of Chicago Press.
Dewey, J. (1934/2005). *Art as experience.* New York, NY: Perigree Books/Penguin.
Florida, R. (2007). *The flight of the creative class: The new global competition for talent.* New York, NY: HarperCollins.
Lassig, C. (2009, October 27–30). *Promoting creativity in education: from policy to practice: an Australian perspective.* In Proceedings, the 7th ACM Conference on Creativity and Cognition: Everyday Creativity, University of California, Berkeley, CA.
McLuhan, M., & Powers, B. R. (1989). *The global village: Transformations in world life and media in the 21st century.* New York, NY: Oxford University Press.
Redfield, M. (2003). *The politics of aesthetics: Nationalism, gender, romanticism.* Stanford, CA: Stanford University Press.
Murphy, P., Peters, M., & Marginson, S. (2010). *Imagination: Three models of imagination in the age of the knowledge economy.* New York, NY: Peter Lang.
Sefton-Green, J., & Soep, E. (2007) Creative media cultures: Making and learning beyond the school. In L. Bresler (Ed.), *International handbook of research in arts education* (pp. 835–854). The Netherlands: Springer.
Taylor, T. D. (2007). *Beyond exoticism: Western music and the world.* Durham, NC: Duke University Press.

INDEX

Academic, 3, 7–9, 26, 64, 68, 77, 78, 82, 88, 102, 103, 105, 106, 110, 157, 178
Aesthetic/s, anti-aesthetic, 6, 89, 93, 115
Affective, 6, 14, 18, 24, 70, 98, 102, 132, 164, 167, 174, 175
Anderson, Benedict, 5, 13, 15, 117, 118, 124, 151–153, 161, 163, 164, 166, 167, 168, 174–177
Animation, 14, 69, 106, 127, 128, 130, 134–139, 142, 144, 147, 148, 152
Appadurai, 4, 5, 11–13, 76, 118, 124, 136, 148, 151, 152, 160, 164–167, 172–175, 177–179
  tournaments of value, 12, 130, 163, 166, 168
  imaginary, 5, 152, 174
  mediascapes, ethnoscapes, 4, 6, 14, 120, 144, 173, 174, 175, 179
Apple, 4, 5, 27, 75, 173
Artist, 2, 3, 4, 10, 40, 42, 49, 67, 74, 106, 132, 139, 146, 147, 152, 164, 173, 180
art, 25–27
  education, 3, 5, 7, 8, 9, 11, 18, 19, 24, 44, 68, 69, 74, 81, 91, 108, 116, 118, 119, 122, 130, 131, 141, 155, 156, 159, 162, 167, 168, 172, 178, 180
assemblage/s, 12
assessment, 8, 9, 20, 22, 45, 67, 68, 75, 77, 120–124
at-risk, 109
aura, 25–28, 108, 130, 131, 146, 147, 174, 175, 177, 181
beauty, 6–7, 13, 79, 84, 131, 132, 146, 171, 179

Barone, 8
Benjamin, 2, 5, 9, 14, 26, 53, 57, 60, 65, 66, 75, 76, 79, 108, 117, 124, 127–135, 138, 145–148, 160, 166, 168, 169, 174, 176–181
Brecht, Bertolt, 21, 22, 84
Bresler, Liora, 9, 81
Brook, Peter, 54, 55–66, 71, 171, 172, 181
Bruner, 7, 8, 68
Business, 2, 4, 8, 12, 21, 23, 27, 41, 48, 49, 54, 57, 58, 59, 64, 68, 78, 81, 114, 120, 143, 152, 154, 158, 164, 168, 173
Butler, 4, 101
Castronovo, 13, 178
capacity-building, 7
CCI (Centre of Excellence for Creative Industries and Innovation), 155, 156, 158
Chaos, 6, 10, 74, 76, 91, 92, 144, 175
Cizek, 7
Collaboration, 10, 25, 26, 44, 50, 61, 63, 76, 88, 98, 105, 110, 134, 135, 137, 139, 158
cormier, Dave, 25, 26, 70, 77
Costantino, Tracie, 67
Craft, Anna, 3, 8, 17, 24, 25, 59, 117, 122, 123, 161–164, 173, 177
Creative/ity
  capacities, 7, 51, 59, 81, 92, 101, 103, 154
  capital, 1–15
  creative education, 3, 56, 57, 59, 64, 71, 77
  creative industries, 151–167
  creative learning, 3, 8, 18, 24, 25, 27, 123, 124, 161, 162

INDEX

creative partnerships, 49, 67, 68, 143, 152, 178
creative pedagogies, 3, 8, 9, 18, 24, 49, 51, 67, 68, 98, 105, 108, 123, 124, 155, 161, 162, 168
creative thinking, 2, 24, 31, 92, 157
  democratisation of creativity, 2, 83, 132
  dispositions, 9, 13, 31, 35, 44, 50, 77, 172, 173
  mastery, 2, 3, 63
  philosophy of creativity, 2
Commodity/ies, 2, 3, 5, 11, 18, 26, 79, 83, 84, 108, 113, 114, 117, 124, 132, 134, 153, 154, 158, 159, 165, 166, 167, 172, 177–181
Consumer, 20, 26, 74, 115, 160
Contingency, 14, 15
creative turn, 17–28
Critical, criticality, 22, 93, 134, 135
Cropley, A., 18, 81
Culture, 127–148
Curriculum, 17, 22, 27, 35, 54, 56, 57, 61, 64, 67, 69, 90, 105, 108, 109, 120–123, 152, 156, 162, 163
Csikszentmihalyi, M., 9, 31, 76, 80, 82, 83, 120, 121
Cyberculture, 128
Cult value, 127, 128, 131, 132
Deadly, theatre, 55–58, 60–62, 147
Deaducation, 53–71
Deleuze, Giles & Guattari, Felix, 2, 14, 21, 73–79, 81–84, 85, 90, 93, 118, 132, 172, 174
Denzin, Norman K., 4, 70, 77, 89, 93
Dewey, John, 7, 56, 74, 75, 77, 84, 130, 172, 173
Digital
  digital media, digital art, 9, 110, 129, 131, 143, 148
Dimitriadis, Greg, 54, 56, 66, 70, 74, 105

Dispositions, 9, 13, 31, 35, 44, 50, 77, 172, 173
Diversity, 12, 13, 17, 26, 83, 90, 133, 134, 138–144
Domains, 9, 83, 99
Economic, 3, 6, 9, 12, 14, 17, 18, 19, 23, 24, 27, 49, 55, 57, 58, 60, 63, 64, 65, 70, 81, 83, 101, 103, 115, 122, 123, 124, 128, 129, 130, 144, 145, 152, 153, 155, 157, 159, 165, 166, 168, 180
Eisner, Elliot, 7, 8, 67, 68, 70, 81, 122, 123, 173
embodied, embodiment, 3, 4, 5, 54, 109, 132, 148, 172
- embodied performativity, 4
Ethics, 73–92, 114, 144, 180, 181
Ethnocinema, 87, 90
Ethnoscapes, 4, 151, 175
Ewing, Robyn, 49
Exhibition value, 128, 131, 134
Failure, 15, 18, 19–21, 23, 25, 90, 103, 120
Fear, 11, 59, 60, 82, 103, 155
fine arts, 2, 11, 76, 113, 116
Florida, Richard, 9, 18, 25, 27, 67, 122, 154, 173
Flow, 5, 14, 61, 76, 80, 83, 121, 145, 166, 167, 175
Future, 2, 4, 5, 15, 17, 28, 53, 54, 68, 108, 122, 143, 146, 155, 159, 163, 165, 172, 175
Gardner, Howard, 7, 8, 9, 24, 81, 91
Gibson, Robin, 49
Giroux, Henry, 23, 167
global, globalised, globalisation, 4–6, 9, 10, 11, 12, 18, 19, 25, 26, 33, 41, 53–55, 57–60, 67–71, 77, 80–84, 101, 103, 114, 117, 118, 120, 124, 128, 129, 144, 146, 152, 155, 156, 158–161, 163–165, 167, 172, 173–181

184

INDEX

pedagogies of creativity, 3, 8, 9, 18, 24, 49, 51, 67, 68, 98, 105, 108–109, 123, 124, 155, 161, 162, 168
elites, 60, 70, 84, 117, 120, 168, 179
economics, 5, 6, 7, 10, 14, 18, 57, 74, 81, 114, 115, 153, 158, 159, 177, 179, 181
global flows, 10, 60, 89, 114, 117, 124, 156, 159, 164, 167, 175, 177
Greene, Maxine, 8, 9, 67
Harris, Anne, 4, 21, 36–40, 45, 54, 59, 67, 69, 74, 77, 88, 98, 103, 106, 131, 134, 136–138, 140, 141, 143
Heath (Shirley Brice Heath), 8
Heathcote, 7
Hickey-Moody, 4, 76, 159, 167
Hunter, Mary Ann, 9
Imaginary
  pedagogical imaginary, 74
  aesthetic imaginary, 6, 15, 74, 108, 117, 124, 148, 154, 159, 168, 169, 171–177, 178–181
Imagine, imagination, 7, 8, 9, 12, 14, 21, 26, 76, 110, 118, 122, 160, 162, 164–168, 175, 176, 179
Imagined communities (Anderson), 5, 12, 15, 117, 151–153, 161, 164, 168, 174–176
Industry, 2–4, 7, 8, 11, 13, 18–20, 22, 27, 33, 42, 45, 49, 50, 54, 55, 57, 59, 62, 65, 66, 67, 84, 106, 114, 116, 119, 133, 152, 155 158, 160, 161, 163, 168, 173, 179, 181
Innovation
Interculturality, 6
Jones, Ken, 8
Learning, 3, 8, 9, 14, 17–19, 22–27, 33, 44, 50, 51, 54, 56, 57, 59–62, 64, 66, 68–70, 82, 83, 91, 98, 101–103, 105–107, 109, 110, 118, 121, 122–124, 128, 161–163, 167, 172

Lehrer, Jonah, 18, 21, 22, 23, 25, 27
Lines of flight (Deleuze), 75, 76, 80, 92, 152
Magic, 56, 121, 127, 171, 172, 181
market, marketplace
Massumi, Brian, 6, 14, 18, 21, 22, 25, 26, 27, 97–99, 109, 110, 165
Mastery, 2, 3, 63
McGarry, 31–33, 43–45, 49, 50
McLuhan, Marshall, 1, 2, 5, 14, 65, 127–135, 143, 145–148, 173, 174, 179, 181
McWilliam, Erica, 6, 9, 11
Mechanical (reproduction), 6, 124, 127, 130–133, 146, 175, 176
media
mediascapes, 14, 173, 174
mobility, 6, 12
muse, 2, 4, 10, 157
myth, 6
neoliberal, 3, 12, 15, 18, 25, 59–61, 63, 74, 79, 84, 89, 92, 114, 154, 163, 168
numeracy and literacy, 2, 7, 14
O'Gorman and Werry, 18–20
Participation, 3, 98, 100, 110, 117, 140, 146, 147
Pedagogy, 3,9, 17, 22, 23, 54, 55, 61, 64, 90, 92, 97, 99, 102, 105, 106, 108, 110, 120, 162–164, 166, 167, 176
Performance, performative, performed, 4, 5, 20, 21, 26, 27, 49, 50, 55, 61, 76, 89
  performative research, 4
  performance ethnography, 5
Pixar, 4, 5, 27, 59, 173
play
playwright, 3, 32, 34, 36, 41, 43–45, 48, 50
  theatre, 21, 32, 33, 34, 35, 37, 38, 40–45, 50, 54–64, 66, 71, 133, 147, 152, 171, 172, 180, 181

185

process, 3, 10, 32, 38, 41, 42, 50, 75–77, 81, 90, 91, 105, 118, 133, 134, 136, 144, 145, 154, 157, 159, 162, 173, 174, 178, 180
product/s, 10, 12, 24, 25, 43, 57, 65, 68, 71, 75, 76, 77, 79, 80, 82, 90, 115, 122, 129, 132, 139, 144, 152, 157, 161, 165–167, 180, 181
   creative products, 10, 65, 68, 80, 82, 180, 181
   productivity, 4, 5, 11, 13, 15, 18, 19, 21, 22, 55, 58, 59, 60, 62, 63, 66, 67, 70, 76, 79, 81, 83, 84, 89, 90, 92, 101, 113, 118, 120, 159, 160, 168, 173, 180
Ranciere, 98, 113, 114, 116, 119, 123, 129, 130, 137, 148, 172, 181
Raunig, 118–119
Redfield, 117–118, 175–177
Renaissance, 1, 131, 132, 163, 173
Reproducibility, reproduction, 2, 5, 6, 12, 63, 79, 131, 132, 160, 176, 180
research, researcher, 3, 4, 6, 8, 9, 13, 14, 17, 20, 25, 45, 69, 70, 74, 75, 76, 77, 82, 87–91, 92, 97, 98, 99, 100–103, 105, 106, 108, 109–111, 113, 114, 121, 134, 135, 138–141, 144, 155, 156, 158, 159, 161, 162, 167
resilient, 103, 123
rhizome, rhizomatic, 75, 77, 78
risk/ risky, 4, 13, 15, 18–20, 24, 59, 61, 66, 71, 79, 80, 82, 90, 91, 102, 109, 118, 120
ritual, 4, 121, 127, 128, 131, 132, 144
Robinson, Ken, 6, 8, 11, 19, 24, 25, 27, 64, 70, 123, 173, 177
Salehi, Soodabeh, 10, 18, 19, 76, 78–81, 83, 84, 89, 91–93, 114
Sawyer, Keith, 45, 49, 51, 67, 78
Schema, 8, 9, 18, 80

School, 2, 3, 14, 18, 20, 21, 23, 34, 36, 38, 39, 41, 48, 50, 54, 55, 60, 67–71, 99, 107, 108, 118, 128, 139, 144,152, 154, 159, 166
   Primary, 6, 60, 103, 122, 123, 130, 139, 154, 180
   Secondary, 9, 11, 18, 21, 25, 27, 50, 82, 102, 103, 106, 109, 113, 118, 122–124, 138, 144, 154, 163, 180
   Tertiary, 9, 11, 97, 105, 118, 122, 161, 180
Seelig, Tina, 23, 49, 67, 98
Sefton-Green, Julian, 3, 8, 24, 25, 27, 45, 49, 67–69, 173, 177
Skills, 2, 7, 9, 13, 24–26, 31, 33, 35, 44, 45, 48, 49–51, 56, 59, 63, 68, 74, 76, 77, 90, 91, 92, 103, 120, 122, 123, 152, 157, 161, 172, 180
Social theory, theorists, 9, 11, 13, 14, 20, 56, 67, 75, 77, 81, 110, 122, 128, 174, 176
Standardization, 3, 14, 18, 19, 54, 56, 59, 60, 63, 66, 70, 74, 76, 81, 82, 92, 123, 160
Sternberg, R., 80, 82, 157
Systems, 9, 13, 19, 31, 56, 59, 64, 70, 71, 74, 76, 82, 104, 118, 119, 121, 122, 152, 157
Teacher, 2, 7, 9, 18, 20, 21–23, 25, 27, 28, 33, 39, 42, 43, 45, 49, 56, 59, 61–66, 68–70, 74, 88, 90–92, 98, 99, 106, 109, 110, 123, 152, 154, 161, 163
   student, vii, 2, 7, 9, 12, 18, 20, 22–28, 33, 39, 50, 54, 57, 60, 61, 62, 65, 66, 69, 70, 74, 84, 87, 88, 91, 99, 100, 103–106, 108, 109, 110, 120, 122, 128, 161, 163
Teaching, 2, 7, 8, 9, 22, 33, 40, 43, 49, 50, 54–56, 60–64, 67, 68, 74, 87, 91, 92, 105, 107, 109, 121, 123, 161, 162, 163

Technologies, 12, 15, 49, 54, 64, 69, 70, 105, 117, 142, 146, 160, 174, 176, 178
Theatre, 21, 32, 33, 34, 35, 37, 38, 40–45, 50, 54–64, 66, 71, 133, 147, 152, 171, 172, 180, 181
Thomson, Pat, 3, 8, 24, 25, 45, 69
Unpredictability, 2, 124
University, 2, 24, 25, 88, 100, 103, 104, 106, 107, 108, 109, 118, 144
value, values, 4, 11, 58, 102, 105, 121, 128, 131, 132, 134, 137, 151, 162, 179
video, ix, 8, 10, 69, 77, 88–90, 98, 100, 114, 128, 135, 138, 140, 143, 144, 152
virtual, 10, 26, 85, 132, 164, 167, 176
vulnerability, 62
Young Playwrights' Festival (New York), 36, 44, 172, 177
Youth, youth arts, 32, 50, 54, 98, 100, 106, 108, 134, 138, 139, 144, 145, 148, 180
Zizek, 116